For Love of a River: The Minnesota

For Love of a River: The Minnesota

DARBY NELSON
with John Hickman, Editor

BEAVER'S POND
PRESS

ISBN 13: 978-1-64343-917-4
Library of Congress Catalog Number: 2019905762
Printed in the United States of America
First Printing: 2019
23 22 21 20 19   5 4 3 2 1

Book design and typesetting by Dan Pitts
Interior illustrations by Lisa Perrin-Kosmo
Maps by Tyler Grupa and Lisa Perrin-Kosmo
Managing Editor: Laurie Buss Herrmann

BEAVER'S POND
PRESS

Beaver's Pond Press
7108 Ohms Lane
Edina, MN 55439–2129
(952) 829-8818
www.BeaversPondPress.com

To order, visit www.ItascaBooks.com or call (800) 901-3480 ext. 118.
Reseller discounts available.

To contact the author, visit www.darbynelson.com.

To Geri,
my paddling companion for life

Contents

Prologue: Boy Meets River

My parents were educators and, like itinerant preachers, they had a hard time staying put in any one town. We flitted from one school district to the next. I was born "up north" in Tower-Soudan, Minnesota, and by the time I was six years old, we had already lived in five small Minnesota towns. At the end of that school year, Dad called the family together and announced that he had taken another new job, this time as high school principal in a town called Morton. It turned out we would live there for the next seven years.

Morton—population 596 then, 411 now—sits on the Minnesota River a little less than halfway between where the river starts its journey at the state's western boundary and its confluence with the Mississippi in St. Paul. Here I would acquire my lifelong fascination with nature and fall in love with the Minnesota River Valley.

Driving south toward our new home on a sunny summer day, it seemed we were forever in farm country—an endless repetition of cornfields and cow pastures dotted with barns and silos and farmhouses. I was lulled by the mostly flat, repetitive nature of the landscape. And then something amazing happened.

Suddenly and seemingly out of nowhere, we began driving down a long, steep slope. I bolted to the edge of my seat for a better view out the windshield—there was no such thing as seat belts in 1947—and held my breath. Down and down we went. Finally, a wide, flat area with a wall of trees across the middle came into view. I could see a bridge—and a river!—and beyond that a long, steep slope going up, a mirror image of the one we had just come down. We were in a valley the likes of which I had never seen. The Minnesota River Valley.

Before we reached the bridge, Dad turned off the main highway and we drove into town. On that first day, even as my parents were hauling our meager family belongings into the white duplex that would be our new home, I began to explore the world around me. A tiny creek flowed along the base of a small hill right across the street! Beyond the creek, a copse of trees gave limited shade to a large park and athletic field. I gawked at the stupendously high bluffs stretching far into the distance, giving me a sense of just how far we had descended from the flat farmland above. I wondered what my new home would look like from way up there.

Over the coming days and weeks, I followed that creek—Morton Creek—all the way across town to the place where it delivered itself into the Minnesota River. I mucked around in the river's backwater ponds, where carp would get marooned after the spring floods as the water seeped ever so slowly into the saturated ground. I climbed the bluffs and was rewarded with a panoramic view of the immense Minnesota River Valley. From that vantage point, the river looked like a tiny little stream as it meandered back and forth across the valley.

Beyond the bluff lay flat farm fields, generally much smaller and more diversified than the vast stretches of corn and soybean we see today. There was corn, yes, but also wheat, oats, and alfalfa grew above the bluffs on some of the richest soil on Earth. Many farms had beef or dairy cattle and all manner of other livestock. From farm-kid friends, I would learn of the delicious taste of prairie chicken and admire the arrowheads some collected from the prairie soil.

My world was overflowing with excitement: frogs in the creek . . . cattle grazing below the bluffs . . . fire in the hills when farmers burned off the slopes in the fall, stimulating new growth for cattle in the spring . . .

pigeons to be chased in a farmer's barn . . . wild onions to be picked from the wet soils along the river . . . a gravel pit swimming hole, the clear water alive with tiny fish and other mysterious underwater creatures . . . salamanders in the quarry . . . wild grapes and plums picked along the river's bank, which my mother transformed into the most delicious grape jelly and plum pudding.

Rocky outcrops and abandoned quarries were scattered around town. Known as Morton gneiss, they were believed at the time to be the oldest rocks on the planet. Huge slabs of waste rock formed large pyramids riddled with chambers, inviting salamanders and little explorers like me into passageways between the immense blocks of stone. Rock collecting became a serious hobby, and I decided to be a geologist when I grew up.

I learned of hunters who captured turtles from the river and sold them commercially for food. I watched in amazement as a man from the Lower Sioux Indian Community just across the river waded across in hip boots. The water was murky, and I admired his ability to read the currents and stay on his feet.

There was an elementary school on the reservation. Students from that school enrolled in the Morton Public School in seventh grade (my last year in Morton), and I became good friends with several but especially Peewee Blue, who I would meet at the river on Saturday mornings to explore. He taught me how to build a no-paper, one-match fire, a skill I have gratefully used to ignite countless campfires over the years.

After seventh grade, my world abruptly changed. Dad took a new job— back in northern Minnesota, a million miles from the Minnesota River. A deep melancholy enveloped me as moving day approached. I could not explain the pain I felt inside.

But life went on. I continued my formal education (culminating in a PhD in ecology from the University of Minnesota); met and married Geri, my paddling companion for life; raised two kids; had a thirty-five-year career as a teacher of biology and environmental science at Anoka Ramsey Community College; and served three terms as a state legislator. Through it all, Geri and I found time for paddling, and lots of it. We have put our canoe in the water in hundreds of lakes and rivers in Minnesota, Wisconsin, New England, Alaska, and Canada from Hudson Bay to the Yukon.

And yet the Minnesota River has continually tugged at my heart and soul. In my twenties, I realized that to satisfy the urge to reconnect, I needed to return to Morton, the place I still call home. I have managed to return almost every year to connect with the river and its natural history and to contemplate the hold that this place has on me.

I've wondered: Is it the pain of separation I experienced as a child that has persisted? Is it a personal weakness to have such emotions? Then I began hearing of "the power of place" and realized that I am not alone in feeling homesick when I am away from Morton.

Comfort came in the words of writer and fellow Minnesota River denizen R. Newell Searle: "In kindly twilight I pondered the mortgage this homely landscape has upon my soul. . . . Southern Minnesota lies so deep in my bones that the farm goes with me everywhere." I am not alone, not the only one who is so attached to this place. Place has the power to profoundly form us, and for me, that place is the Minnesota River Valley. It has instilled in me an intense love of the natural world and so my life's direction. And it insistently, persistently calls me home.

Is there something special about rivers, perhaps? Bill Mason, Canadian paddler, author, and conservationist, wrote, "For those who travel [rivers] by canoe, they become living things that speak to the soul."

If I am to understand the power that this place called the Minnesota River holds on me, I am compelled to pull on my scruffy tennis shoes, assemble our paddles, canoe, and tent, and hop in the car with Geri. Together, we decided to paddle the entire 335-mile length of the river, to camp on its sandbars and fall asleep to its music. And to share our experience with as many people as possible, hoping to inspire them—you—to explore, appreciate, and work to protect this precious place.

This place has a long, complex, and sometimes controversial history, and this book covers it all in roughly chronological order. The opening chapters describe the unique, 3.6-billion-year geological history of the place, a fascinating story that is still unfolding. By geological measure, the Minnesota River Valley we see today is very young and changing before our eyes. The book continues with an account of the area's first human inhabitants as well as more recent human activity, including the displacement of the indigenous population by Euro Americans and the development of commercial agriculture. Nine chapters chronicle the canoeing adventures Geri and I took over a five-year period in our successful effort to paddle the Minnesota River. Unlike our actual itinerary, these chapters are arranged so as to take you from the source of the river to its confluence with the Mississippi. In the table of contents, these chapters are marked by paddles ⌒▭▭ . The voyage is punctuated with six "Voices for the River" stories of inspirational people who share my passion for this special place and who have worked tirelessly to protect and improve it.

I began writing this biography of the river fully aware of the human tendency to see what we want to see and ignore what we don't want to acknowledge. Henry David Thoreau, the nineteenth-century naturalist and author of *Walden* and *Civil Disobedience* and a major influence in my life, took an excursion up the Minnesota River a century and a half ago. In one of his essays, he wrote, "A man sees only what concerns him. . . . How much more, then, it requires different intentions of the eye and mind to attend to different departments of knowledge. How differently the poet and the naturalist look at objects." Henry, I will do my best to see and describe the Minnesota River through the eye and mind of both the poet and the naturalist.

One need not go to the ends of the earth to discover new things. It is my hope that you will open your eyes, heart, and mind to the Minnesota River's remarkable history, serious challenges, and promising future. Over the years, I have been puzzled and occasionally frustrated that so many people, including my colleagues in the Twin Cities conservation community, do not share my passion for the Minnesota River. Far too prevalent is the uninformed opinion that the entire area contains nothing but corn and bean fields cultivated by farmers who callously pollute the river for their own short-term profit. Not true! There is a much richer story to tell, and this book is my way of telling it. My hope is that you, too, will come to love the Minnesota River.

Panorama

Identity of space, or sense of place, if you like, cannot be discon-
nected from time. Time gives character. A place without a history
is harder to grasp, harder to characterize, harder to love.

—PAUL J. RADOMSKI

Looking at a topographical map of south-central Minnesota, a casual observer who had never visited the area might expect it to be flat and boring—corn and soybean country. But look more closely; there is a slender yet deep wrinkle running across the map. Herbert E. Wright, geology professor emeritus at the University of Minnesota, described it in *Geology of Minnesota: A Centennial Volume* (edited by P. K. Sims and G. B. Morey):

> The Minnesota River Valley is truly the most striking and scenic
> feature of all of south-central Minnesota. It is a narrow sliver of
> wooded hill slopes in the vast plains to the north and south, and
> it holds within it a diversity of geological features such as rugged
> granite knobs, boulder-gravel river bars, broad sandy terraces,
> gentle colluvial slopes—and a stream along the axis that is al-
> most tiny in the context of these major features.

The Minnesota, a river of modest size, flows from border to border across the southern half of the state. The region is known as Mnísota Makhóčhe—Land Where the Waters Reflect the Clouds—by the Dakota people who lived in these environs long before white folks showed up.[1] The Minnesota River itself is Mnísota Wakpá. Seventeenth-century explorers led by Pierre-Charles Le Sueur, among the first white people to see the Minnesota River, named it Rivière St. Pierre because they came upon it on St. Peter's Day (June 29) and because three members of the party were named Pierre. It wasn't until the mid-1800s that the river got its current name, perhaps at the recommendation of Joseph R. Brown or Henry Hastings Sibley.

The western boundary that separates Minnesota from the Dakotas runs nearly straight north and south. That line, however, is interrupted near its midpoint by a stubby knob that protrudes some twenty miles west into what one might think ought to be part of South Dakota. The small town of Browns Valley sits at the tip of the thumb; that is where the Minnesota River and its grand valley and watershed[2] begins.

Compared to its extraordinarily wide valley, the Minnesota River looks like a small stream meandering its way southeast for a little over two hundred miles and then, abruptly, northeast for another hundred miles or so through the heart of the state. At the end of its sinuous route, it releases its waters to the Mississippi River in St. Paul.

The Minnesota River Basin encompasses approximately fifteen thousand square miles (about eleven million acres). It drains nearly 20 percent of the state and small chunks of South Dakota, North Dakota, and Iowa. All or parts of thirty-seven Minnesota counties are in the watershed. Agricultural activities account for about 80 percent of the land use in the basin; this is some of the richest farmland on the planet.

As concerns about the environmental impact of human activity have

---

1. The Dakota language existed only in spoken form until 1834, when missionaries Samuel and Gideon Pond developed an alphabet based on the English alphabet. See the glossary at the back of this book for pronunciation.

2. A watershed is an area of land with well-defined boundary lines. Unlike the boundaries of cities, counties, states, and nations drawn by people for political purposes, the boundaries of a watershed are drawn by nature. All the surface water in a particular watershed runs off (sheds) into a particular body of water. For example, much of the land around Morton sheds its water into Morton Creek, so that area is called the Morton Creek watershed. The Morton Creek watershed is one small area within the Minnesota River watershed, which is itself an area within the Mississippi River watershed. The term *watershed* is roughly synonymous with *basin*.

grown, we've learned more about the nature and well-being of rivers. What happens upriver does not stay upriver. The waters of the Minnesota River, with its burdens of chemicals, fertilizer, organic matter, and sediment, travel via the Mississippi River all the way to the Gulf of Mexico. Everything is connected to everything else.

To fully understand the river's story, one must understand the interwoven relationships between changes in climate and terrain on a geological and current time scale, episodic events such as floods and droughts, and terrestrial and aquatic plants and animals, including humans. The perspectives and insights of geologists, ecologists, botanists, historians, and other experts must all be taken into account in order to produce a comprehensive, holistic biography of the Minnesota River.

The biography of the Minnesota River and its watershed is created through layers of time and place in a series of connected events, where one happening begets another in an unbroken narrative stream. The stories begin long before there was a Minnesota River with its broad valley and immense watershed.

These stories speak of shallow, salty seas covering land near the equator. Of glacial ice, ponderous and plodding out of the north, carving landscapes in its wake, landscapes from which the river would ultimately arise. Of a slow warming of the climate, the coming of giant mammals and, soon after, human beings who ventured forth as the ice receded.

More recent stories speak of explorers and fur traders, settlement on a massive scale, cultural conflict, and tragedy. There are stories of prairie landscapes with their uncountable lakes and ponds and potholes. Of land survey crews laying out townships and sections. Of steamboats, then railroads moving farmers' crops to market. Of pollution in the form of silt, pesticides, and fertilizer, and too much water. Of recent attempts to clean up the river and expand its recreational opportunities.

A river is not simply a single flow of water. It gets its lifeblood from water traveling underground and from tiny seeps and rivulets, creeks, and streams that flow into it. These flows carry nourishment from the land— soil and sand, organic matter from plants and critters. People from urban and rural areas alike make their own contributions—fertilizers from lawns and farm fields, chemicals from commerce, bacteria from leaky septic systems and feedlots. The content of this lifeblood reflects both the natural influences of the river and its basin and our cultural values. To understand the story of a river, one must learn about not just current events but history.

The story of the Minnesota River begins more than three billion years ago, with a special kind of stone I first became familiar with in my hometown of Morton.

Stone

The earth on which we live is essentially a huge, bulging ball of rock. . . . Man draws from the earth many materials which are necessary for life and happiness.

—GEORGE M. SCHWARTZ AND GEORGE A. THIEL

A massive pile of broken boulders—waste rock from a quarry—rests in a jumbled pyramid as you enter Morton some hundred miles west of the Twin Cities. Similar rock piles dot the landscape, several of which are visible from the road as you pass through town. Appropriately, this rock is named Morton gneiss (*nice!*). Gneiss is formed when granite partially melts under intense pressure and heat in the presence of water; it eventually recrystallizes into its distinctive, banded pattern. This is ancient rock; at 3.6 billion years old, it's a mere 1 billion years younger than the earth itself. Until a discovery in Australia in 1999, Morton gneiss was the oldest known rock on the surface of the earth.

Morton gneiss is everywhere in Morton. An engraved sign of polished Morton gneiss welcomes travelers into town. A five-foot-tall post of gneiss with a metal ring stood on the boulevard in front of our house; Dad explained that it was a hitching post from the time when horses were the main form of personal transportation. City streets were periodically treated with a seal coating of tar mixed with crushed gneiss. Random, rounded outcrops of gneiss protrude in front of the schoolyard and elsewhere around town. A popular supper club at the outskirts of town, the Rocks Club, drew patrons from all over the valley in the town's heyday.

Holding a piece of Morton gneiss is truly a touchstone to the ancient past.

Today, a piece of Morton gneiss sits on the desk in my writing shack. It reminds me of those carefree boyhood days crawling through passageways among the huge slabs of rock comprising that jumbled pyramid. My stone is ten inches long and ten wide. Bands of gray, pink, and black undulate across its face like partially stirred ingredients in a mixing bowl. The mix of colors and sparkles in gneiss, and its hardness, give the stone commercial value. It is polished and sold as decorative stone on buildings throughout Minnesota and North America under the trade name Rainbow granite.

* * *

It was no surprise to my parents when, soon after settling into our new surroundings, their inquisitive young son began collecting rocks. When they observed that this hobby of mine had staying power, they gave me a book for my eleventh birthday, *Rocks and Their Stories*, and then, for Christmas, *A Field Guide to Rocks and Minerals.*

I learned that rocks are composed of substances called *minerals* that in turn are composed of various chemical elements. Minerals are distinguished from one another by their color, hardness, and other attributes. Each mineral has its own structure and chemical features, which affect the shape and fracture patterns of the rock they comprise. Quartz is the most abundant mineral on Earth and is found in nearly every type of continental rock; it is less common in rocks that underlie the seafloor—the basalts and their metamorphic equivalent, greenstone. It is nearly impervious to weathering,[3] which is why most beaches and river sands are composed mainly of resistant grains of quartz. It comes in a wide variety of colors and, together with the mineral feldspar, is the main component of gneiss.

From another book, *Minnesota's Rocks and Waters: A Geological Story,* I learned of the importance of rocks and minerals to society, such as road aggregate, building stone, jobs for quarry workers and stonemasons, landscape stone, crushed rock to support railroad beds, and the conversion of sand to glass, among other uses. Geologists like to say, "If it can't be grown, it has to be mined." But in a sense, the growing of crops is also taking advantage of the mineral nutrients that remain in deeply weathered rocks. So in fact, it all leads back to our rocky substrate.

* * *

There are three categories of rock, based on how each is created: *Igneous* rock is formed from magma, the superheated stuff that spews out of volcanos (or sometimes doesn't make it all the way to the surface and solidifies slowly underground). *Sedimentary* rock originates as broken-down or weathered bits of rock that settle in a particular place. The sediment can be transported by the wind, left behind by a glacier, sink to the bottom of a body of water . . . any place where sediment gathers by any means is a potential birthplace of sedimentary rock. *Metamorphic* rock starts as either igneous or sedimentary rock and changes under intense pressure or heat into something new. Morton gneiss is a hard, metamorphic rock formed from the igneous rock granite. It is also, of course, my favorite rock.

All three categories of rock can be found in the Minnesota River Basin, and they all contribute to our understanding of the geological and cultural history of the area. Here are examples of each:

---

3. In the geology dictionary, *weathering* means chemical breakdown of minerals in rocks that result from the temperature and moisture conditions at the surface being so different from the deep, hot places where they originally formed. *Erosion* refers to physical removal by water or wind of weathering products or bits of rock.

Granite is an igneous rock. Isolated, well-rounded outcrops of granite and gneiss, sometimes with well-rounded boulders perched atop them, punctuate the upper stretches of the river.[4] They inspired place-names such as the city of Granite Falls and Big Stone County. Note to paddling enthusiasts: in some places in the upper stretch of the river where an outcrop is close to the water, the scene is virtually indistinguishable from sites in the Boundary Waters Canoe Area (BWCA) Wilderness.

In 2012, a company that for decades has operated a small quarry just outside Big Stone National Wildlife Refuge sought rights to expand to other locations in the area. The company estimated that, through expansion, they would be able to continue blasting and crushing rock for 130 years. Advocates for preserving the scenic value of the river and surrounding land organized to block issuance of the mining permit, and they were initially successful, as the township board sided with the citizens and passed a moratorium on such projects. But the county board overrode the township board's decision and approved the permit. A twenty-first-century battle over a rock that counts time in billions of years. In this case, Big Business crushed the Big Stone preservationists.

Kaolinite. As a boy, I once explored a small tributary of the Minnesota River close to town and spotted something unlike anything I had seen before: a mottled green-and-gray rock. And it wasn't just the color that was peculiar—unlike the unyielding gneiss I was familiar with, this rock was soft and slippery. Not only could I cut the stuff with a jackknife, I could actually scratch it with my fingernail. It kept me carving for days. So what exactly was it?

Years later, I learned that there are deposits near Morton of a type of clay mineral called *kaolinite.* I went to see this soft white material;[5] it crumbled easily in my hand. Its presence in Minnesota seems incongruous because kaolinite is formed under hot, moist, tropical conditions—not exactly typical Minnesota weather. A universally accepted theory called *plate*

---

4. This type of outcrop is called a *corestone.* Corestones form as the softer rock around them dissolves.
5. Kaolinite comes in a variety of colors, depending on the types and amounts of other compounds it contains.

tectonics provides the explanation: the earth's crust consists of several sections (plates), which are in constant, if exceedingly slow, motion (tectonics). The geological record reveals that hundreds of millions of years ago, what we know today as Minnesota was much closer to the equator, at about the same latitude as present-day Rio de Janeiro. The tropical conditions provided the necessary warmth to soften the rock to a gritty paste that was capped with a crusty soil. Kaolinite is still mined in a valley near Sacred Heart, and sometimes you can see piles of it by the railroad tracks there.

That soft green rock I had carved as a kid was actually a chunk of something that hadn't quite completed that weathering process. I've learned the science, but I still find it incredible that tropical warmth, water, and time are able to turn super-tough gneiss sitting near the equator into slippery kaolinite in Minnesota.

I had actually been introduced to kaolinite years before, in northern Minnesota. As a college kid, I worked in a paper mill in International Falls. My job was to sit in a chair in a boxcar filled with a purified and refined kaolinite waiting for a lone lightbulb to switch on—my signal to trigger a large vacuum tube to suck kaolinite out of the boxcar en route to the paper-making room of the plant. When mixed with paper pulp, the fine clay produces the glossy paper for magazines and other specialty papers. The kaolinite used by the mill had been imported from China; kaolinite from the Minnesota River Valley was used to make bricks and the sturdy tile of silos that dotted the region. When you see the *Ochs* name on an old silo, you're looking at a structure made from local kaolinite.

Sioux quartzite, two billion years younger than Morton gneiss, was deposited in shallow basins along a former sandy shoreline in southwest Minnesota from New Ulm west and south into South Dakota and Iowa. The three main areas of sand accumulation now form highlands of resistant quartzite because time and pressure made this the hardest rock around. This quartzite can be pink or various shades of red and even purple, making it relatively easy to identify. Sedimentary features still preserved in the layers of quartzite indicate it began its metamorphosis when an ocean invaded the land. A shoreline setting such as a beach, tidal flat, or river delta is suggested from the combination of shallow-water features (ripple marks) and exposure (mud cracks and impact from raindrops). In places, the accumulated sand is more than five thousand feet thick. For millions of years, less resistant rock around it has been deeply weathered and eroded away, leaving the former pink sand basins high in the topography.

Skipping ahead a few hundred million years (sometimes there is no geological record of what happened in a particular place), during the Cretaceous Period, some of these highlands formed islands in a vast sea that covered the continent from the Rockies to eastern Minnesota. Fossils indicate that sharks, turtles, and even swimming dinosaurs circled it and perhaps came ashore. During a much later glacial period, these uplands were scraped and polished by ice and wind, but they remained the resistant quartzite uplands. One upland near Luverne, Minnesota, is called Blue Mounds for the appearance of the bedrock from a distance. Climbers like to ascend the near-vertical face of an old quarry along the southeast margin of the Sioux quartzite outcrop in Blue Mounds State Park, clinging to the cracks in the fused sand layers of an ancient shore. Another deposit lies near Fairmont, Windom, and Jeffers. The outcrop at Jeffers Petroglyphs historic site[6] is a testament to the appeal of the smooth pink rock. Early people must have spent long hours here as they pecked out the forms that offer glimpses into their way of life. The third deposit lies along the river valley at New Ulm, where quarries were established in 1859 and remain in operation today. Chickens of the region are offered finely crushed pink grit from this quarry to store in their crop to help them digest grains.

Pipestone, a.k.a. Catlinite, is a softer layer within the very hard Sioux quartzite. In an area of southwestern Minnesota now protected as Pipestone National Monument, this thin layer is exposed and represents a finer-grained sediment layer in the mostly sandy deposit. It was most likely a clayey and silty layer deposited by slack water, and when it metamorphosed, it produced a softer red layer. Carvers would dull their tools on quartzite, but they can readily work pipestone, at least when it is fresh out of the ground. It hardens slowly when exposed. The rock is called *pipestone*

---

6. About the Jeffers Petroglyphs, the Minnesota Historical Society writes that "American Indian ancestors left carvings—petroglyphs—[of] humans, deer, elk, buffalo, turtles, thunderbirds, atlatls, and arrows. They tell a story that spans more than 7,000 years." You can also see the names and initials of nineteenth-century explorer/mapmaker Joseph Nicollet and his party carved into a rock at Pipestone National Monument.

in English because it has been used for generations by indigenous peoples to carve ceremonial pipes; the Dakota name for it is Íŋyaŋ ša (red stone). For centuries, indigenous peoples from around the continent have been coming to extract and carve the red stone in a spiritual quest. Much later, it was named Catlinite in honor of American artist and journalist George Catlin, who visited the site in 1835. Geology can tell us much about the 3.6-billion-year history of this corner of Minnesota, but we need other ways to explain the attachment and reverence of humans for these sites.

Limestone. The people who built Fort Snelling in 1820 used limestone from the river bluffs nearby. By 1850, limestone, a sedimentary rock, was also being quarried in the Mankato area. A variant containing the mineral dolomite was quarried around Mankato and the small community of Kasota by 1868. Limestone is formed by the settling of particles of dead organisms (no, not limes) such as coral and mollusks[7] as they dissolve or break up in shallow ocean water. The presence of these rocks around Mankato reveals that this part of the Minnesota River Basin was under a sea that flooded the continent hundreds of millions of years after the sea that deposited the Sioux quartzite and hundreds of millions of years before the sea with swimming dinosaurs that lapped on the shores of the quartzite islands.

A yellow to pinkish-yellow variation of dolomitic limestone is particularly attractive and became known as Kasota stone after the town that had rich deposits of it. Kasota stone is prized for its beauty and durability; it's used in buildings and facades all over the United States, including the Minnesota Capitol, the Smithsonian Museum of the American Indian in Washington, DC, the Philadelphia Museum of Art, and the Chicago Botanical Gardens.

Shale. The Cretaceous Period started about 145 million years ago and ended with a bang when a giant meteor crashed into the Yucatan Peninsula in Mexico some 65 million years later, triggering an instantaneous and devastating change to the environment. During the Cretaceous, the ocean

---

7. Mollusks are members of a phylum that includes a wide variety of organisms, including snails, slugs, octopuses, and, as used here, mussels and clams. These last two critters tend to look very much alike—they both have hinged shells and so are known as *bivalves*—but they have significant, harder-to-see anatomical differences. In common parlance, both tend to be called *clams*.

invaded the center of North America from Mexico to Alaska and the Canadian Yukon coast, and from the Rockies to Minnesota. That ancient seabed spans the area that we know today as the Great Plains. The sea deposited clay, silt, and a little sand in southwestern Minnesota, as well as much of the western half of the state. Most of the deposits in Minnesota formed a soft, dark gray shale, composed primarily of tiny clay-sized particles that were compressed by pressure but not changed significantly from the original mud.

Most Cretaceous deposits in Minnesota are buried beneath glacial till. In the few places where shale is exposed at the surface, it doesn't form a striking outcrop because of its softness, but it does yield a rich collection of plant and animal fossils, including tree leaves, clam shells, and sharks' teeth. The minerals in the shale limit the ability of plants to take root and allow people and animals to enjoy tasty, clear water. Take a trip northward along the shores of Big Stone Lake and note where the cottages decrease and the woody hillsides open up to prairie. The shale is very close to the surface here, and the presence of sulfur and other minerals in the rock that dissolve in the water change the whole feel of the place.

* * *

I think about my geology teacher in college presenting the central axiom of geology: *The present is the key to the past.* In other words, because the laws of physics and chemistry are fixed, we can apply what we know about the present to help us understand the past. But is not the past also the key to understanding the present? Unraveling the history of granite, gneiss, quartzite, and the other rock formations of the Minnesota River Basin reveals a dynamic and ever-changing Earth. The relationship between rivers and geology is intimate. Geology determines where a river flows, the nature of a river's bank, the myriad substrates created on river bottoms, and the economies of civilizations that dwell there.

Back for yet another visit to Morton, I sit on a rounded prominence of gneiss a bit west of the school and contemplate the valley below. I can barely see the river through slim breaks in the crowd of trees that line its banks. I caress my smooth stone seat and think of its origins and its incredible age—that it was weathered into its pleasing roundness in tropical climes as the tectonic plate that held what we now know as Minnesota slowly moved from equatorial latitudes to where I sit on it today. How patient and serene it feels. I give thanks to this ageless rock at Morton that is our touchstone to the ancient earth. Touching the rock connects me to the birth of the earth itself.

Ice

Everything is flowing—going somewhere, animals and so-called lifeless rocks as well as water. Thus the snow flows fast or slow in grand beauty-making glaciers and avalanches.

—JOHN MUIR

June is in full swing as I hike onto a plateau known as the Coteau des Prairies and set my field notebook on top of a weathered fencepost wrapped in rusty barbed wire. A solitary Black Angus bull grazes downslope from me on the far side of a stock pond. He turns to watch me watching him. Below me, the rolling, grassy landscape extends to the distant horizon. A thin copse of trees stands to the north, and I get a glimpse of the Cottonwood River through the leaves.

The Coteau des Prairies (named by French explorers; *coteau* means *hill*) is enormous: one hundred miles across at its widest point, two hundred miles long, and as much as nine hundred feet high. Towering over the surrounding prairie, the Coteau played—and plays—a leading role in shaping the landscape of southeastern South Dakota and northwestern Iowa as well as southwestern and south-central Minnesota through its influence on the area's flow of wind and water. The Coteau is the source of several significant rivers that release their waters into the Minnesota, including the Redwood, Cottonwood, Yellow Medicine, and Lac qui Parle.

I close my eyes to engage in a game of time travel. A chill wind is blowing over a vast, frozen plain. Tiny specks of windswept silt catch in my hair and dance across the snow. Some specks land in slight depressions for a brief moment, only to be blown back into the air to continue the dance. I sense an endless world of white with splotches of gray. There are no sounds save the howling wind. My toes enter the game, chilled to the bone. That does it, game over! I open my eyes to bring back the green, radiant early-summer day.

* * *

There have been ice ages periodically since the beginning of time. The most recent one began about two million years ago. Land in Minnesota that had felt the warmth of the equator 250 million years earlier now felt a distinct chill—the onset of a glacial age. A mass of ice accumulated in regions east and west of Hudson Bay in northern Canada. Ice built up and flowed south. The entire state of Minnesota was covered at one time or another, but the southeast and southwest corners escaped the final glaciation. The thickness of the ice sheet varied. It would have been up to two miles thick at the source, thinner as it spread but still thick enough to bury today's urban high-rises and rural grain elevators across the state.

For virtually all those two-million-plus years, the ice sheet dominated the northland, advancing and retreating from what is now Canada, as though unable to make up its mind where to go. The first foray to the south took it as far as Nebraska before it ran out of oomph and ice. But that was merely the opening act. Ice pulses flowed periodically through Minnesota and farther south until very recently on the geologic timeline. Glacial geologists see the deposits of many distinct ice advances into southwest Minnesota, the most recent of which began between sixty and seventy-five thousand years ago and ended a mere twelve thousand years ago.

The Des Moines lobe was the last tongue of glacial ice to invade southwest Minnesota during this glacial period. Its western border, Buffalo Ridge, lies atop the Coteau. But for the most part, the erosional power of this lobe created the escarpment (steep slope) of the Coteau as it formed the lowland to the east, advancing south to present-day Des Moines, Iowa. The ice lobe most likely followed the path of earlier ice lobes and rivers, deepening and broadening the lowland with its passage. The central axis of this lowland eventually became the path of the Minnesota River. On the west side of the Coteau, the James lobe was hard at work, most likely also following a riverine lowland. It created a great trough and beveling that extends to where Sioux Falls is now. The Coteau is just a lucky accident, a freak of nature if you will, spared by the ice lobes and carved from the thick layers of debris left behind by earlier glaciers and the soft sedimentary rock (the shales of the Cretaceous Period described earlier) that lay beneath.

The protruding Coteau forces the prevailing west winds upward, generating energy that is now being converted to electricity by a growing number of wind turbines. Most are on Buffalo Ridge, the moraine of the Des Moines lobe that forms the highest ridge on the Coteau. Driving near there on this bright, bright sunshiny day, Geri and I spot nearly a hundred of the giant blades plying the wind—about half the total in the area. They can be used to map the edge of the Des Moines lobe as it lapped up onto the Coteau—and it was a windy place then too. Southwest Minnesota just pancake-flat land? Not true. Not everywhere.

* * *

The glaciers I have seen in Alaska and the Rocky Mountains are inadequate to convey the magnitude of a continental ice sheet like the ones that once covered Minnesota and much of North America. But a few years ago, Geri and I did get at least a sense of what it must have looked like. We flew to Greenland to undertake a kayak expedition along the huge icy island's west coast, well north of the Arctic Circle. We paddled and camped among the behemoth ice walls for eleven days. How spectacular, not to mention scarily loud, were the walls of ice calving bergs into the sea. We hiked up to see parts of the immense ice sheet that air travelers see when flying the northern route to Europe in cloud-free skies. We curled into sleeping bags each night, awakening in the morning to an orchestra of ice songs: low, distant booming thunder; the crunch of ice cracking; and sporadically a sound like a rifle shot reverberating against an immense ice wall across the fjord.

* * *

Glaciers carry a wide assortment of rocky material, from grains of silt to boulders as big as a bus. The inexorable movement of the ice grinds away at this amalgam of rocky debris. Grinding, grinding, grinding—turning boulders into cobbles, cobbles into pebbles, pebbles into sand, sand into tiny particles of silt called *glacial flour*. Taken as a whole, this rocky mix, when spread across a landscape, looks like a freshly tilled field, explaining the name given to it: till. Glaciers spread their load of till like spackling compound, leaving broad, gently undulating plains and squeezing up ridges at their margins (moraines). The segment of the moraine of the Des Moines lobe that has survived subsequent erosion, Buffalo Ridge (Poverty Ridge on some maps), is about sixty miles long.

Think of till as a glacier's version of a Kilroy-was-here sign. In the course of their travels, ice lobes acquire and drop various kinds of sediment and loose rocky debris (plus peat, trees, plants, bugs, and anything else that can't get out of the way fast enough), thereby depositing freshly ground rock laden with minerals that are conducive to the development of fertile soil. The Des Moines lobe carried to Minnesota fragments of gray shale originating in the Dakotas and limestone from Manitoba that helped form a fine-grained, nutrient-rich substrate (called *loam* by soil scientists) for, first, prairie vegetation and, later, agriculture.

What might a till plain left by the Des Moines lobe have looked like just after the ice had receded? I saw a retreating glacier years ago near Valdez, Alaska, that had very recently melted back, revealing freshly exposed glacial terrain. Stones of all sizes lay spread over the ground. The rocky ground was dark gray; as they weather—that is, chemically change—rocks will oxidize and turn brownish or yellowish. Some sparsely scattered fireweed and small clumps of alder—pioneer plants—dotted the otherwise bleak landscape. They were helping the till take its first steps toward soil formation. Imagine the area of a parking lot that's piled high with plowed snow and the sod, sand, bits of pavement, road salt, and litter mixed in. Let it slowly melt over March and April, and come May, the debris left behind embodies the randomness of glacial stagnation deposits.

Stones in Minnesota's till were the bane of early farmers trying to plow up the prairie, and they continue to pose a challenge to farmers today. One can see stones piled at the corners of fields. Approaching the small town of Lynd, I was struck by the sight of two large piles of immense boulders in a field just west of the highway. I stopped the car and walked over to take a look. Several boulders were at least four feet across. Some were granites of different colors. Many were metamorphic rocks ridden with stripes and bands revealing a past life under immense heat and pressure. None of the rocks had rough edges; they were rounded, most likely indicating their origin as corestones formed as granite and gneiss weathered during the long period of tropical weathering earlier described. A few were more angular and had a lighter color; some had an identical color and texture of the limestone that I had brought home from a kayak trip on the northwest shore of Lake Winnipeg years ago. I stood stunned. I knew glaciers scraped the earth over which they flowed and carried rock debris with them to eventually be deposited elsewhere. But four-foot-diameter boulders? All the way from north of Winnipeg to here?! Wow! I walked away from those rock piles with a greater appreciation for the power of glaciers.

A few miles south of Marshall, I stopped at Camden State Park. I wanted to hike across a prairie there that had recently been acquired from a neighboring farmer. The park ranger told me that there was no traditional signage to guide visitors on their hike; rather, I would find the trail marked by a series of cairns—human-made piles of rocks. Now, nobody would want to carry rocks this size any farther than absolutely necessary, so I surmised that they had all been collected on-site. As I walked the path, I also discovered that rocks were the best crop that could "grow" in this field: the landscape was replete with the tops of partially buried stones looking like so many emergent plants. I quickly understood at least one of the farmer's motivations to sell the land. New stones rise to the surface every year as the winter's frost heaves them up. The farmer had fought those cussed stones for cropland long enough and was happy to enable the state to add it to the park. There are places in the Minnesota River Valley near the Swede's Forest, Homme-Kollin Unit Scientific and Natural Area in Yellow Medicine County, where early farmers couldn't even dig holes for fenceposts and instead were forced to make wire baskets filled with corestones to serve the purpose.

* * *

Approaching Redwood Falls one day, I about drove off the road when I saw a line of immense boulders stacked higher than six feet tall and stretching what looked to be at least three football fields long. While Geri took pictures, I visited with an employee of the rock supply company. They were in the business of selling these boulders as landscape stones. They had acquired the rocks from farmers within a fifty-mile radius. A two-foot-diameter boulder weighing half a ton fetched twenty-five dollars—not including the cost of hauling it to the customer's home. Who were the buyers? City folk from places such as Minneapolis, Des Moines, and Omaha. "Yup," the man said. "We are moving part of Minnesota to Nebraska." We're transporting rocks just as the glaciers did.

* * *

A warming climate beginning some sixteen thousand years ago led to a lobe of ice advancing quickly southward atop a layer of slippery meltwater into spruce forests in Iowa, where it stagnated and eventually began to retreat. As glaciers melt away, they sometimes create lakes when the retreating edge creates a dam and prevents water from draining away. Glacial Lake Benson was one of those ice-dammed lakes. It covered the area now home to the communities of Benson, Appleton, and Montevideo along the upper Minnesota and Chippewa Rivers. Farther south, a lake formed in a similar setting a couple of thousand years earlier when the ice lobe front was in present-day North Mankato. This water of glacial Lake Minnesota stretched almost to the Iowa border. Both lakes were about fifty miles long and forty miles wide, dwarfing modern-day Mille Lacs, but they lasted only a few decades before their ice dams pulled away, removing the source of water and one of the lakeshores.

With canoe atop the car en route to paddle the headwaters of the Minnesota, we take a short detour to Benson. Except for an occasional swale, the terrain is flat as a pancake, revealing the location of the lakebed. That we are on the ancient lakebed is confirmed by a map in Richard Ojakangas's book, *Roadside Geology of Minnesota*. We pull to the roadside along a field of corn. Deep, lush green extends as far as I can see, interrupted only by a few farmsteads in the distance. Occasional patches of yellowish cornstalks reveal that those plants are in a swale and are under stress from excess moisture in the soil. Most of the land around Benson has been drained for agriculture. The ditches are dug deep to drain this table-flat land and expose the thin, alternating layers of silt and clay. These were deposited as mud settled to the bottom of glacial Lake Benson each season that it existed: silt in the summer and clay in the winter when lake-ice formed, stilling the water so that even the finest particles could settle out to the bottom.

I'm an aquatic ecologist, so I can't help but ponder what kind of fish may have swum in the icy, silty waters of Lake Benson. As the glaciers retreated, considerable quantities of meltwater were released, creating countless streams in which hardy fish could progressively move north. The notion is not as farfetched as it might seem. Fisheries biologists have labeled lake trout as a "glacial relic," a holdover from the Ice Age. Lake trout distribution today is closely associated with the boundaries of the Wisconsin glaciation. Natural lake trout populations exist in northern Minnesota, and it is almost certain they would have gotten there by following the waterways created by the glacial-melt streams. Some ichthyologists believe other fish species such as whitefish and cisco now present in lakes of the upper Midwest and Canada got there the same way. Today, there are plenty of popular recreational fishing lakes near Benson, such as Green Lake, Norway Lake, and Lake Minnewaska.

Isolated pebbles, called *drop stones* by glacial geologists, indicate that icebergs may once have been present in glacial Lake Benson. I want to travel back in time with Geri to explore the lake in our kayak, making sure to steer well clear of the temperamental bergs. I would climb a moraine ridge to get a lay of the land.

* * *

Truth be told, I have a long list of things I would dearly love to go back in time to experience. At the top of my list would be to see what Morton looked like as the last of the ice disappeared. The Minnesota Geological Survey has recently provided a vicarious opportunity to do just that by publishing a geological atlas of Renville County, where Morton is situated. I have pored over this atlas for days, and the picture of the land after the glaciers left is becoming clear.

The maps offer a kaleidoscope of glacial features. The ice obtained its rocky material from the southwest corner of Manitoba and deposited it unevenly in Minnesota. Loam here, gravel there. Pockets of ice. And water everywhere. Scattered broadly, silt and clay suspended in glacial lakes settled out to form seasonal layers. I see over a dozen long ridges from twenty to fifty feet high. These are moraines, marking a temporary margin as the retreating ice lobe left the state. In an interesting symmetry, nearly all these moraines are aligned perpendicular to the Minnesota River. I see another group of ridges from three to five miles long running parallel to the river. These ridges are composed of both sorted and unsorted sediments. Sand and pebbles, silt and clay. They formed as debris squeezed up into or fell into cracks in the ice—crevasse ridges. Some ridges represent the paths of streams the flowed on the surface of the wasting ice lobe. The map makes sense of a jumbled terrain that formed as far-traveled, debris-covered, and highly fractured ice slowly wasted away, depositing its load in what I now comprehend as a predictable yet peculiar way.

* * *

The warming climate eventually won out, bringing an end to the glacial age in Minnesota about eleven thousand years ago. The ice retreated to Canada, readying for the next pulse. Melting ice created a very watery landscape, and much of that water would have ponded, forming lakes of all sizes. One of those lakes was so big it triggered an event that created the Minnesota River Valley itself. The lake, appropriately, was named after Louis Agassiz, the famed biologist-geologist-founder of glaciology, who convinced the scientific world in the mid-1800s that many of Earth's landforms were created by the movement of glaciers.

As the ice front retreated farther and farther north, the lake impounded in front of the ice grew to an enormous size. For a thousand years, the ever-growing glacial Lake Agassiz dominated the landscape and grew to be larger than all our current Great Lakes combined. It ranged, at different times, from west-central Minnesota to the edge of Hudson Bay. One fateful day, a moraine constituting the southern bank of the lake collapsed. An immense whoosh of water poured out, instantly creating glacial River Warren,[8] which sent a giant wall of water in a southeasterly direction, tearing through the stacked glacial tills from previous glaciations and removing

---

8. Named after General G. K. Warren, who first explained the event in 1868. He was on an expedition to identify possible routes for a railroad.

the rotten rock beneath, leaving behind only scattered corestones on the undulating rock surface. In the blink of a geologic eye, it created what we know today as the Minnesota River Valley, as much as five miles wide and up to 250 feet deep. Imagine! The Minnesota River Valley we know today was once filled to the brim with a raging river.

Once Lake Agassiz had drained, the huge valley left on the landscape was used by the much smaller Minnesota River. The tributaries were stranded above the broad valley and instantaneously became waterfalls. Water seeks its own level, the adage goes, and tributaries to the Minnesota have been seeking to level themselves with the Minnesota River ever since Lake Agassiz drained. Their waters cut through the valley walls, creating steep ravines where glacial till lay beneath them, or forming slowly retreating waterfalls where bedrock was exposed. They continue down-cutting and back-wearing until they find the gently descending gradient to the river they are seeking. This is one of the major reasons why there is so much sediment in the Minnesota River today and why many tributaries feature spectacular waterfalls over the resistant bedrock; they are out of adjustment and working slowly to get back in balance. Slowly in geologic terms, that is, but over the last 150 years or so, we have greatly increased the rate of adjustment by draining wetlands and plowing up the prairie for agriculture (the other major reason for there being so much sediment in the river). And why did people plow up the prairie? Because that prairie was growing in some of the most fertile soil on the planet.

Soil

It is a subsoil of unsurpassed fertility, absolutely inexhaustible,
and on it is superimposed the wind-formed soils [loess], the dark
loam of the prairies. Not even the Valley of the Nile can boast of
such soil as this.

—UNNAMED FARMER, YELLOW MEDICINE COUNTY, 1870

Though my dad spent his career in education, I suspect he was always a farmer at heart. The year we moved to Morton, he persuaded the Lutheran minister to let him plant a garden on the back lot of the church. When we built a new house in town a year later, Dad made sure the back yard had space for a substantial vegetable garden. What huge rutabagas, beans, tomatoes, carrots, cabbages, raspberries, and onions came out of that soil! Dad tended the garden, and Mother canned the produce. We had bumper crops every year, and we had "summer in a jar" to sustain us in the fall, winter, and spring. My cells and yours are nourished by plants that are themselves nourished by soil.

* * *

The University of Minnesota Extension Service is not overstating the case when it tells us that "soils are the basic resource upon which all terrestrial life depends." In terms of its potential for large-scale agricultural output, however, much of the world has low-quality soil. But the 16,770-square-mile Minnesota River Basin is exceptional; it has incredibly rich soil, soil that is the foundation of Minnesota's economy, feeds millions of people (either directly, or, as in the case of Minnesota's corn and soybeans, as food for animals that are processed into meat for people), and produces a great variety of non-food products (most notably, corn that is converted to ethanol). You cannot understand the Minnesota River Basin—or the history of the state, for that matter—without understanding the importance of the basin's soil.

The story of soil begins with rock, with stone. James Hutton (1726–1797), considered the father of modern geology,[9] perceived soil as the living bridge between rock and life, where worms and myriad other life-forms mix dead plant and animal matter with minerals to build a fertile soil. Minerals come from rock fragments. Physical weathering, frost wedges, water freezing and thawing in cracks, and glaciers grinding rock into smaller and smaller bits release locked-up minerals to create a complex mixture of inorganic particles. In descending order of their size, the particles that make up soil are sand, silt, and clay.

Clay, with its superfine particles, is of particular importance in creating rich soil because it has a huge amount of surface area. There can be as much as two hundred acres of mineral surface in half a pound of clay, delivering important minerals like potassium, magnesium, and calcium to plants. Clay holds water well; so well, in fact, that it can seriously inhibit today's farming practices in the Minnesota River Valley. Wet soil can take longer to thaw in the spring, drown plant roots, and prevent farmers from driving heavy equipment on their fields. That's why underground drainage systems, commonly referred to as *tile drainage* or simply *tile,* are so prevalent here; they carry excess water away. In the words of Minnesota geologist Dr. Carrie Jennings, "You have to tile it to farm it."

Tile drainage may help solve the problem of "excess" water in soil that is otherwise suitable for row-crop farming, but the way we tend to handle that water introduces another problem. "No matter what we do on the surface," Jennings elaborates, "whether it's urbanizing an area . . . or draining

9. Hutton developed what came to be called the *doctrine of uniformitarianism,* which asserts that the geological processes we observe now are the same processes that have always existed. In other words, by understanding the present, one can piece together what happened in the past.

agricultural fields, it all has the same effect, which is to hurry water to the stream, to get it there as quickly as possible. . . . [When] you give a river more water to work with, it becomes more erosive." More erosive means more sediment in the river, which degrades water quality and eventually deposits that sediment in places it's not wanted. As a society, we must either increase storage of water on the land or grow more crops that don't require so much water to be moved so quickly.

Soil consists of more than just minerals; it is full of life and so can be thought of as the frontier between geology and biology. A mere handful of soil has more living organisms than there are people on Earth; soil scientists see it as the stomach of the earth, consuming, digesting, and cycling nutrients and living organisms. Rock fragments eventually are covered with moss and lichens, and soon organic life begins to overwhelm the stony material. Vegetation dies and decays to the point where plant structures can no longer be discerned, mixing with the soil-in-the-making and ending up as a dark brown-to-black material called *humus*. Bacteria, fungi, and algae invade tiny spaces between the particles of this young soil. Centipedes, millipedes, earthworms, ants and beetles, round worms, ground-dwelling rodents, slugs, nematodes, single-celled creatures called *protozoa*, snails and slugs and mites—an abundance of life eventually makes mature soil. A tiny percentage of what is produced by green plants is consumed by above-ground animals; most is consumed by the profusion of life-forms below the surface.

All of this life exists in the uppermost of three layers that comprise soil. Naturally enough, the top layer of soil is called *topsoil*. Below topsoil lies *subsoil*, the repository for accumulated water and fine particles from above but containing no organic matter. This is where moles, badgers, and other burrowing mammals carve out their homes. And below the subsoil is a layer called *parent material*, consisting of larger particles—that is, sand, rocks, and pebbles.

Soil provides important nutrients that enable plants to convert solar energy and carbon dioxide to carbohydrates. In the process, they produce oxygen and retain water. The amount and variety of nutrients; sunlight and temperature; and the amount and timing of precipitation determine the level of productivity of the ecological system that we call topsoil. Growing and harvesting plants can deplete minerals and other elements of the soil and change its character. Fertilizer supplements of phosphorus, nitrogen, potassium, and other trace elements are available, of course, but at a steep cost.[10] Soil science is more complex than one might think, as any farmer will tell you.

* * *

How did the incredibly fertile topsoil of the Minnesota River Basin come to be? As one might expect, its origin can be traced to glaciation.

The sheer weight and inexorable force of the advancing glaciers swept up some of the material (till) that had been at the surface. Then, as the glaciers retreated, the till was plastered across the landscape. Some till got left behind in big piles called *moraines,* and a thick layer of the stuff—typically ten to fifty feet deep—was spread across the landscape. Over time and with the contribution of growing and decaying prairie grasses, this till weathers into the three layers of soil, inch by inch, year by year. Ten thousand years after the glaciers, the topsoil layer in the Minnesota River Basin can be as much as ten to fifteen feet deep. That may seem like an "absolutely inexhaustible" amount, as the unnamed 1870 Yellow Medicine County farmer I quoted earlier exclaimed, but it's not. In some places, unsustainable farming practices over the last 150 years have resulted in the loss of as much as half of the topsoil. At that rate, future generations will be dirt poor.

Conservation-minded farmers today employ a wide variety of techniques to save their precious topsoil. They build terraces on sloped land, install grass waterways to collect and move water safely, and plant cover crops to protect ground before, during, and after the cash-crop growing season. Drainage systems that were thought to improve water quality may save topsoil on the farms where they are installed because they reduce water flowing over the surface at certain times of year. However, we have learned that because it accelerates the removal of water from the field that

---

10. Minnesota exports agricultural commodities, such as corn, soybeans, and pork, but to sustain that economy, we must import nutrients and fossil fuels. This scheme can continue to work only so long as we take care of our topsoil and water and so long as we are willing to pay the economic and environmental costs of the imports.

would otherwise soak in, tile drainage has made our streams much more erosive. Moreover, we do not know its effect on the longer-term storage of deep groundwater. So although about the same amount of topsoil is eroded directly from fields despite an increase in the number of acres farmed, in the Minnesota River watershed where tile drains are installed in most fields, an average of eighty acres of land is eroded away from stream banks. Decades ago, about two-thirds of the sediment washing into the Minnesota River came from farm fields, and one-third originated from ravines and stream banks; today, there is seven to ten times more sediment washing into the Minnesota, and most of it is coming from stream banks and ravines. In solving one problem, we created another.

* * *

Water isn't the only thing that can carry away soil; wind can do it too. It happened in the aftermath of the Ice Age; it happened in the 1930s; and it happens today.

When the glaciers retreated, there was little to no vegetative cover to hold the ground in place. Fierce winds blew sand and silt to new locations. Over time, the settled particles made the type of soil called *loess*.

In the 1930s, drought gripped much of the United States, including much of the Minnesota River Basin. Wind lofted the dry loess into the air, sometimes to such an extent that the airborne particles almost completely blocked out the sun. The aptly named Dust Bowl devastated fields and scarred a generation of farmers. In response, the US government created the Soil Conservation Service (now called the Natural Resources Conservation Service), which helped develop many of the soil-saving practices mentioned above.

Today, during winter in the western part of the basin, there is often very little snow cover, and much of the land is bare. Wind picks up the topsoil and blows it across the landscape. The soil is captured in places where there is snow, and the combined snow-dirt is called *snirt*. It's a vivid, black-and-white reminder that we need to take care of our soil year-round.

Glacial till is the parent material of our soil, but factors such as variations in the types and amounts of minerals, slope, and vegetative coverage mean that soils evolve differently over time. In fact, while there are five basic types of soil in Minnesota,[11] those five types have more than three thousand subtypes. A single farm field may have several variations of soil, posing a challenge to farmers who want to maximize the productivity of the land. What plants are best suited? How much and what kind of fertilizer should be added? Sophisticated and thorough analysis of soil is an essential component of a farm's profitability. These days, that analysis is often incorporated into a system called *precision farming*. In their tractor cabs equipped with digital soils maps and satellite positioning systems, producers can customize application rates as the tractor moves across a varied landscape. Getting just the right amount exactly where it's needed maximizes yield and minimizes wasteful—and harmful—runoff.

* * *

Water and soil are intimately interconnected. Depending on when, where, and how fast it falls, some precipitation may soak into the soil to slake the thirst of plants, and some may stay on the surface, forming rivulets that move soil and water to new locations. These are natural processes, of course, but our modern agricultural practices and urban stormwater systems have fundamentally changed them, sending water and soil to bodies of water such as the Minnesota River at a much more rapid pace. Aquatic organisms and water quality suffer.

As a society, we are taking steps to keep and enhance our topsoil, but we need to pick up the pace. Millions of tons of topsoil as well as deeper sediment layers are eroded annually from field and town, not just in Minnesota but throughout the corn belt of the Mississippi River Basin. Every second, North America's largest river carries another dump truck's load of soil to the Gulf of Mexico. We are exporting our soil, dumping it on people who don't want it. We need to be keeping it here at home.

---

11. The five types are till/bedrock (in the Arrowhead region of northeastern Minnesota), loess (in extreme southwestern Minnesota and the Driftless Area of the southeastern region), lacustrine (the bed of glacial Lake Agassiz in the Red River Valley and northwestern part of the state), outwash (till washed by waters released by the glaciers, scattered in the Minnesota and Mississippi watersheds), and till (Minnesota River Basin and much of north-central Minnesota). The US Department of Agriculture uses the term *major land resources areas,* not *soil types.*

Land of Lakes

Lakes are like sparkling jewels in their effect on humans.

—JOHN R. TESTER

Especially among metro-area residents, the Minnesota River Basin is commonly perceived to be nothing but a dirty river flowing through corn and soybean country. When you're driving along mile after mile with corn on one side of the road and soybeans on the other, it's easy to be lulled into thinking that the entire basin is nothing but one giant farm field. But the people who live here can tell you something else: it's also lake country.

As our license plates remind us, Minnesota is the Land of 10,000 Lakes. Less well advertised is the fact that the Minnesota River Basin is the land of more than a thousand of those lakes. They lie within a vast area known as the Prairie Pothole region, which extends from the central part of northern Iowa into Minnesota and the eastern Dakotas and well up into Canada. Just as the Minnesota River Valley was created by glaciers, so, too, was the Prairie Pothole region. As the glaciers receded, they left behind countless depressions of varying depths, commonly referred to as *potholes*. These holes in the ground, naturally, collect water. Some potholes are so shallow that they hold water only temporarily, for a few days or weeks during the spring melt. Others are deeper and permanently intersect the water table, which is to say, they are lakes. All are naturally landlocked; they have no outlet, no connection to a stream or river. The only ways that water can escape a landlocked lake are evaporation and seeping into the ground.

In the Minnesota River Basin, more than 90 percent of these potholes have been drained, and more than 99 percent of the prairie has been plowed. Prairies hold water too. One acre of mature prairie can soak up 350,000 gallons of water. If we are to be serious about improving water quality in the Minnesota River, these numbers are going to have to change. We need to restore some of those potholes and the uplands surrounding them. Lost water carries lost nutrients, and it is all money down the drain, especially when you think about how much society spends trying to improve surface water quality after we've polluted it.

* * *

Lakes have been classified into four basic types based on the relative amount of nutrients[12] and oxygen they contain. *Oligotrophic* lakes have low nutrient levels and high oxygen content, which generally result in low vegetative productivity and thus very clear water. In Minnesota, you're most likely to find an oligotrophic lake in the northern part of the state. *Mesotrophic* lakes are moderately productive and still have clear water. *Eutrophic* lakes are those with excess nutrients and somewhat clear water. *Hypereutrophic* lakes have extremely high productivity—dense, oxygen-sucking algae and markedly brown or green murky water. Sunlight cannot penetrate deep enough to support beneficial, bottom-rooted aquatic plants, carp or other rough fish tend to stir up the bottom sediment and make the water even murkier, and there is little oxygen available.

In Minnesota, the Pollution Control Agency and other state and local governmental bodies concerned with water quality rely on the Citizen Lake Monitoring Program to help them collect data. With a little training, volunteers aptly called *citizen scientists* are able to gather accurate infor-

---

12. Here, *nutrients* refers to phosphorus (P) and nitrogen (N), which feed plants. Another name for nutrients is *fertilizer*. Farmers apply P and N to cornfields, and city folk spread N on their lawns (the soil already contains enough P to grow grass, and in 2004, the Minnesota Legislature enacted the Phosphorus Lawn Fertilizer Law, prohibiting P). When P and N run off into lakes and streams, they stimulate the growth of aquatic vegetation.

mation by using a simple tool called a *Secchi disk*. The disk, attached to a string, has four alternating quadrants of black and white. Citizen scientists submerge the disk in a lake to determine the greatest depth at which they can see it, thereby determining the clarity of the water. (A similar device, called a *Secchi tube*, in which the disk is contained in a calibrated, clear plastic tube, is used to measure water clarity in rivers and streams.) Knowing water clarity enables one to assess the general condition of a body of water, revealing insights on sedimentation and vegetal productivity. If you love a lake or river near you, consider becoming a citizen scientist yourself. Go to the MPCA website, search for "citizen water monitoring," and sign up!

* * *

As an aquatic ecologist, I have conducted most of my Minnesota lake studies "up north," and I figured it was about time to explore some lakes in the southern part of the state. Geri and I undertook a grand expedition; over a two-week period, we surveyed about forty lakes from the Chippewa River watershed in the upper part of the Minnesota River Basin to the Le Sueur River watershed in the lower part of the basin.

No matter where we were, we were not far from a lake. The lakes of the Minnesota River Basin are not pristine like those in the Boundary Waters Canoe Area, but then again, the basin is not a federally protected wilderness area like the BWCA, nor does it have similar bedrock. On our survey, Geri and I encountered excellent recreation amenities, gorgeous scenery, soothing solitude, charming communities, and much evidence of significant efforts at stewardship. We also encountered some lakes that lacked most of these characteristics. The healthier lakes provide critical habitat for waterfowl and countless other critters and offer fishing on a par with the best lakes anywhere in the state.

All Minnesotans love their lakes. The next time you're contemplating a trip up north, fighting traffic all the way, why not set your sights down south? To help you decide which lakes to visit, see the chapters on the lakes of the upper, middle, and lower parts of the basin later in this book.

People

The time of the Ice Age is of utmost importance to humanity,

for it is our time of origin. We began this interval as . . . ape-

like forms living and dying among the other wildlife of Africa.

We ended the Ice Age, only 10,000 years ago, as humans. . . .

For humanity the Ice Age was the crucible of evolution.

—PETER WARD

My interest in stone artifacts began when a school friend showed me several beautiful arrowheads he had found buried on his parents' farm. That interest was rekindled as an adult when I discovered a small, sharp-edged stone in a gravel pit near a river close to my home in the northern Twin Cities area. Natural weathering could not have shaped this stone; it's apparent that the edges were made by adept human hands. A reverence comes over me as I hold this object in my own hands. It is a rich, glossy brown and as smooth as glass. Ten chips have been flaked off the edge, and there is a shallow groove across its length. It's obviously a tool of some kind. I regard it as a touchstone that connects me to the deep human past. I cannot hold such a stone in my hand without wondering about the hand that shaped it.

In the Dakota belief system, the creation story is centered at Bdoté, translated as "the place where two waters meet." The two waters are the Minnesota and Mississippi Rivers, and the place is where Fort Snelling sits now. This is where, untold thousands of years ago, the Dakota were born of the land and, tragically, where they were imprisoned under brutal conditions in the aftermath of the Dakota–US War. The human story told in this chapter is based on scholarship from modern-day, non-indigenous archeologists.

* * *

Archaeological evidence indicates that human beings arrived in North America at the end of the last Ice Age, about sixteen thousand years ago. That's when small groups of hunters, called the Clovis people, left Siberia and made their way across the Bering Land Bridge that joined the far eastern tip of Asia with the far western tip of Alaska. They spread into the Americas as the glaciers retreated. Archaeologist Guy Gibbon cites radiocarbon data showing that present-day Minnesota became ice-free about fourteen thousand years ago and that humans were likely residing in the state as early as thirteen thousand years ago.

Clovis people were followed by the Folsom people, who used a new kind of projectile tip found at bison kill sites. In Minnesota, their artifacts are in greatest density in the southwest part of the state. During bridge construction in the southern metropolitan area of the Twin Cities in the summer of 2013, archaeologists were ecstatic to discover an eight-thousand-year-old campsite long buried in wetlands along the Minnesota River. Although no human remains appeared at the site, the discovery could provide a mother lode of insight into how such ancient inhabitants of the Minnesota River region lived. Analysis will go on for some time, and as one archaeologist told me, it's too early to tell what we might learn.

Two books have answered many of my questions about the early history of humans here: *Southwest Minnesota Archaeology: 12,000 Years in the Prairie Lake Region,* by Scott Anfinson, retired Minnesota State archaeologist, and *Archaeology of Minnesota: The Prehistory of the Upper Mississippi River Region,* by the aforementioned Guy Gibbon, professor emeritus of archaeology at the University of Minnesota. Even so, I would love to travel back in time and talk to the original Minnesotans. Where did they come from? Why did they leave their homeland? Did they witness glacial River Warren?

Our current understanding of human migration is that human beings, *Homo sapiens,* started moving out of Africa as long as 120,000 years ago, and we have been on the move ever since. Some people are pushed and others pulled to pick up and go to a new place. Is the pursuit of the unknown embedded in our genes? Are we all wanderers at heart?

My Norwegian grandfather got on a boat for America in 1890 because, as one of the younger children in his family, Grandpa Ole would never inherit the family farm; on the death of his parents, his oldest brother would take charge. There was little to no unclaimed arable land in the vicinity, so Ole was compelled to pick up and go—he was pushed. Aware of glowing letters from countrymen who had left home for greater opportunities in the New World, he was also pulled. Like Ole, many Norwegians and other European Americans came to Minnesota and established farms in the Minnesota River Basin. They did so by forcibly pushing out the Dakota people, who had been living there for centuries.

But what possible pull or push would have drawn people to come to the edge of an ice sheet in the middle of a continent? David J. Metzer, author of *First Peoples in a New World: Colonizing Ice Age America,* probes the question. One reason he proposes is that sheer curiosity has an adaptive advantage. Who knows what new prospects may lie over the next hill or around the next bend in the river?

* * *

At first glance, it might seem that archaeologists face an almost impossible task in understanding people who lived here over ten thousand years ago. How can we know anything about these ancient people when their bones and most belongings became dust, lost to history?

One critically important substance did not turn to dust: stone. For ancient people, some kinds of stone were a godsend, a hard, multipurpose material, a tool. For archaeologists, stone tools are akin to the Rosetta Stone: enigmatic, but, when properly interpreted, they open gates of understanding into the past. *Chert, flint,* and *jasper* are different words for the same thing: microcrystalline quartz, that, when struck by a harder rock like gneiss, produces a curving, glass-like break known as a *conchoidal fracture.* That type of fracture enables a person, with tutelage and practice, to create sharp edges by chipping off thin flakes in a process called *knapping.*

I have watched knappers at work. I once tried it myself at an archaeology exhibit at Gustavus Adolphus College in St. Peter, just a few miles north of that ancient gathering spot. After watching the instructor for a time, I struck a piece of chert to try making a flake myself. I failed miserably. Suddenly I had a much deeper appreciation for the skill of early toolmakers.

To look at a spear point knapped by an experienced toolmaker thousands of years ago is to look at a work of art as much as a useful tool. How valuable such artisans would have been! They produced a variety of tools from spear points to scrapers, adzes, and knives.

Gibbon writes that, to date, seventy-five distinctive types of stone artifacts have been found in Minnesota. Seventy-three are weapon points (of which there are four basic varieties), one is a scraper, and the other is a drill. Folsom points are particularly clustered in the southern half of the state and are dated to around 10,500 BP (Before Present).[13]

* * *

The oldest human remains discovered in Minnesota—about nine thousand years old, according to radiocarbon dating—were found in 1933 during a gravel-mining operation in Browns Valley near the headwaters of the Minnesota River. The site sat on a gravel ridge between Lake Traverse and Big Stone Lake in the valley carved by glacial River Warren. The bones included the cranium, several arm and leg bones, and the collarbone of an adult male between twenty-five and forty years old.

Although the site experienced significant disturbance during the mining operation, a number of artifacts were recovered. A burial pit, stained in red ochre, was found four and a half feet below the surface. Projectile points, pieces of sandstone used to wear away material, and stone knives were also uncovered.

Given that people first arrived not long after the glaciers had retreated, food would have been scarce. The rich assemblage of fish and other aquatic food sources that exist today would not yet have populated the ice-cold streams and scattered potholes filled with melted ice. Edible terrestrial plants would not have been present in abundance. Gibbon estimates that the diet was likely made up of 70 percent land animals, 20 percent aquatic foods, and 10 percent land plant material. As populations grew, pressure on food resources increased, leading inevitably to changed behavior patterns. Gathering food required greater effort, and food choices were forced to broaden, ultimately leading to early phase agriculture and reliance on other available natural foods such as wild rice.

13. *Before Present* means before 1950, the year that radiocarbon dating was standardized.

A number of other important sites have been discovered in the Minnesota River Basin. In 1988, a landowner digging with a backhoe not far from Granite Falls discovered a pit containing the skeletal remains of five bison with butchering marks. Two stone-chipping tools and a hammer stone were also uncovered. The animals were *Bison occidentalis,* larger than the species we know today. Radiocarbon dating revealed the bones to be around 6,700 years old.

A second site, known as the Hildahl site, was discovered not far from the Granite Falls site. Here, archaeologists identified thirty-seven bones, including those of bison, raccoon, turtle, muskrat, bird, and fish. The site is considered to be 4,500–8,500 years old.

Archeologist Scott Anfinson describes a Middle Prehistoric Period starting 3,000 BP and continuing almost up to contact with Europeans. Called the *Mountain Lake Phase,* it is located southwest of Mankato. It was a time of cooler, moister climate when large bison herds moved farther west. The Lake Benton phase, located southwest of Marshall, illustrates a more recent cultural transition about 1,500 years ago. It was during this phase that the bow and arrow replaced the spear as the weapon of choice.

Another site, J Squared, was originally called Jackpot Junction—the name of the casino owned by the Lower Sioux Indian Community across the river from Morton. The site was examined by archeologists attached to a highway construction crew; they discovered stone flakes as well as bones from bison, turtles, small mammals, and fish. No projectile points were found, however. The carbon date from bone established an age of around 3,600 BP. As I read about the site, I thought of my boyhood days exploring the countryside, including Saturday morning rendezvous with my Dakota friend Ronald Blue, better known as Peewee. Had I known about the presence of such ancient secrets so close, certainly I would have become an archaeologist. It's humbling to consider that my Dakota classmates could be descendants of those intrepid people who first populated the lands of the Minnesota River so many thousands of years ago.

Dakota still call the Minnesota River Basin home, but only through extreme tenacity. They faced an existential threat about a century and a half ago: the occupation of their homeland by Euro Americans led to war.

War

The task remains to listen to all the voices that called this land home, to comprehend what was lost, as well as what was gained—and at what cost. It is a complicated story and a discomforting one, the history, not just of Minnesota but of America itself, and the work to fully come to terms with it has only just begun.

—MARY LETHERT WINGERD

The anger and hatred is so bad I don't think we'll ever find the truth about what happened.

—DAVID E. LARSEN (H̆PUʹH̆PU)

At the end of our family's first year at Morton, school done for the year, my mother packed a picnic lunch and drove my sister and me the mile and a half from town to Birch Coulee Park. Mother stopped alongside the gravel road, and we walked onto a grassy prairie, spread out our lunch on a blanket, and, under a bright blue sky, basked in the unique joy that only the start of summer vacation can elicit.

The place was alive. Butterflies flitting and fluttering in their rich hues, other insects of all kinds flying and hopping and crawling, birds singing their own sweet songs, wild roses infusing the air with perfume, a redheaded woodpecker flying from a lone prairie tree into the woods and disappearing down the ravine. And flowers, flowers everywhere. It was a blissful afternoon, one that I can still see, smell, and hear to this day.

Birch Coulee Park became a favorite playground for boyhood friends and me. Some years on the last day of school, our teacher would put us on the bus, bring us to the park, and release us to frolic in the fields and wade in the creek looking for salamanders and minnows.

It was not until sixth grade that I was introduced to the dark history of the place.

Soon after school began that year, our teacher informed us that, once a week, she was going to tell us a story, an adult kind of story. Her purpose was clear: to prepare us for the new classmates we would have the following year who had different histories, different cultures, from us white kids. That's because, when I was growing up in Morton, students from the Lower Sioux Indian Community across the river attended the reservation's Bishop Whipple Indian School until seventh grade, when they enrolled in the Morton public school.

The adult stories were about a war in Minnesota between white people and Dakota Indians. The war had been waged mostly in the Minnesota River Valley, and one of the teacher's stories was of a significant battle fought in a place I knew and loved—Birch Coulee. Suddenly, I had a whole new perspective on that place and on life itself. One story that made a particularly strong impression on me was about what a white trader had said shortly before the war began. My teacher's recounting of the words *Let them eat grass* is etched indelibly in my mind.

Let them eat grass was a paraphrase of a chilling statement by trader Andrew Myrick, who was in charge of the storehouse at the Lower Sioux Agency. When some famished Dakotas asked him to give them food on credit because their treaty-promised annuity payments were late in arriving from the federal government, Myrick turned them down. His full statement exemplified the harsh attitude toward the native population that had evolved since the relatively peaceful, interdependent relationship between the two cultures during the fur trade in Minnesota in the late 1700s and first half of the 1800s. "You will come to me and beg for meat and flour," Myrick told the supplicants, "and I will not let you have a thing. You and your wives and children may starve, or eat grass or your own filth."

When the Dakota students joined our seventh-grade class, I don't recall our teacher telling us more adult stories; I just remember liking my new classmates. The first time I ever had a crush on a girl, it was a Dakota girl (she never knew, or so I've always believed), and Peewee Blue became my best friend. Years later, I learned that another classmate, David Larsen, was a descendent of Chief Wabasha. David grew up to become the tribal chair and historian. I reconnected with him when he gave the commencement address at Anoka Ramsey Community College and also at the dedication of the bust of Chief Wabasha III[14] at the state capitol.

* * *

Many authors and recorders of oral histories have shared accounts of the Dakota–US War. The more you read, the more viewpoints you will encounter and the more you will recognize the complexity of this story. But don't limit yourself to books and the internet. By visiting historic sites such as the Treaty Site History Center, Lower Sioux Agency, Reconciliation Park, Fort Snelling, and Birch Coulee Battlefield, you can gain a fuller appreciation of the history by seeing artifacts, talking to staff and fellow visitors, and immersing yourself in the landscape where history was made.[15]

The following is my understanding of the war and, in particular, the Battle of Birch Coulee. I encourage you to do your own research, visit the sites, and form your own understanding.

A fundamental aspect of American history is the inexorable westward expansion by European Americans. In the 1850s and early 1860s, thousands upon thousands of settlers were moving into the rolling prairies of southern Minnesota, which the Dakota called home. Seeing they had no choice, the Dakota signed treaties that ceded almost all their more than twenty million acres of land to the whites, agreeing to retain only ten-mile wide strips on each side of the upper Minnesota River (in 1851) and then only on the south side (in 1858, by which time thousands more land-seeking settlers had arrived).

---

14. Chief Wabasha III was a signatory of the Treaty of 1851 at Traverse des Sioux (see the chapter "A River Bends") and the Treaty of 1858 in Washington, DC, in which the Dakota were obliged to give up about half the land they had been granted in the 1851 treaty.

15. In addition to the interpretive centers at historic sites, there are also several excellent museums operated by historical societies in Brown County (New Ulm), Renville County (Morton), and Sibley County (Henderson, which is also home to the Joseph R. Brown Minnesota River Center), among others.

The Dakota could choose to live primarily off annuities promised in the treaties or learn to farm the way white people farmed. The latter choice was antithetical to the Dakota way of life, in which it was women who tended the cultivated crops and the soil was not tilled. It also tended to be risky, as it often brought harassment and even death from those Dakota who thought it imperative to perpetuate their traditional ways. By 1862, over two hundred indigenous families had become farmers and there was a waiting list for the program, which included provision of a barn, livestock, and a house.

Issues in the dispensing of annuities, food, and supplies caused restlessness on the reservations. There was still periodic conflict between Dakota and Ojibwe in certain hunting areas (known as the "contested zone"), which often prompted intervention by the US military and federal Indian agent. At the same time, large numbers of settlers kept coming, many of them on steamboats on the Minnesota River, which was the major westward highway. Some Dakota traveled by steamboat to get to St. Paul or Fort Snelling, a small example of multicultural assimilation.

Times were unsettled—to say the least—in southern Minnesota and complicated by the onset of America's Civil War. Many white Minnesota men went off to fight in that war, which limited the number of military personnel available to serve at Fort Ridgely, Fort Snelling, and other military outposts.

In mid-August 1862, a group of young Dakota men killed a farm family near Acton, east of present-day Willmar. When this incident was reported to the men's chief, Little Crow (Thaóyate Dúta, "His Red Nation"), the chief knew his tribe's tenuous situation was about to get worse. He convened a council of Dakota elders and warriors, who eventually convinced him that war was the only option. Predicting that "we will all die together," the reluctant chief launched the war on August 18.

One of the first attacks was at the Lower Sioux Agency, where food supplies were kept under guard. Military men, including Captain John Marsh, as well as traders and their families, were among those killed. Andrew "Let them eat grass" Myrick was found dead, his mouth stuffed with grass. From there, attacks were made on individual farmsteads, which sent survivors running for safety at Fort Ridgely or the town of New Ulm while warriors were gathering under the direction of Chief Little Crow to attack those very locations. Two attacks on each location were repelled in part because the defenders had cannons.

Monday evening, September 1, a group of US soldiers and raw volunteers led by Major Joseph R. Brown headed to Birch Coulee to camp for the night. They had been assigned to bury the dead from the battles at Lower Sioux Agency and Redwood Ferry and to be on the lookout for Dakota warriors. They hadn't seen any Indians in two days, and when they arrived at Birch Coulee, they neglected to set up the camp in a typical defensive stance despite the fact that the area had many trees and much tall grass, ideal terrain for an ambush. Colonel Brown set off on a reconnaissance mission, leaving Captain Joe Anderson in charge.

That same evening, 340 Dakota led by Gray Bird (Ziŋtkáda Ȟóta) arrived at Lower Sioux Agency. They looked across the river and saw a column of soldiers that looked to them like a line of ants. Chief Gray Bird dispatched five scouts to find out what they were up to. The scouts reported back that there were only seventy soldiers (about one hundred of the contingent had not yet arrived) and that it looked like they were heading to Birch Coulee. Gray Bird and other chiefs quickly understood their advantage. They planned a surprise attack on the soldiers at dawn with groups of men positioned at strategic locations, some with double-barreled shotguns and others with bows and arrows.

Captain Anderson asked the cook, who always rose early to prepare breakfast, to wake him if he heard anything unusual. Early in the morning, the cook crawled to the captain's tent and whispered, "The camp is surrounded by Indians!" The shooting began at dawn and lasted into the next day.

Private Charles Watson had been recruited two weeks before the attack and was stationed at Fort Ridgely, sixteen miles from Birch Coulee. Inexperienced though he was, Watson thought he heard distant gunfire and rushed to the fort's commander, Henry Sibley,[16] who had not heard

---

16. Henry Hastings Sibley was the State of Minnesota's first governor (1858–1860) and had deep connections to the Dakota. At the request of the second governor, Alexander Ramsey, he commanded the forces responding to the uprising.

anything. Again Watson heard the sound, and again Sibley could not hear it. The third time, Sibley heard it and immediately understood the risk to the burial detail. He sent 240 troops, a howitzer, and a six-pound gun from Fort Ridgley to reinforce battle-worn men in desperate need of water. The battle finally ended with thirteen US soldiers killed and forty-seven wounded, and two Dakota killed. Jerome Big Eagle (Waŋbdí Tháŋka)[17] related the following account:

> Both sides fought well. Owing to the white men's way of fighting they lost many men. Owing to the Indians' way of fighting they lost but few. The white men stood up and exposed themselves at first, but at last they learned to keep quiet.

On September 22, Sibley's troops were camped at Wood Lake, not far from the Upper Sioux Agency. Only three hundred of the one thousand Indians gathered at Upper Sioux were willing to fight. Fourteen Indians died that day, as did seven of Sibley's troops. Two hundred warriors followed Little Crow in retreat onto the plains. For all practical purposes, the war was over.

* * *

The day after Christmas 1862, the largest mass execution in American history occurred in Mankato. Thirty-eight of the 303 Dakota warriors convicted of capital crimes were hanged. The others, spared by Abraham Lincoln, were sent in shackles to a military prison at Camp McClellan at Davenport, Iowa, while captured women and children were interned at Fort Snelling. Many of these prisoners succumbed to sickness or frigid temperatures. A policy of exile or extermination of all Dakotas was adopted by the State of Minnesota and had some "success." But little by little, some exiled Dakotas returned, and today there are three Dakota tribal lands along the Minnesota River.

---

17. Waŋbdí Tháŋka was named chief of Black Dog's Mdewakanton village near Mendota in 1857. The next year, he went to Redwood (Lower Sioux) Agency and joined the farmer band there. When the war started, he reluctantly took up the fight, leading his men at Birch Coulee and elsewhere.

* * *

While eating raspberries near Hutchinson, Minnesota, Little Crow was caught on July 3, 1863, and shot. When I pick raspberries in my garden, I think of this strong leader who struggled to find a realistic alternative to war.

* * *

On Labor Day of 1930, a crowd of several thousand people gathered at Birch Coulee to commemorate the battle. Eighty-five-year-old Robert K. Boyd stood on a wooden stage as the featured speaker. Boyd had taken a bullet through his right arm. He was one of the first soldiers to have been shot in the Battle of Birch Coulee, and in 1930, he was the last survivor. He began his talk by saying, "I came to tell you of events that took place here a long time ago. . . . It was a story that was older than history and always the same, when a poor, ignorant, defrauded, and downtrodden people rise up in their wrath." He paused to let the weight of his opening remark set in before continuing. "The whole reservation system was tainted with fraud that left Indians with a smoldering resentment. There are some who might expect me to describe the outrages committed by the most desperate and depraved of these Indians. But I shall not do so." He ended his talk by saying, "I think the people of western Minnesota should preserve all places of historic interest." Birch Coulee was added to the National Register of Historic Places in 1973, and the site is now maintained by Renville County.

* * *

It is a beautiful blue-sky day in Birch Coulee Park. Geri and I are back for one of our many visits to this place the Dakota people call Thaŋpá yukháŋ, or "place of the white birch." A warm wind blows into my face. I inhale perfume from a cluster of prairie rose bushes. A swallow flies overhead. Young trees and sumac with climbing wild grapevines have taken over much of the grassy area. Scattered piles of brush signal an effort to cull the trees and return the land to prairie.

The Minnesota Historical Society's trails and informational signs help me visualize how the battle unfolded. I see where Big Eagle (Waŋbdí Tháŋka) "led my men up from the west through the grass and took up a position 200 yards from the camp behind a small knoll."

I myself wander off through the grass into the woods of birch, ash, oak, and basswood. Around a bend, I come upon a majestic, gnarled oak. It appears to have an old fire scar. Might it have been a witness tree, perhaps a sapling in 1862? I sit at the base of this great-great-grandfather of a tree, close my eyes, and listen. Listen.

Transformation

There are two things that interest me: the relation of people to each other, and the relation of people to land.

—ALDO LEOPOLD

Back when I was in graduate school, I obtained what remains a prized possession to this day: a copy of a huge map, measuring forty-eight by fifty-five inches, which opened my eyes to what the Minnesota River Basin looked like before Euro American appropriation. Titled "The Original Vegetation of Minnesota," the map was made in 1930 by one Francis J. Marschner, research assistant in the Office of Agricultural Economics, US Department of Agriculture.[18] Strangely, no other state map of "original" vegetation has been made in such detail. Stranger still, Marschner apparently never visited Minnesota; he developed his map from information provided by the US General Land Office surveys of Minnesota townships that took place between 1847 and 1907.

Marschner identified sixteen vegetation units for the state, eight of which occur in the Minnesota River Basin, where the "Prairie" designation dominates. Superimpose a map of Idaho with its boot-like shape onto the western half of Minnesota, resting the sole of the boot along the southern

---

18. A fascinating account, "The Mystery of a Map and a Man" by Tim Brady, appears in the January–February 2003 edition of the *Minnesota Conservation Volunteer;* it's available online.

border. The upper part of the boot rises all the way to the Canadian border, and it is prairie all the way.

Throughout the prairie are sprinkled splotches of what Marschner labeled as "Wet Prairies, Marshes and Sloughs—Marsh grasses, Flags, Reeds, Rushes, Wild Rice, with Willow and Alder in places." Today, these areas are better known as the "potholes" of the prairie-pothole region. They were repositories for rainfall and snowmelt and havens for a multitude of critters, including mosquito larvae, which made them a royal pain in the prairie for Euro American settlers.

All along the Minnesota River and its tributaries were "River-Bottom Forests" with a mix of elm, ash, cottonwood, box elder, oaks, basswood, soft maple, willow, aspen, and hackberry.

Scattered at the eastern edge of the prairie grew patches of "Oak Openings and Barrens," featuring fire-resistant bur oak. Other patches included "Aspen-Oak Land" with some elm, ash, and basswood, and elsewhere there is "Brush Prairie," comprising grass, brush of aspen, balm of Gilead (balsam poplar), and hazel.

In an eighty-mile-wide swath from Mankato all the way to northern Hennepin County, the extensive "Big Woods" covered over two million acres. This forest was dominated by American elm with a mixture of basswood, maple, ash, four species of oak, hornbeam, aspen, birch, and several other species.

* * *

Researchers using radiocarbon dating tell us that some 11,500 years ago, when the Holocene epoch began, the Minnesota River Basin became a landscape of mostly spruce and ash. By 8,000 BP, the basin was dominated by oak and elm, and by 6,800 BP, prairie had become the dominant vegetation unit.

The Holocene is marked by a warming trend that had major consequences for the Minnesota River Basin, most significantly the retreat of the glaciers. The warmth also brought a drier climate—conditions that no longer favored trees, but rather grass, resulting in prairie. Several types of prairie emerged: shortgrass prairie in eastern Montana, mixed-grass prairie in the Dakotas, and tallgrass prairie in Minnesota as well as northern

Iowa and the eastern edges of Nebraska and Kansas.

Think of a tall grass prairie as a rich assemblage of plant species; start with big bluestem with its six- to eight-foot stems (and roots of equal length), Indian grass, little bluestem (two to four feet high), prairie cord grass, switch grass, and buffalo grass. Then add an array of non-grassy plants (collectively called *forbs* in the lexicon of botanists), such as prairie clover, numerous goldenrods, pasqueflowers, and shrubs such as lead plant, wolfberry, and prairie rose. A native Minnesota prairie contains as many as nine hundred species of plants, not to mention three thousand species of insects.

What a lovely early sign of spring is the pasqueflower!

Some small prairie flowers bloom early in spring to reduce competition from the grasses soon to grow tall. The pasqueflower is one of the earliest to bloom. One Easter, my mother took me on a walk to the base of the bluff near our house in Morton to show me one of these whitish flowers cuddled around glacial till partly covered in snow.

July and August are prime times to see tallgrass prairie flowers. It is a sublime pleasure to walk through a field of prairie blazing star, sweet black-eyed Susans, pink prairie smoke, golden Alexander, and the rich orange butterfly weed, better called *butterfly flower*. It is the sweet fragrance of the wild rose and its simple pink flowers that most enthrall me.

Typical prairie grasses spread horizontally by sending out new shoots and roots, resulting in the formation of a dense mat of plants and roots, which form the best natural soil anchors on Earth and can store large amounts of water. A cubic meter of big bluestem sod may contain more than twenty linear miles of rootlets and root hairs. One acre of established prairie can produce twenty-four thousand pounds of roots and can absorb buckets of rain. Big bluestem roots penetrate down nine feet, Indian grass roots ten, switch grass eleven, and leadplant roots fourteen feet. Above ground, leadplant is a three-foot-high shrub. Conservationist and journalist John Madson wrote about one old rose plant that set roots down into the soil some twenty-one feet.

Significant amounts of carbon are stored in a prairie's biomass, up to 90 percent of which is underground. As the organic material decomposes, the soil becomes progressively richer and deeper year by year. No wonder the farmers who settled in the Minnesota River Basin were willing to break their backs to break the sod.

* * *

So how have native plant communities fared since the General Land Office surveys interpreted by Marschner? The Minnesota Department of Natural Resources embarked on a major project in 1987 to answer this question, using Marschner's map to guide their efforts. The DNR's Minnesota Biological Survey deployed experienced field crews to gather data and map how changes have occurred among native plant communities since the time of Euro American settlement. Working county by county, it took them fifteen years to complete the survey for the entire state.

A helpful DNR ecologist provided me with six Biological Survey maps covering parts of seventeen Minnesota River counties from Big Stone at the headwaters to Ramsey near the confluence at St. Paul. Each map measures sixty-two inches wide by thirty inches high. A checkerboard of thin red lines demarcates township boundaries, precisely six miles apart.

I unrolled the first map, which covers Brown, Redwood, and my home county of Renville, and I was sobered by what I saw. Instead of a rainbow of colors depicting different types of vegetation as on Marschner's map, the Biological Survey map is virtually all white—indicating zero native vegetation—except for the land hugging the Minnesota River. Along the river through Sacred Heart, Redwood Falls, Morton, and Franklin to New Ulm, the DNR surveyors found hardwood trees (denoted in green on the map) and some splotches (brown) indicating the presence of dry, fire-dependent oak woodlands. Red spots identify bedrock outcrops that show up around Franklin, Morton, and cities upriver. But where is the prairie that dominated Marschner's map? I scanned township after township. The first contained Linden Lake, but no native plant communities. The next two townships had Lake Hanska (described in the "Lakes of the Middle Minnesota River Basin" chapter of this book), but no native plant communities. At the fourth township, I finally found a forty-acre plot of wet prairie.

The long, narrow strips of floodplain forest and areas of oak openings that cling to the Minnesota River and its tributaries are dominated by such canopy trees as silver maple and cottonwood, and there is also an assemblage of sub-canopy trees, including hackberry, box elder, green ash, American elm, and basswood. Also present in bright green are the mixed hardwood forest communities of bur oak, basswood, green ash, red elm, ironwood, American elm, prickly ash, and chokecherry trees, as well as forbs like bloodroot, wild ginger, Virginia creeper, and wild grape. Plains cottonwood is the most massive and fastest-growing tree species in Minnesota, often growing to 120 feet high. It lives along streams and lakeshores and on the floodplains in southern and western Minnesota. I often visit the gigantic cottonwood at the Treaty Site History Center just north of St. Peter whose trunk is wider than I am tall.

Geri took over the analysis. In each of the seventy-seven townships on her map, she counted the number of acres that had color—native vegetation of one kind or another. Forty-four of the townships had no native vegetation. Almost all of the colored areas followed the snaking turns of the river. All the native vegetation added together came out to three thousand acres, which would cover only 22 percent of one six-mile-by-six-mile township. Out of the one million total acres on the map, only 0.3 percent of the land is currently covered by vegetation that was present before Euro Americans arrived. So, what is on the rest of the land, the stark white dominating this map? The prairie and wetlands have been transformed into land used for commodities farming, pastureland for grazing, logging, and residential and commercial development.

I unrolled the remaining maps and discovered very similar patterns throughout. Aside from the land along the rivers, there remain but a few scattered patches of native vegetation. Only parts of townships in Big Stone, Lac qui Parle, Chippewa, and Yellow Medicine counties have sizable tracts of extant prairie.

Nearly all of the Big Woods, which occupied the south-central part of the state, has been cleared, first for building material and then agriculture and urbanization. Carver County was totally covered by the Big Woods, but today, only one stand of seventy-four acres survives there. Other notable remnants are found outside the Minnesota River Basin in Nerstrand Big Woods State Park near Northfield, at Wolsfeld Woods in Long Lake, and in a small segment near our home in the north metro. Geri and I visit periodically and enjoy walking on the wide-open forest floor under the maple-basswood canopy.

Although precious little remains of Minnesota's grand, dominating prairie, not all has been lost. A few areas that never saw the plow have been preserved in state parks and the basin's two national wildlife refuges. And a few fortunate farmers have maintained patches of prairie bequeathed to them by their ancestors.

In addition, Scientific and Natural Areas (SNAs) have been established to protect the state's natural features of exceptional scientific and educational value, including prairies. Managed by the DNR, they are scattered around the state and open to the public for free. As a legislator in the state's House of Representatives, I carried several bills enhancing SNAs and prairies. There are more than twenty SNAs in the Minnesota River Basin, from Bonanza Prairie in Big Stone County to Savage Fen in the southwest metro. In addition, nonprofit organizations such as Pheasants Forever, Minnesota Land Trust, The Nature Conservancy, and Ducks Unlimited do much great work to acquire, protect, and restore our native prairie (and wetlands too).

* * *

The contrast between Marschner's map of "original" vegetation and the maps of the DNR's recent Biological Surveys could not be more vivid. So what happened? How did this transformation take place?

Essentially, a whole lot of people showed up who were intent on using the resources of the Minnesota River Basin in ways that were in all-encompassing conflict with the ways the native population had been using them. The goal was to extract resources, not sustain them. Several pivotal events, methodically building one upon the other, drained the color from Marschner's Map.

The first Europeans to visit what is now Minnesota (generally accepted to have been members of a 1659 expedition led by Frenchmen Pierre-Esprit Radisson and Médard Chouart des Groseilliers) encountered a native population whose lifeways were based on the area's varying geography, biodiversity, and seasons. In winter, the Dakota made their homes in the sheltered Big Woods, where they could harvest big game, such as deer and elk. In spring and summer, they lived near rivers where women collected naturally occurring foodstuffs, such as maple sap, berries, roots, and herbs, and tended gardens of beans (omníča), maize (wamnáheza), squash (wamnú), and sunflowers (waȟčázizi). According to an interpretive sign at the Upper Sioux Agency, the four plants worked interdependently—bean plants convert nitrogen from the atmosphere into a fertilizer other plants can use; cornstalks are a trellis to support the bean vines; squash plants cover the soil to retain moisture and, with their spiny stems, ward off predators; and sunflowers attract pollinators. Sounds like a system that everyone from backyard gardeners to row-crop farmers could learn from today. Meanwhile, the men hunted and fished. In the fall, the Dakota moved to areas near shallow lakes and backwaters where wild rice (psiŋ) flourished; it was a major component of their diet because it can be preserved and eaten year-round—not to mention it's nutritious and delicious. In late fall, they went on bison-hunting expeditions.

Just as natural resource professionals do today, the Dakota of the past employed strategic use of fire to maintain the vitality of prairies. Fire burns most of what grows above ground and stimulates new growth at the surface. By periodically regenerating the prairie, the Dakota ensured that bison, which eat prairie vegetation, would stick around.

In this way, the Dakota lived with the seventh generation in mind. From the perspective of nineteenth-century Euro Americans, however, the indigenous population was letting the land go to waste. To make the land productive, they believed, it had to be converted to agriculture. For this to happen, the native people and animals would have to be removed from the landscape.

The first Europeans and Euro Americans to establish permanent residence here were fur traders. Their heyday was from the late 1600s to the early 1800s. Most fur traders integrated themselves into Dakota culture through marriage. They provided such items as metal pots and pans, wool blankets and clothing, guns . . . and whiskey. In return, the natives brought them furs, with beaver being the most valuable. The Dakota adapted to the fur trade without changing the ecosystem of their homeland.

In 1805, soon after the Louisiana Purchase transferred ownership of what's now Minnesota from France to the United States, an expedition led by army officer Zebulon Pike arrived at the confluence of the Minnesota and Mississippi Rivers. A magnificent bluff overlooking both rivers was the ideal spot for a fort, and Pike persuaded the Dakota to sell land that included the confluence and the bluff and, significantly, extended north to the Falls of St. Anthony, which would become the driving force powering development of the region. Construction of the fort was completed in 1822, and it was named after its first commander, Colonel Josiah Snelling. The United States had a foothold in Dakota Territory.

Even before Fort Snelling was constructed, the fur trade was petering out. The value of the furs procured by the Dakota typically fell short of what they owed to the traders, and the traders often didn't make enough to pay what they owed their creditors, enterprises such as the American Fur Company. Eventually, it became apparent that the only way the traders and their employers could make good on their investments was to convince the Dakota to sell their land to the US government.

These land-ownership transactions were called *treaties* and often included provisions such as government payment coming in the form of annuities that would be paid for a number of years. The construct of land ownership (let alone money) was foreign to the Dakota, whose philosophy can be summed up in the term they use to describe the earth and all its inhabitants: mitákuyapi, "my relatives." The terms of the treaties stipulated that the Dakota would be paid for the land, but typically the fur traders insisted the Dakota turn over a substantial portion to them as repayment of debt. The traders, in turn, used a portion of these monies to pay their debts to the fur-trading companies. The Dakota, naturally, did not want to give up their land, but they were well aware that whites had overwhelmed tribes to their east and eventually came to terms with the inevitable.

Invariably, in Minnesota and elsewhere, the indigenous people got the short end of the stick in treaties, and invariably, the United States reneged on its end of the deals. The most notorious of the treaties involving the Minnesota River Basin were the 1851 Treaties of Traverse des Sioux and Mendota, in which the Dakota ceded virtually the entire basin for 12.5 cents an acre. Accounts differ, but the consensus is that at Traverse des Sioux the Dakota were duped by fur trader Joseph R. Brown into signing a separate document requiring them to turn over a large percentage of the payment to the traders, which included Brown and the man who would become the first governor of the state of Minnesota, Henry Hastings Sibley. The Dakota were allotted ten-mile-wide strips of land on both sides of the upper Minnesota River from Big Stone Lake to what is now New Ulm. Then, in 1858, they were forced to sell the land on the north side of the river, where Morton is, because there was so much demand for land by settlers. Where would I have grown up if the government had honored the 1851 treaties? It's likely I never would have written this book.

The US government had been planning for settlers to populate Minnesota for some time. Remember those thin red lines denoting townships on the DNR's Biological Survey maps? They were drawn by surveyors beginning in 1847 following the guidelines of the original Public Land Survey System of the United States. The perfectly straight lines of townships, six miles apart and themselves divided into thirty-six one-mile squares called *sections* (often divided into 160-acre quarter sections), comprise an artificial grid drawn over the landscape. The purpose? To facilitate real estate transactions. While they were at it, the surveyors also mapped out the native vegetation; that's what Marschner used to make his map.

Having acquired the land and mapped it out in easily measurable units, land offices were opened and the government was in business. The 1851 treaty lands began to go up for sale in 1855.

In 1850, there were just over six thousand white people in Minnesota Territory. Minnesota became a state in 1858, and by 1862, the population was about 175,000, with more than twenty thousand Euro American settlers in the Minnesota River Basin, most of them in farm families. They—and the businessmen in the burgeoning urban area that would grow to become the Twin Cities—set about transforming the landscape for a type of agriculture they were familiar with, which was wheat farming. The prevailing belief among whites was that the native population was squandering the potential productivity of the rich prairie soil.

When men like Cadwallader C. Washburn and Charles Pillsbury learned of the awesome power of the Falls of St. Anthony, the ready availability of timber, and the fertile soil of the Minnesota River Basin, they saw dollar signs. They recognized it would be possible, with enough laborers, to transform the prairie into flour they could sell at a profit. In his 1860 inaugural address, Minnesota's first governor, Alexander Ramsey, put it like this: "Give us the capital of more men, of more people, and we will vivify, infuse the breath of life, into the dead capital of millions of acres now growing only prairie flowers."[19]

In the early days, many towns across the basin had their own mills to make flour out of wheat to serve mostly the local population. With the laying of railroad tracks, it became possible to transport wheat to centralized processing facilities. The nascent city of Minneapolis became the thriving "Mill City," and the Minnesota River Basin became "the breadbasket of the world."

A lot more has happened in the last century and a half—the Homestead Act, which incentivized white people to settle here; inventions of increasingly efficient farm implements such as the moldboard plow and steam-powered threshers; the introduction of dairy farming and its gradual consolidation into fewer and fewer hands; development of new strains of maize, some of which occurred in Morton's Renville County, that have

---

19. As quoted in episode 2 of the documentary "Minnesota: A History of the Land," produced by the College of Natural Resources, University of Minnesota, 2005.

A moldboard plow is on display in the Renville County
Historical Society and Museum in Morton.

dramatically increased yields; construction of a nine-foot channel in the
Mississippi River to increase its capacity to transport grain and other commodities; the post–World War II introduction of fertilizers such as nitrogen, another innovation to increase yields—and all of it has been a variation
on the theme of transforming the natural resources of the Minnesota River
Basin into commodities that can be sold at a profit. The unaccounted-for
costs—the downstream costs, if you will—include eroded soil, excessive
amounts of water, and unused fertilizers ending up in the river.

Today's descendants of the Euro Americans who began the transformation of Minnesota's natural resources represent the fifth and sixth generations. I wonder: What will we bequeath to the seventh generation?

Voices for the River:
Clyde and Shirley Ryberg

People who boat the river, either for fishing or cruising, can't help but be impressed with its sense of wilderness, its lack of people, and the variety of wild creatures who live along its banks. Such pilgrims should be naturals to learn the conservation story which they can carry back to their communities and translate into conservation support at the polls on election day.

—SHIRLEY RYBERG

Geri and I are by no means the first to have paddled the entire length of the Minnesota River. I would imagine that countless indigenous people have done it over the centuries and that some 1800s fur traders did so as well. In 1930, teenager Eric Sevareid and his friend Walter Port achieved the feat—traveling upriver—as part of their incredible Minneapolis-to-Hudson Bay journey documented in Sevareid's *Canoeing with the Cree.* For many years, starting in the 1980s, Montevideo high school biology teacher Richard "Butch" Halterman led students from near the headwaters to the confluence with the Mississippi on summertime learning adventures. *Mankato Free Press* writer Tim Krohn and photographer John Cross did it twice—in 1998 and 2008. Also in 2008, another pair of teens, Colton Witte and Sean Bloomfield, essentially retraced Sevareid and Port's journey, starting their expedition in Chaska, about forty river miles from the confluence. Three years later, recent college grads Natalie Warren and Ann Raiho did the same, becoming the first women to accomplish the feat. In 2017, Michael Anderson and Paul Twedt embarked on a mission to remove trash from the river, collecting nearly five thousand pounds of it from Odessa to the confluence. And in 2018, Jay Gustafson, a.k.a. Waterway Jay, paddled from headwaters to confluence as part of his epic—and successful—effort to paddle every mile of every Minnesota state water trail (then thirty-four, now thirty-five) "to galvanize Minnesotans to take pride and ownership of the freshwater ecosystems that make our state unique."

But were it not for the contributions more than half a century ago by husband-and-wife river enthusiasts Clyde and Shirley Ryberg, there may well have never been any Minnesota water trails at all.

In 1962, Evan Jones published *The Minnesota: Forgotten River* for the acclaimed Rivers of America series. He named the book after watching a documentary film, *Forgotten River*, produced by the couple who were instrumental in helping Minnesotans discover the recreational value of their state's rivers.

While the Minnesota River may have been forgotten by most non-indigenous residents in 1962, it was well known to Clyde and Shirley. In 1957, they fashioned a custom catamaran (two canoes lashed together and topped with a platform). Powered most often by a small outboard motor and occasionally by paddle, they embarked on an eight-day excursion from Big Stone Lake to the confluence. Shirley noted, "Muddy or not, the Minnesota is a resource for recreation, transportation, and navigation that the people of this state are almost wholly neglecting. . . . Every bend in the river is different—and every bend is beautiful. And it's all public waters, all 330 miles of it, from Ortonville to St. Paul, for us to freely use."

* * *

A growing interest in outdoor activities had emerged after World War II. Attendance at state parks boomed, as did participation in hunting, fishing, and other forms of outdoor recreation. Many Minnesota lakes became overcrowded with pleasure boats. At about the same time, some US citizens and public officials who were drawn to rivers and canoe recreation pressed for action and, in 1958, the US Congress established the Outdoor Recreation Resources Review Commission (ORRRC), which presented over thirty recommendations to President Kennedy in 1962. The report specifically highlighted canoe and boat routes.

By the time that report was published, the Rybergs and others had already begun promoting river recreation. In 1960, a group of prominent citizen activists, including Clyde and William F. Dietrich, established the Minnesota River Recreation Development Association. They developed a rapport with legislators, the commissioner of the Department of Conservation (later renamed the Department of Natural Resources), the commander of the US Army Corps of Engineers, and others interested in developing the river's recreational potential.

Though elected officials and agency professionals had begun to respond to public interest in outdoor recreation, progress was too slow to satisfy the Rybergs. Clyde urged local communities to not wait for the state but to utilize their own resources to tap into the economic potential of their rivers. One major need he recognized was to remove woody debris from the river. Huge trees that come sailing down the river with most of their branches submerged are a hazard to watercraft. Safety demanded their removal. Support grew, and the legislature allocated some funds, but, again, progress was slow. Clyde took control, heading up a crew to remove snags from the river.[20]

Clyde and Shirley worked with other activists to produce the film *Forgotten River,* which inspired author Evan Jones. The film presented a persuasive case for developing a recreational paradise on the Minnesota as well as the Mississippi and St. Croix Rivers. *Forgotten River* was screened hundreds of times throughout the state and is credited with generating significant enthusiasm for the recreational features of Minnesota's rivers.

Although created primarily to stimulate parts of the country depressed by unemployment, the federal Area Redevelopment Act (ARA) of 1961 directed some money for the out-of-doors. It included strong recommendations highlighting water as a "focal point for outdoor recreation."

Governor Elmer L. Andersen (1961–63) supported an outdoor recreation system in the state and established the Minnesota Natural Resources Council, which, combined with ARA and ORRRC, encouraged recreation on rivers that had otherwise received scant attention.

---

20. At the same time, it must be noted that snags provide a valuable ecological service: they create temporary dams, sometimes even islands, that capture sediment in the channel and create habitat for a variety of plants and animals. Geri and I will be exploring some snags later in our river journey.

Andersen's successor, Governor Karl Rolvaag (1963–66), was himself an avid paddler. He got caught up in the public interest in rivers and declared, "Arouse this sleeping recreational giant—canoeing!" The following year, legislators put forth a bill that identified four rivers—the Minnesota, St. Croix, Big Fork, and Little Fork—to be established as canoe and boating routes and authorized the commissioner of conservation to develop the rivers for recreational purposes. The commissioner was given the authority to mark the routes and work with landowners to acquire land and develop recreational facilities, but there was no funding mechanism. Although stymied financially, the commissioner laid the groundwork. Implementation of the plans was slow, such that some observers felt it would have taken decades to complete the work had it not been for ordinary citizens doing extraordinary things, particularly in the Minnesota River Valley.

The indefatigable Rybergs then went on a mission to finance a survey of the four designated rivers. After finding support from the governor and the conservation commissioner, Clyde approached the Central Marine Association Board, which listened to his plea and gave him $2,000 to begin the work. This resulted in Clyde's "Report on the Minnesota River for the 1963 Legislature" that explained the feasibility of canoeing the rivers; provided a list of services in towns on the river; and identified potential campsites, portages, and access points. Clyde, with Shirley's constant support, was leading the charge for Minnesota's first water trail program.

Also in 1963, the legislature passed a one-cent-per-pack cigarette tax and created the Minnesota Outdoor Recreation Resources Commission (MORRC) to make recommendations for projects from this new source of funding. Little was known about the conditions on the rivers and the degree of public safety concerns, but now citizen involvement, government support, and funding converged to address challenges, identify opportunities, and take action. By 1968, the Minnesota River State Water Trail was well established.

The Rybergs have passed on, but the people they worked with tell us that they deserve considerable credit and acclaim for their leadership in establishing our state's canoe and boating routes. They understood the potential for water recreation and played a major role in the establishment of a water trail system that now includes the Minnesota and thirty-four other waterways throughout the state. I encourage everyone to experience a water trail and, from personal experience, offer a friendly reminder that preparation is key to enjoyment. Two excellent sources of information are the Minnesota Department of Natural Resources' online and printed maps of state water trails and *Paddling Southern Minnesota: 85 Great Trips by Canoe or Kayak* by Lynne Smith Diebel and Robert Diebel. And find out what the current conditions are before you go!

* * *

Nearly sixty years after Clyde and Shirley Ryberg navigated the river from Ortonville to St. Paul, Geri and I did the same. Shirley wrote an article for the *Minnesota Conservation Volunteer* about the Rybergs' experience,[21] and we were excited to look for similarities and differences. We traveled by canoe paddle; they traveled on "a raft which was a platform built on two canoes, powered sometimes by the quiet river current but more often by a seven h.p. Johnson motor." They were thrilled to see a lone pelican; we saw several flocks of them. They saw ducks everywhere; we saw almost none. They never saw a deer; we saw several. They continually encountered cows where pastures bordered the river; the ones we saw were relatively few and far between (though vexatious every time). They also saw sheep, pigs, and a few horses; we saw not a one of these farm animals. We all saw people fishing all up and down the river.

The Rybergs' 1957 river journey brought attention to the challenges and potential of the Minnesota River, and their contributions live on to this day. A tip of the paddle to these evangelizing pioneers. Geri and I are honored to follow in their wake—and we can't wait to get started!

---

21. "Floatin' Down the River" (November–December 1957). The article opens with "There's an untravelled wilderness pathway close to 75 percent of Minnesota homes—and almost no one uses it." It's available online.

Starting at the Source . . . If We Can Find It!

I have made . . . surveys of this same river [the Minnesota] from

its junction with the Mississippi up to its sources; which are

not, as was supposed, at the foot of the Coteau des Prairies, but

among a magnificent group of lakes upon the plateau.

—JOSEPH NICOLLET

The town of Browns Valley, Minnesota, population 589, sits on two boundaries: one political and one geographical. Its city limits share a boundary with the Minnesota–South Dakota border, and it sits on a continental divide: to the north of the divide is the Red River Basin and to the south is the Minnesota River Basin. Nearby, the moraine dam that contained giant glacial Lake Agassiz burst, releasing its torrents of water—the glacial River Warren—and carving out the Minnesota River Valley we know today. Browns Valley is in the middle of the River Warren channel on a low feature that formed after the floods waned—a small alluvial fan deposited by the Little Minnesota River that flows from South Dakota and empties into the Ancient River Warren Channel where the river is no longer large enough carry away the sediment.

What is an alluvial fan? One of the many unusual features of the Minnesota River Valley, an alluvial fan is a deposit of sediment and silt that builds up at the confluence of a tributary and a larger river. It forms a partial dam, backing up the water in the larger river to form what looks and acts more like a lake than a river. Rivers elsewhere typically don't have alluvial fans forming every time a sediment-laden tributary enters, but in short order after Big Stone Lake, we will encounter Marsh Lake and Lac qui Par-le, both partially dammed by tributaries that are carrying more sediment than the modern Minnesota River is able to carry away—and in recent times both dammed by people who wanted to exert more control on the flow of the river.

Geri and I have arrived in Browns Valley with great anticipation and no small amount of preparation. The car is topped with canoe and loaded with tent, sleeping bags and pads, paddles, water bottles, bush clothes, camera, a dented, blackened cook pot, food, and other paraphernalia, including our Secchi tube for measuring water clarity. My childhood dream to paddle the Minnesota River from its source to its confluence with the Mississippi in St. Paul is about to get under way.

After an obligatory stop to read the Browns Valley Man historical marker (see "People"), our first task is to try to figure out precisely where the Minnesota River begins. Before we left home, I had asked a DNR water recreation director if he knew the actual source of the river. He was not sure. I also contacted the US Army Corps of Engineers and asked them what they consider to be the official headwaters of the Minnesota River and how they make such a determination. The reply? They do not have a technical process to make such a decision and that it is often driven by historical events rather than scientific evaluations. The Corps has accepted Big Stone Lake, just south of Browns Valley, as the headwaters. I got a similar answer from a scientist with the Minnesota Geological Survey. I was also aware of a sign at the foot of the dam at the outlet of Big Stone Lake near Ortonville, some forty miles south, that declares the river begins there.

As I look at my US Geological Survey map, it appears there are two other contenders. In the northeast corner of South Dakota, the Little Minnesota River meanders southeast, gaining water from the modest Standfast Creek and Jorgenson River. It flows a few miles past Browns Valley before emptying into the top of Big Stone Lake. Based on the map, I suspect the Little Minnesota might qualify as the Minnesota River's source. Another South Dakota river, the Whetstone, flows farther southeast than the Little Minnesota and releases its waters at the bottom of Big Stone Lake. In fact, an alluvial fan deposited by the Whetstone is what created Big Stone Lake.

We drive to the west end of Browns Valley on the South Dakota border, park the car at the US Army Corps of Engineers wayside rest, and begin exploring. We are at the southern tip of Lake Traverse, on the continental divide. Water here flows north from Lake Traverse into the Red River of the North to Winnipeg and ultimately to Hudson Bay. A concrete dam, maybe a dozen meters wide, replaced earlier natural conditions. No water flows south toward the Little Minnesota this day. A depth marker stands at the western edge of the dam, an indication that sometimes water here spills into the Minnesota River Basin.

I set out on foot in search of other water sources that might have a connection to the Minnesota River. There is a small wetland across the road from the wayside on the south side of the dam. Though I see no water flowing there, the south end of the pond narrows and turns west out of view. Along the highway, a drainage ditch runs for over half a mile where I discover a pond rimmed with cattails. A gravel road there turns south, marked by a sign that says, "Travel at your own risk. Road minimally maintained. Bridge out." Just our kind of road! Perhaps it will lead us to the source. We hop back in the car and drive down the deeply rutted road only to discover it dead ends in a farmer's field. We see no bridge. We do see another grown-over drainage ditch heading south in the direction of the Little Minnesota River. We find ourselves at marshy places at every turn.

Lacking strong scientific consensus and failing to find an obvious place ourselves, Geri and I decide that, for our goal of paddling the entire length of the Minnesota, the Little Minnesota River shall be considered the source of the Minnesota River. The first practical place to launch our canoe appears to be where it flows past Browns Valley. We will begin our journey there and paddle upstream toward the source as far as we can get.

We drive to the south edge of town, pull the car off the road, don life jackets, and carefully step downhill toward the slick, muddy bank of the Little Minnesota. We put paddles, rope, and water bottles into the canoe as usual, as well as our Secchi tube for periodic measurements of water clarity.

We slip the canoe into the chocolate-brown water and begin paddling. The Little Minnesota is flowing furiously here, and the racing current quickly swings us downstream. We paddle hard to work our way back upstream. The river here is perhaps twenty-five meters wide. Tree branches lean out over the water, making paddling tricky and progress slow. We make it to a bridge, under which there's a bit of calmer water. Facing us are two long branches protruding far out over the water and more branches stretching out from the opposite bank. Beyond them, the river bends out of sight. To continue, we would have to swing wide, out into the racing current. We paddle in place, pondering our predicament. Given the force of the current and the lurking, leaning limbs, we decide continuing upriver is not prudent. This is as close to the source as we can get. We turn around and continue downstream, on the lookout for an appropriate place to get a reading with our Secchi tube.

A short stretch of smooth water appears. I back-paddle to hold us in place while Geri submerges the Secchi tube, filling it with water. She lowers the disk into the tube until it is no longer visible, notes the depth, then slowly raises the disk until she can see it again. She averages the two values and records the clarity at 17.5 centimeters, about seven inches. Dirty water.

The river widens and we continue downstream, eager to get a better feel for the Little Minnesota, but what we see around the next bend changes our mind. A veritable canopy of low-lying branches arches across the water from both sides, making further travel difficult if not downright unsafe. We made it up the Little Minnesota from Browns Valley as far as we could get to the source and were thwarted from paddling a meaningful distance downstream. Out of necessity, we revise our goal from paddling every mile of the Minnesota River to paddling every *possible* mile. We will drive south to the first safe spot to put in, set up camp, and paddle from there up the Little Minnesota as far as we can back toward Browns Valley. Consulting the map, we see that the Little Minnesota flows south and east out of Browns Valley. It meanders through four or five miles of wetlands then widens considerably, so much so that the name of the river changes from the Little Minnesota to Big Stone Lake. The first place to launch a canoe is at Big Stone Lake State Park, about twenty miles south of where the Little Minnesota ends and Big Stone begins. We decide to set up camp at the park and in the morning paddle as far as we can from there upriver toward Browns Valley. Sometimes, in order to reach one's goal, it's necessary to take a step back.

From Big Stone to the Little Minnesota and Back

You must live in the present, launch yourself on every wave, find your eternity in each moment.

—HENRY DAVID THOREAU

Morning has broken. We launch onto Big Stone Lake and paddle fifty meters offshore for a Secchi measurement. Geri can see the disk a full meter down. The contrast with the river measurement from the day before is stark. While flowing rivers stir up sediment, creating turbidity, lakes are more sedate, allowing all but the finest grains of silt to settle to the bottom. Today, this lakelike part of the river is dead calm, smooth as glass.

After a few miles of paddling, we notice a narrow point of land projecting out into the lake. There is a sandbar just off the point, and it is covered with huge, white birds. American white pelicans! I do a quick count and estimate there must be at least sixty of these magnificent creatures with their preposterous, yet practical, pouched bills. I am thrilled but not surprised to find them here; they are drawn to large lakes. All stand stoically, staring at us. They start to fidget, uncertain as to our intentions. We keep our distance. Any closer, and the flock could take flight. While I would love to admire their nine-foot wingspans in action, I don't want them to waste precious calories just to distance themselves from us, so we back away. The pelicans settle down, and we watch them through binoculars.

The epithet *birdbrain* certainly does not apply to pelicans (nor to birds in general). Geri and I have watched groups of pelicans band together in a circle, surrounding their aquatic prey, then suddenly plunge heads beneath the water in unison, returning to the surface with captured fish in their gular pouches. We have seen pelicans on a wilderness Canadian river line up on a narrow rock ledge by a rapids and take turns diving for fish. The bird at the head of the line slips into the water, gulps down a fish, and returns to the back of the line. Pelicans often fly in formation with wings spread wide, gliding a mere inch above a placid surface. It is a magical sight, one we hope to observe sometime during our river journey.

In the distance, we see the north end of the lake, and as we approach, its shoreline turns to green and splotches of tan left by last year's broken cattail stalks. We land at a beach covered with organic debris, flotsam[22] left by waves. We watch several cows amble down the bluff to drink from the lake. Like the pelicans but less nervous, they stop to look us over. Posts supporting a wire fence imply a farmer's intent to keep his animals away from the lake. But the animals all seem to know about the hole in the fence and head to the water to relieve themselves, dropping urine and cow pies with the nitrogen, phosphorus, and *E. coli* bacteria they contain, adding to the chemical load the Minnesota River must bear. The bank is lined by a curtain of cattails with tall, thin, dark green blades. These appear to be the invasive narrowleaf species, which tend to dominate areas where they grow, crowding out other plants, including the native broadleaf cattail. The leaves of both species are long and cylindrical, resembling, as you might expect, a cat's tail. Narrowleafs have negligible nutritional value, while the broadleaf is nutritious—not to mention tasty as Geri and I can attest. Its leaves make for a good salad green; the stems are tasty when roasted; young shoots can be boiled like asparagus; even the pollen can be used as an ingredient in pancakes. The two species often hybridize; unfortunately, the hybrid is also not nutritious.

We continue paddling slowly along the shore and finally encounter breaks in the cattails where channels reveal themselves. The South Dako-

---

22. One often hears the terms *flotsam* and *jetsam* used together. *Flotsam* is debris from natural sources or ship-related accidents. *Jetsam* is debris deliberately tossed overboard.

ta shore is looming larger as we wend our way north and west. At some point, we will have crossed the invisible boundary in the middle of the lake that separates our two states. Then a much larger channel appears; we have reached the confluence of the Little Minnesota and Big Stone Lake.

We paddle up the river awhile—nice little river!—but a loud siren emanating from we-don't-know-where prompts us to turn around. Revised mission accomplished: we have paddled every possible mile of the upper end of the river.

Within sight of the confluence, where the chocolate-brown water of the stream joins the clear blue water of the lake, we see a bright yellow object. A plastic yellow ducky is bobbing happily along with the current. Geri captures it and shows me the number 91 indelibly marked on its bottom. In Browns Valley, we had heard folks talking about a ducky race for kids on the Fourth of July, shortly before our visit. Summertime water levels are often so sluggish that the ducks must be nudged along by their owners to make a race of it. But this year, the water was so high and the current so vigorous, it wasn't possible for kids to wade the stream to guide their ducks, and the plastic creatures raced off for parts unknown. I expect many eventually got hung up in vegetation and dead-end waterways. Perhaps Number 91 is the leader of the flock.

At the confluence, the sediment is settling out in similar fashion to the alluvial fans we encountered. This is a natural process, although farming practices that involve sending runoff from land to river as quickly as possible are accelerating it.

A brisk wind is whipping up whitecaps. I turn the canoe into the waves, and we work our way toward the Minnesota shore. It will take vigorous paddling to get back to camp. We are relieved to reach "Pelican Point" (now unoccupied), where we can get closer to shore, more protected from the waves. We pull into the landing at the state park as the wind calms. Our campsite is a few steps away from where the vegetation of the land meets the water lapping at the shore—a good place to rest and reflect.

Around the campfire, my thoughts turn to Joseph Nicollet, a scientist-geographer who, in 1843, produced the first map of the hydrological basin of the Upper Mississippi, including the entire basin of the Minnesota River. I own a copy of this map that has been called the greatest contribution made to American geography. Compare it to modern maps, and you will see that Nicollet's map is remarkably accurate. It shows what he considers to be the headwaters of the St. Peter's River (the early European American name for the Minnesota): a small river carrying water off the north end of the Coteau des Prairies. That stream on today's maps is called the Little Minnesota. One can track on Nicollet's map the Little Minnesota as it leaves the Coteau initially flowing southeast, then picking up a small feeder stream as it bends east. One can see where the Little Minnesota is subsumed into Big Stone Lake. Nicollet's credentials as a geographer are impeccable. His conclusion is confirmation for me. A bit reluctantly, I must admit that the source of our state's namesake river is in South Dakota. Oh well. I swallow my Minnesota pride and smile knowing that "our" river carries its name into a neighboring state. Tomorrow, we will wave good-bye to South Dakota, and the rest of our journey to the confluence will occur well within the borders of Minnesota.

* * *

Morning comes. I emerge from the tent and set two bowls of Geri's home-made granola on the table, add powdered milk and water, and let the mixture soak until it's ready to eat.

Well nourished, I go sit for a moment of reflection in the silent, moored canoe. I hear tiny water droplets falling—*drip . . . drip . . . drip*—from the stem of a sedge leaning out over the river, making the tiniest contribution to the river's flow. Every drop counts. I contemplate how the flow will grow as we make our way toward the confluence. Gradually, I come to the realization that my search for the very beginning of the Minnesota, or any river, is misguided. A river is less a specific place, a single geographical location, so much as it is a gathering of myriad contributors that give and sustain the life of a river. Every drib or driblet brings coherence to the flow, becomes the flow.

We break camp and drive south on a beautiful road along the lake (it's the first stretch of the Minnesota River Valley National Scenic Byway) to a city park that lies just below the dam in Ortonville. A sign proudly proclaims that this is the source of the Minnesota River. I won't dispute the point with the local officials or anyone else in town. And they do have a legitimate claim to the distinction, at least as far as the name is concerned; the river isn't called the Minnesota River until it flows past the dam. Up to this point, Geri and I have been paddling on the Little Minnesota River and Big Stone Lake.

Just downstream from the dam, the mouth of a tired Whetstone River yawns from the South Dakota shore. A line of steel pipes stands guard in the water, dissuading boaters from traveling upstream. A gaggle of pelicans bob up and down below the dam, and we watch as they organize themselves, plunge in unison, and pop to the surface, with a surprisingly high percentage of pouches containing a wriggling fish. Suddenly I'm hungry again.

A thin, weathered man bikes into the park toting fishing rod and tackle box. We invite him to join us for lunch. He works for a landscaping company and comes here nearly every day to fish. He says he and his friend are particularly fond of walleye. I sense life has been tough for him and that fishing is his outlet.

"Time to fish," he says. He walks to the dam and casts into the river's turbulence a bit downstream from the pelicans. A few minutes later, he returns to our spot and asks, "Do you like northern pike?"

"We sure do!" exclaims Geri.

"I've got one here," he says. "Do you want it?"

He pulls a two-pound pike from a plastic bag and hands it to us. We thank him, talk a bit more, then he returns to fishing and we hop in the car to seek out ice for the fish, which we will enjoy for dinner tonight somewhere downstream. A lovely man and a lovely fish. Geri and I have received a double gift from the river this day. We look forward to a fine fish dinner and to dreaming about what new gifts tomorrow may bring from the Minnesota River and the generous people who love the river as much as we do.

Refuge

A national park is not a playground. It is a sanctuary for nature and for humans who will accept nature on nature's own terms.

—MICHAEL FROME

Just south of Ortonville, the Minnesota River meanders for about forty-three river miles within Big Stone National Wildlife Refuge. Our original plan was to launch at the upper end of the refuge and work our way downstream. But both DNR and Wildlife Refuge staff warned us of logjams and snags in the first thirteen river miles, making it risky for paddlers. They strongly suggested we avoid that segment.

In my youth, I was a bit of a daredevil on the water. But getting married changed my perspective. On my first few paddling adventures with Geri, I was cautious. How could I live with myself, let alone face my father-in-law, if imprudence had led to disaster? But I soon learned, to my delight, that Geri is not averse to a little risk-taking herself. Through many years and thousands of paddling miles, we have always balanced risk with safety. Today, as usual, we will heed the advice of the experts. Our maps reveal that we can get on the river just west of the tiny community of Correll and paddle upstream to the south end of the obstructions.

We drive west from Appleton and turn off "the tar" (as folks who live where there are lots of gravel roads often refer to a paved highway) onto one of those gravel roads heading south. We soon reach a concrete bridge spanning the Minnesota River and park at a tiny boat launch. I carry the canoe to a gravel shore, and we begin loading the gear.

A pickup hauling two men and a boat pulls up, and we stop to chat. They are surprised at our plans to paddle upriver, apparently believing that going up the creek without a motor is an arduous undertaking. Actually, it's not as difficult as it may seem, I explain. A river's edge has irregularities along its banks: a jutting point, a protruding rock or fallen log can slow a small portion of the river's main flow. These obstructions create eddies (swirling currents) that can literally reverse the water's flow, giving paddlers a bit of a boost upstream and a moment of rest.

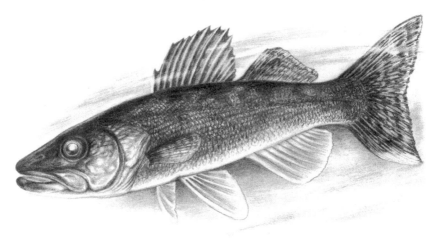

Minnesota's state fish, the walleye, is a popular target for anglers throughout the Minnesota River Valley.

The fishermen tell us they are angling for walleye. Now Geri and I are the ones who are a bit skeptical. Walleye? In this shallow, chocolate-colored stretch of the Minnesota River? They assured us they are usually successful, but I can't help feeling they're just having a little fun with a couple of city slickers.

The fishermen get on the water before we do and pause to give us one last bit of advice: Not far upstream, the river splits into two branches. We must keep to the right to avoid the twisting channels and backwaters on the left. We thank them and will try to memorize landmarks to keep from getting lost on our return. We launch, paddle up to them, and wave. One is already reeling in a fish. He holds it up for us to admire and exclaims,

"Walleye!" Well, I never! But in the coming days and weeks of paddling, Geri and I will learn that walleye are commonly caught most everywhere on the Minnesota River.

Our arms can sense the tug of the current against us, but paddling is far from strenuous. As always, we are happy to be underway. The river here is maybe 250 feet wide. It will get progressively narrower as we travel upstream today.

We're staying on the right as instructed, but nevertheless our channel periodically bifurcates, sending off side channels that we quickly discover are dead ends surrounded by dense islands of dark green cattails. The Minnesota River here wanders, seemingly aimlessly, within a large wetland complex. Its world seems one of endless clusters of cattail islands within passageways of open water that branch, then disappear. In places, the cattails are ten feet tall. Their long leaves bend over our narrow waterway, creating welcome shade on this sultry July day.

As we paddle, we come upon stands of reed canary grass and *Phragmites,* a common reed. Both are unwelcome invasive species that crowd out native plants. In some places, I find spaghetti-like tubes with elliptical leaves swaying just below the surface. They are members of the *Polygonum* genus, smartweed. I have seen smartweed in rivers when it's in bloom, with beautiful pink flowers emerging at the surface. We're too late in the season to see the floral show on this trip.

Reed canary grass is a perennial, cool-season grass up to six feet tall that forms large, single-species stands. It spreads rapidly and is a major threat to native wetland species. It was introduced here in the 1800s as forage for stock animals and erosion control. *Phragmites* also outcompetes many native wetland plants. It can spread by runners up to sixteen feet per year, gets upward of fifteen feet tall, and has very long leaves for a grass— eight to nineteen inches. The native version of this plant does much less damage to wetlands than the type that came to America from Europe. We are seeing only a few scattered groupings of these two species. I wonder if they cannot tolerate the water levels along the cattail littoral zone.

I am puzzled that we have seen only a few ducks, but Geri reminds me it's not migration season. Her father, an ardent hunter and fisherman, often regaled me with stories of traveling from their suburban Minneapolis home in the 1940s and '50s for the fabulous hunting in this part of the Minnesota River watershed. The water level in these cattail clusters also looks good for birds such as American coots, pied-billed grebes, and sora, but we aren't lucky enough to see any.

A significant decline in wetland habitat across the continent, including a devastating 90 percent loss in the Minnesota River Basin, has greatly reduced the number of waterfowl even during migration. Wetlands have been drained, ditches have been dug, prairies have been plowed, and subterranean drainage systems have been installed to make the land suitable for large-scale agriculture. We grow huge amounts of such commodities as corn and soybeans, but we destroy habitat and despoil water in the process. A balance must be found.

We paddle backward out of a dead end and return to the main flow. How wide is the river here? Only an airplane pilot or a bird could say.

Carp are ubiquitous. We hear them snorting along the banks. They often jolt us as they bump into our paddles or swirl away from the canoe in a panic. They are so plentiful I believe one could fill a washtub with a net in no time. At one spot, we hear a commotion at the shore and paddle over to discover a carp yanking on a root, apparently trying to drag the whole plant into the water.

Carp! And to think we brought them on ourselves. I rue the day in 1883 when railcars arrived in St. Paul from Washington, DC, with live fish. Word has it that these fish were considered to be such delectable eating that guards were posted to keep people from stealing them. When young, carp eat mostly vegetation. As adults, they eat almost everything else—aquatic insects, crayfish, minnows, the list is long. They can survive in degraded waters where most species can't. By stirring up lake and river bottoms, they block sunlight for aquatic plants. With their hose-like mouths, they vacuum up food, including seedpods. These fish have very keen senses and are adept at detecting both predators and prey. They prefer muddy and sandy bottoms. The warmer the water, the more active they become. This scorching-hot day that is rapidly draining my water bottle is to their liking and helps explain why we are seeing so many.

We meet small flotillas of mayflies drifting downstream. Mayflies and numerous other insects play major roles in aquatic food chains. Most mayfly species do not tolerate polluted waters, so their presence here is encouraging; it means the water is clean enough to support them. I think of the walleye the fishermen caught back near the landing. Clean water = more mayflies = more walleye. As John Muir wrote, "Everything is connected to everything else in the universe."

* * *

As we go farther upriver, we encounter fewer cattail side channels and more open riverbank. The place where river meets land, the riparian zone, is a narrow strip that is the meeting point of two ecological systems. The riparian zone serves as a transition between water and land and is critically important to the well-being of a river. By buffering the river from runoff laden with sediment, fertilizer, and other pollutants, and by helping to establish rooted plants, the riparian zone plays a major role in holding soil and other materials in place and slowing down the water flowing overland into the river. As a paddler and camper, I find riparian zones delightful. They give a place character and an aesthetic presence. And they are a magnet for wildlife. Water levels can fluctuate dramatically in a riparian zone, so different types of wildlife may occupy it at different times.

Periodically, we pull the canoe to the bank to explore the riparian zone. The ground is flat as can be; it's a floodplain, created by the river when it overtops its banks and the slack water releases its sediment. The composition of riparian vegetation ranges widely, from clusters of tiny green plants with threadlike roots penetrating the soil to large stands of reed canary grass and *Phragmites* six-plus-feet tall. Shade-tolerant wood nettle is also common and stands a few feet tall in dense patches, their leaves forming an unbroken canopy. Just a touch gives a sharp sting that thankfully dissipates quickly. Nettle tends to thrive where there has been an invasion of earthworms, dumped by fishermen, that restructure the soil, allowing only species that are tolerant of the changed conditions.

The riparian zones in this stretch of the river reveal evidence of very recent flooding, troubling in July. Farmers have explained to me that, for them, flooding in the early spring may disrupt their planting schedule, but a summer flood that leaves water on the land for more than a couple of days will destroy their crops. I silently express hope it was a short-lived flood that left behind the detritus I'm seeing along the banks today. Still, I know and farmers know that tile drainage, installed now in agricultural areas throughout the basin, is a significant contributor to flooding. Even small rain events at inopportune times can cause major damage as water rushes through the tile directly to the river.

We paddle past a stand of dead trees scarred by fire high up their trunks. Fire in such a wet environment is curious. I surmise that in a dry year, lightning or a careless fisherman's match triggered the burns. We also observe that the wet-soil habitat attracts a particular cohort of tree species. Sporadically, clumps of willow adorn the banks. In Minnesota, we have more than a dozen willow species, and they are notoriously difficult to distinguish. But the sandbar willow is almost certainly the species we are seeing. Welby Smith, in his book *Trees and Shrubs of Minnesota,* describes the sandbar willow as a large shrub, common in the prairie region, and found on riverbanks, sandbars, floodplains, and prairie swales. On occasion, we also see cottonwoods and silver maples. In the vast grassland of the upper Minnesota River Basin, trees near water can survive, protected from windswept prairie fires. But even some of these riverbank trees seem to have narrowly escaped.

* * *

The river swings back and forth. On an outside curve, the flowing water eats away at the bank, while on an inside bend, there is an accumulation of mud and sediment and occasionally a small bit of sand, building a protruding bulge. Periodically, we hear a splash as a chunk of mud plops into the water. Erosion. The recent floods saturated the banks. As the water level drops again, the sodden banks are weakened and susceptible to calving off in chunks.

We round a sharp bend and eye an immense rock the size of a Volkswagen Beetle that takes up half the river's channel. We pull to the bank to admire this huge monolith. Its surfaces are well rounded, well worn. You might think, as some early geologists did, that it suffered a long journey in a slow-moving glacier or the icy waters of glacial River Warren to reach this spot. But in fact, it was most likely revealed by floodwaters washing away the saprolith—the rotten rock—that buried this corestone that has been in this valley for billions of years. Geologists today can tell because it matches the type of rock that is exposed in the valley here instead of a type from some distant place.

As we work our way upriver, we occasionally get a glimpse of the bluffs, way off in the distance, that rim this great valley. Sometimes we see the South Dakota side, sometimes the Minnesota. The temperature is well into the nineties and the humidity feels the same. The river bends sharply to the north. Our map tells us we are nearing the thirteen-mile risky section authorities warned us about. The river has narrowed markedly; the closer you get to its source, the smaller a river gets.

There's a lot less water in my water bottle too. Definitely time to turn around. I take a sip, and we point the canoe downstream. Before long, we're back in those confounding cattail side channels. But we follow the current, tick off our landmarks, and are able to navigate the maze with few wasted paddle strokes. As the river widens, the proper direction becomes progressively more obvious.

* * *

A squadron of cormorants, black as pitch, flies above us heading downriver. They use any open water for capturing fish. Decades ago, in the era of the deadly pesticide DDT, populations of cormorants (as well as bald eagles and other birds) plummeted. When the lethal pesticide was banned, populations of cormorants rebounded rapidly. Now some fishermen express irritation that their avian counterparts are taking too many fish away from humans, and in some places, the DNR takes active steps to reduce the number of cormorants. I expect other fishermen actually appreciate cormorants for gulping down significant poundage of carp, which is good for the native walleye.

The Minnesota County Biological Survey assessed breeding birds in the Minnesota River Valley counties and found 167 species. We have heard a variety of birds on the river, many of them little songbirds. One that would have been easy to identify, had we seen it, is the brilliant-yellow prothonotary warbler. They're found in floodplain forests, particularly in stands of silver maple, where they nest in cavities in trees hanging out over the water.

Keeping a canoe on course while fumbling with binoculars and trying to identify birds all at the same time is a recipe for capsize—something we have never done, in part because when one of us wants a magnified view, the other steadies the canoe.

With its striking appearance and raucous call,
the yellow-headed blackbird must be seen and heard to be believed

Sometimes birds afford us both a good, naked-eye look. While we're drifting toward the landing, a large flock flies across the river in front of us and lands in a tree with a cacophony of clamoring. Yellow-headed blackbirds! A favorite of mine. My quick count is around sixty. Yellow-headeds are birds of the marsh. I am overjoyed at finding them here on the wetlands of the Minnesota River. Their screeching call has been described by ornithologists as like the sound of a rusty gate turning on its hinges, but it's music to my ears.

* * *

We round a bend to refind the fork in the river the fishermen had directed us to avoid, and the bridge comes into sight. And not a moment too soon: my water bottle is dry, the pangs of dehydration are setting in. I promise myself not to let that happen again.

As we drift under the bridge, a massive flock of cliff swallows takes flight from the mud nests they've built on the underside of the structure.

We reconnect with our fishermen friends. The high water this year gives motorboats more river to explore than would normally be the case. When I ask if they had caught more walleye, they smile. "More than enough to take home," came the reply. What they wouldn't have been able to eat for dinner they released back into the river for the next angler—whether human or cormorant.

Voices for the River:
Lemuel Kaercher

*It is the long history of humankind (and animal kind, too) that
those who learned to collaborate and improvise most effectively
have prevailed.*

—CHARLES DARWIN (ATTRIBUTED)

The Whetstone River, a tributary on the west side of the Minnesota, deposited sand and silt at its mouth, creating an alluvial fan. It backed up the water on the main stem, creating what we know today as Big Stone Lake. After a long period of drought in the 1930s caused a severe drop in water levels, public pressure to do something to stabilize Big Stone grew. Minnesota's response was to obtain funds from the federal Works Progress Administration (WPA) to build a dam at Ortonville. The idea was to replace the natural alluvial-fan dam at the outlet of the Whetstone with a controllable structure that could hold back water during periods of drought and release it when the lake reached capacity. The mouth of the Whetstone would be moved to prevent sediment from accumulating on the upstream side of the dam. The WPA completed the dam in 1937, establishing an average lake depth of eight feet and a maximum of sixteen.

With a relatively stable depth, Big Stone Lake and Ortonville became popular fishing and resort destinations. As time passed, however, the quality of the water began to suffer. Silt deposition, runoff from agricultural operations, and municipal, industrial, and resort wastes led to severe eutrophication, a term derived from the Greek for "well-nourished." It's a condition in which excessive amounts of phosphorus and various forms of nitrogen, referred to collectively as *nutrients,* stimulate aquatic algal and plant growth. Mixed with bottom sediment, the nutrients can transform a relatively clear lake or stream into one that looks more like pea soup. In 2002, Minnesota became the first state in the nation to enact a law severely restricting the use of phosphorus for residential lawns for this reason.

But use of phosphorus for agricultural purposes was (and is) not restricted. Nutrients run off into rural waterways and fuel the growth of aquatic plants. With increasingly dense algal blooms degrading the aesthetic qualities of Big Stone Lake, people were put off by the smell and frustrated by a buildup of sand and silt that inhibited boat traffic. The concerns were exacerbated by several years of high water levels and serious flooding. Some folks argued that the "improvements" should be removed to redirect the Whetstone back into its natural flow into the Minnesota River. Others worried that altering the Whetstone might have negative consequences downstream for Lac qui Parle and for agricultural operations.

In stepped a man named Lemuel Kaercher, editor of the Ortonville *Independent* newspaper. Lem, as he was known, was concerned about the increasing degradation of Big Stone Lake's water quality and the subsequent decline of fishing and resort business. The lake had become a smelly pool of green scum. Frustrated with the absence of action, Lem began advocating for collaborative solutions. He convened a meeting in October 1955 that drew an impressive crowd, including congressional representatives, legislators from Minnesota and South Dakota, the chief of planning and development from the US Soil Conservation Service (now called the Natural Resources Conservation Service), officials from the US Army Corps of Engineers, and concerned citizens. Lem's persistent activism eventually led to action: in 1965, the Corps was given authority to address the problem. They developed a plan for transforming and expanding a marshy area into a twelve-thousand-acre lake—Marsh Lake—by building a dam on the Yellow Bank River, which flows from the west to the Minnesota, and, to mitigate for the loss of inundated habitat, a national wildlife refuge a few miles north but still in the Minnesota River watershed. Big Stone NWR was established in 1975, one year before the Minnesota Valley National Wildlife Refuge was established at the other end of the river.

Kaercher used his newspaper to keep the authorities on their toes by publicizing goings-on and providing full coverage of every problem and potential solution confronting citizens, agencies, and elected officials. For fifteen years, Lem scheduled meetings, flew to Washington to testify before congressional committees, drove to St. Paul to meet with state and federal officials, and kept local interests involved in the project. He was successful in securing funding, often before agencies were prepared to spend the money.

When the dam was dedicated in 1974, Lem was eighty-two years old, and there was still much work to be done to clean up Big Stone Lake. Challenges remain to this day, including an excess of nutrients especially at the north end of the lake. But water quality overall has improved from hypereutrophic to eutrophic, resulting in shorter algal blooms and increased recreational use of the lake. Thank you, Lem, and everyone who has carried on his legacy of Big Stone Lake stewardship. We will keep you in our hearts as we continue our journey downstream.

Lakes in the Middle of the River

Time spent on rivers is more than recreation; it can be re-creation in the finest sense—a renewal of the spirit, a refreshment of the mind, a reinvigoration of the body.

—TIM PALMER

Our experience of Big Stone Lake behind us, Geri and I now prepare for Marsh Lake. After a trip to Appleton for water, food, rest, and time in the city library gathering local history, we decide to drive west from town back to the same gravel road and concrete bridge from where we had paddled upriver yesterday, only this time we will direct the canoe south onto Marsh Lake.

Marsh Lake is well named. With a maximum depth of five feet and water clarity less than a foot, it is essentially a huge, 4,500-acre wetland complex and reservoir. Lakes have an established shallow near-shore area, the littoral zone, where most of the plant and algae growth occurs. It begins where land meets water and extends out to where sunlight can still penetrate to the bottom and sustain rooted aquatic plants. This productivity creates the food web that supports the rest of the aquatic creatures. All of Marsh Lake's 4,500 acres are littoral zone, where floating leafed plants, submerged plants, and algae can produce huge quantities of organic matter, rich in nutrients, which die and decompose on the lake bottom.

Life jackets on, paddles cutting the water, we become part of the transformation of a river into a lake. The river lake broadens quickly as we leave the landing, initially forming a flow perhaps the width of a football field but widening considerably after about three-quarters of a mile. The current slows, and the river begins to look and feel much more like a lake. We have to paddle to maintain our forward progress.

Numerous islands stretch out before us. This was one of my father-in-law's favorite places to hunt ducks, and at this moment, I vividly recall his stories of rescuing less experienced hunters who had gotten lost in the seemingly endless green byways. Geri and I make careful mental notes about landforms and other features to help us avoid a similar fate. A light wind blows from the south, and we paddle a short distance along shore to get our bearings, although it's not altogether apparent exactly where the shore actually is.

We come upon our first cattail-bordered bay and note it as a landmark to help us find our way back. We move offshore to explore two elongate cattail islands that look like emerging submarines. The wind has picked up, creating choppy water and bouncing the canoe along, so we head to the sanctuary of a small bay and stop to get a bead on where we are. As we look for landmarks, nothing is immediately recognizable. Apprehension subsides when we spot a farm with two tall silos that we had noticed upon first entering the lake. Bearings regained.

Numerous corestones jut out at and just below the surface, presenting an obstacle course that could chew up the blades of a boat motor. Anglers and recreationists in gas-powered vessels can enjoy the lake when the water is higher, but today, only watercraft like the ones first used millennia ago can ply these waters. Oh, the time-honored joy of a canoe with its three-inch draft.

Although we have not yet seen any fishing boats on the lake, its rich organic mass supports a food web that produces sustenance for aquatic life in great abundance. It is not for want of fish that the lake is without fisherfolks this day. Indeed, another two-legged fish lover, the American white pelican, is a frequent sight here. Nesting mostly on islands in the lake, pelicans here form one of the three largest colonies in North America (the other two being in North and South Dakota).

Minnesota DNR netting data for Marsh Lake reveals the presence of eight game species and six rough-fish species. Ranking the number of each species caught by nets puts common carp at the top of the list.

Given all the carp we saw upriver of the lake and the ideal habitat here, I am not surprised.

Second in rank is bigmouth buffalo, a member of the sucker family. It prefers the slow-moving, shallow water of rivers, lakes, and streams. It is also tolerant of warm water and can survive extremely low oxygen levels that would kill nearly all other Minnesota fish. Netted commercially for food, the bigmouth buffalo can grow to well over fifty pounds. Ironically, these behemoths subsist on tiny tidbits of food—microscopic zooplankton.

The walleye fishermen we met at the landing upriver a day ago knew what they were doing; the third-most caught species in the DNR nets is walleye. Walleye populations in Marsh Lake are sustained by both natural reproduction and stocking and vary year to year.

Other fish species of interest to anglers are channel catfish; northern pike; freshwater drum; black and white crappie; bluegill; northern pike; largemouth, white, and rock bass; and black and brown bullhead.

The ecology of a lake is different from that of a river in many ways. For one thing, a river's current adds a continuous rich supply of oxygen to the flowing water. Without this turbulence, oxygen levels in lakes can vary greatly and are less reliably sufficient for aquatic life.

Food webs also differ. In lakes, the food web is based on photosynthesis that produces organic matter that feeds a rich variety of aquatic creatures called *plankton,* an assemblage of tiny organisms no larger than a carrot seed. Plankton are eaten not only by bighead buffalo but also by small minnows that, in turn, are eaten by larger, carnivorous fish such as walleye. In rivers, the food web comprises an incredibly rich diversity of animal life, including crustaceans, aquatic worms, and aquatic insects. The main energy source powering life in the river is detritus, partially decomposed organic matter such as leaves that provide food for aquatic insects such as mayflies that, in turn, become food for fish.

In a river, what's here today will be gone downstream tomorrow. Nothing is stable. I think about the river species that leave their turbulent habitat in the river and flow into this lakelike environment. The dramatic reduction in velocity must befuddle river creatures.

The wind dies down, and we meander to the north side of the lake to explore several large bays and more clusters of cattail islands sprinkled among patches of open water. While the lake is a mosaic of interwoven cattail islands and open water, it is broken occasionally by scattered clumps of reed canary grass and *Phragmites* where the lake and river have gathered together a patch of soggy organic soil.

As we begin paddling back into the mouth of the river, we encounter a jungle of sapling willow trees rooted in wet, black organic soil at the edge of the water. We work the canoe onto a narrow sandy shore and eat lunch among this dense grove of willows an inch in diameter and standing over ten feet tall. Though the ground is littered with dead willow stems, a canoe party could camp there for the night. We make a mental note of that but decide to end our day by paddling back to the car.

* * *

The next day, we drive a short distance out of Appleton on Highway 119 to a landing by twin bridges over the Minnesota River and paddle two and a half miles upriver to the base of the Marsh Lake dam. It's slow going as we work our way through dense plant coverage, our paddles continually getting hung up. In some places, skinny tree limbs lean out over the river ten feet above the surface. They are covered with dead leaves, twisted twigs, and other debris forming a sort of canopy—revealing that the flow of the river last spring was a good ten feet higher than it is today. Paddling would have been a real challenge had we been here when that torrent rushed through.

Besides the encumbering vegetation in the water, our paddling is slowed by numerous gatherings of carp. We have apparently arrived at their spawning season this warm July day. I should have expected as much. Carp are particularly attracted to flooded backwaters. Photoperiod and water temperature inspire these grand gatherings. Carp, carp, everywhere. The fish continually bump into one another and the canoe, evincing no fear of our presence. They break the surface and dance around with noisy, writhing splashes, sometimes even piling on top of one another. Each female can carry up to a million eggs, and she can reproduce several times a year when conditions are right. Eggs and hatched young are rapidly devoured by birds, aquatic insects, crayfish, and fish, including carp themselves. Despite this intense predation, carp populations remain robust.

An hour later, we stop underneath a railroad bridge and examine the immense superstructure. I wonder what it would be like to look up at the belly of a moving train from the seat of a canoe. There's no such serendipitous moment today, so we paddle on.

As we round a bend in the river, we see the Marsh Lake dam. Like other dams along this part of the Minnesota River, it was built to hold water and thus reduce flooding downstream. We paddle to the west side of the dam, rope the canoe to a tree branch, and climb onto the dam to explore. Its structure is unlike any I am familiar with. Two mounds of stones protrude fifteen feet above the level of the lake. They are separated from each other by a 150-foot stretch of flat stones over which a trickle of water dribbles out of the lake and meanders downslope to the river below. At the east end of the dam, a sluiceway funnels the lake water in a rush of whitecaps to the river channel below. Two hundred feet downstream, a pod of pelicans rides the waves, anticipating fish for lunch.

We walk back along the base of the dam to the canoe, cross the river to the east shore, beach the canoe, and start eating lunch as a man in a pickup drives up. He tells of high water this spring that flowed well above the picnic table where we're eating. This confirms my interpretation of the source of the debris we saw suspended in the trees earlier in the day, and I suspect the lake may have even overflowed the dam. Just FYI, the man in the pickup adds, this side of the dam is a popular place to fish.

Back on the water, the river's flow carries us downstream from the dam to the railroad bridge, and we retrace our route as the river spreads itself into the expansive wetland. Given the density of aquatic plants, one wonders if a river even exists here. The carp bump into the canoe like drunken sailors.

When we get to the car, we are just a few miles northwest of where Highway 40 crosses over the last big river lake, Lac qui Parle. We quickly stash gear into the car and head to the Milan Bridge. What a great opportunity to see miles of lake in both directions.

At the bridge, we find a boat access and twenty camper trailers spread out along the lakefront, but no people. We park the car in a tiny gravel lot across the highway from the campground. Several paths lead from the parking area down to a series of beach lines, fine sand above, coarse sand below, and well-worn gravel half above the waterline and half below. A fishing dock extends out over the water with a fisherman waiting patiently for a bite. Two fishermen stand above us on the bridge, kibitzing and dangling bait in the water below, occasionally giving a tug. Moments later, one of them pulls up a fish—a freshwater drum.

Lac qui Parle is about half the size of Big Stone Lake and, at 574 acres, about one hundred acres larger than Marsh. Its water clarity varies from 1.3 to 5 feet, somewhat clearer water than on Marsh, but less clear than Big Stone. With a maximum depth of 15 feet, the entire acreage of the lake is littoral zone, making it eutrophic: highly productive. The Lac qui Parle Dam at the foot of the lake adjusts water levels to minimize flooding, so spawning is highly successful some years but a bust in others. This happens to be a good year; the DNR reports that natural reproduction of walleye has produced some of the strongest year classes on record, with similar results for white bass and freshwater drum. Fish populations have their ups and downs over the years; sometimes crappie, channel catfish, northern pike, bluegill, and yellow perch are also present in the lake.

Suddenly, I am aware of a disgusting flotilla of algae and aquatic plants in the eddy current just downstream from the highway. A strong smell of feces emanates from it. I am puzzled. We have experienced nothing like this since we set out from Browns Valley. What explains the presence of this obnoxious odor? I suspect there is no proper disposal of sewage back at the trailer camp, enabling waste to find its way into the lake. A sign in the small parking lot exhorts, "Keep our river clean."

We drive back to Appleton to replenish food, then return to the library to learn more local history. From there, we walk a few blocks to a park where the Pomme de Terre River, a major feeder stream to the Minnesota, meanders through town to release its flow into the Minnesota River.

We park again at the twin bridges and unload the canoe on the south side of Highway 119, where the lake begins along a narrow, passive flowage that parallels the highway. But to get to the open lake, we must penetrate a dense stand of cattails that extends several football fields long and as much wide. Conventional wisdom has it that one ought never stand up in a canoe. I beg to differ. In circumstances like this, one simply must stand in order to look out over the terrain and spot passageways. Geri and I paddle hard at multiple slots in the cattails but to no avail. We back up to the flowage, carry the canoe across a gravel strand beside the road to escape the cattail thicket, and paddle out into open water.

A gray sky and choppy waves come at us from the southeast. Occasionally, a larger wave sprays the canoe's bow. In light of these conditions, we decide to work our way into the northeast corner of the lake, where small channels with aquatic plants will keep us close enough to shore in case conditions get worse. We discover rocks just beneath the surface the hard way and move farther out from shore to prevent further scrapes.

Although we feel able to handle the waves, we notice that much larger ones are appearing farther down lake. A light rain sets in, and out comes our rain gear. Given the increasing frequency and intensity of those white-caps, we decide to turn back toward the landing as rain begins to fall more heavily and distant thunder rumbles out of the west, soon followed by lightning. We paddle furiously. I notice a car has stopped on the highway and the driver is watching us. He drives off only when he sees we are out of harm's way. Good Samaritans live in rural Minnesota.

By the time we get the canoe back across the gravel bar, the heavens have really opened, and two waterlogged paddlers scramble into the car. Rainstorms are tolerable on the water. Lightning storms are dangerous. Wet as river rats, we head shivering for Appleton and a motel room's hot shower and spend the rest of the day ensconced in the library.

* * *

Our son and daughter-in-law, Per and Margie, and their children, five-year-old George and two-year-old Ingrid, have agreed to join us on a day's paddle to explore the southern end of Lac qui Parle. Geri and I arrive at Lac qui Parle State Park early and look over the map of campsites. The park has a campground up on the bluff and another down in the floodplain, close to the lake. The staff person at the desk senses my attraction to the water and quickly, strongly, advises us to take the high ground. "Mosquitoes," she intones. "Mosquitoes are pretty bad down along the lake." Geri immediately says, "We'll take the upper." Our family joins us in late afternoon at our campsite, which has a spectacular view of the lake and the magnificent bluffs that frame the valley of the Minnesota River. The grandkids, already veterans of paddling trips in northern Minnesota's Boundary Waters Canoe Area, are excited. Our plan for the next morning is to drive west over the Lac qui Parle Dam and then a few miles north to Boyd Landing, launch our canoes, and paddle back across the lake to the campground.

As we're finishing our oatmeal breakfast, the wind picks up considerably, and Per and I decide the two of us should go check out the conditions at our planned launch site. First, we drive down to the lower campground, where we'll be able to see the Lac qui Parle River as it flows into the Minnesota. We get out of the car, and immediately we are swarmed by the most aggressive mosquitoes I have ever encountered, more so even than the hordes that assaulted me in Alaska's far north. A missionary, Dr. Thomas Smith Williamson, established Lac qui Parle Mission in 1835. He lamented, "This country where the mosquitoes in summer and the cold winds near all the rest of the year render comfortable meditation . . . for the most part out of the question."

With no hesitation let alone meditation, Per and I retreat to the sanctuary of the car. Arriving at Boyd Landing, our intended launch site, we see large whitecaps pounding away at the shore. Not good. We return to our camp on the east side of the lake, where the water is calm as glass as far as we can see. Our family spends the day paddling Watson Sag and circumnavigating Rosemoen Island and other smaller islands near the dam. We steer the canoes into every dead-end bay and swag. Unlike most sections farther up the lake, the lower reaches have extensive wetland shores and small wetland bays.

Geri and I began taking our kids canoeing when they were still in diapers and discovered that toddlers and older kids alike can have great fun in a canoe. We are delighted that George and Ingrid can accompany us this day. Their fun begins with paddles made by Grandpa tied to the canoe, allowing them to swish away. But the real joy for the kids is all the new "toys" they discover: floating things, flying things, swimming things, jumping things, and a rich array of newly discovered aquatic plant life with their diverse shapes, smells, textures, and designs.

We end the day out on the big lake on water mirror-smooth, silently watching a group of pelicans and another of cormorants resting on a tiny offshore island. Three generations of the Nelson clan are spellbound.

* * *

After a few days of R&R back home, Geri and I return to the Milan Bridge. The conditions are favorable, so we launch and paddle north to where the rain and big waves ended our first try. This time, to my surprise, the odor of sewage—so prevalent when we were last here—is gone.

As we head north, we are pushed along by a tailwind. A flock of cliff swallows, fifty birds or more, darts past us over the water. We probe a backwater bay dotted with a long line of floats apparently supporting a massive net. We paddle over, pull up a float, and find there's no net attached. Is it for fish capture for only certain times of the year? I don't know. Anglers work in mysterious ways.

In a marshy bay, we pull to shore. I walk up the bank and discover a cattle trail. A herd of Black Angus watches me a football-field distance away. They seem perplexed at my presence. Farther up the slope, I discover two signs that share a single post. The east-facing sign says, "Wildlife Management Area / Hunting allowed." The west-facing sign says, "Hunting not allowed." I wonder if the deer and other critters know which side is which.

Willows dominate the shore with a flank of cottonwoods standing farther back from the water. We find much wild grape and honeysuckle, a few ash, and some small trees in the cherry family. Box elder and a few soft maples dominate the canopy. Wild gooseberry bushes grow in the shade of the riparian forest.

The wind continues to push us along among modest waves and, after exploring several indented bays, we can see just ahead where we were forced to turn around that rainy day. We turn south to face a headwind, but the canoe cuts the waves like a champ. We have no trouble making steady headway. We reach the bridge and continue downstream until we come to where we had paddled with Per and Margie and the grandkids. The big lakes in the middle of the river are now behind us. As the author of *For Love of Lakes,* I begin to muse about what other lakes there are in the Minnesota River Basin that Geri and I might one day explore.

Lakes of the Upper Minnesota River Basin

A lake is an archive of all that we do. What we do to the land and to the air, we do to the lake.

—DARBY NELSON IN *FOR LOVE OF LAKES*

It is July, warm and with more than enough hours of daylight to do plenty of exploring each day of the two weeks Geri and I have allotted for our examination of Minnesota River Basin lakes. We've been planning this trip for a long time, and we're itching to get started. Working off our checklist, we load canoe, life preservers, paddles, lunch sacks, water bottles, sunscreen, and water-quality instruments, including the trusty Secchi disk, and head out.

Lake Amelia is in Pope County, near the top of the Minnesota River watershed. It's the source of the east branch of the Chippewa River, which flows southwest to join the Minnesota River at Montevideo. As we drive north from Olivia on US Highway 71, we notice we are getting out of the relatively flat corn-and-soybean country of southern Minnesota and into much hillier terrain. The retreating glaciers bequeathed a much different landscape here.

At Amelia's large, well-maintained launch site, two boats are being detached from their trailers. Seeing several powerboats down lake, we decide to paddle the other direction. Amelia is 934 acres, making it one of the larger lakes on our itinerary. The shore is ringed by seasonal cabins and year-round homes. We make our way far out onto the lake. Our eyeball test indicates that the water's clarity is excellent, and the Secchi reading confirms it: two meters (6.5 feet). Geri also measures the depth: fourteen meters (45 feet). The Minnesota DNR's LakeFinder website, an invaluable resource, reports similar water clarity and a maximum depth of twenty-one meters (69 feet).

Back along the shoreline, Geri gleefully shouts, "*Chara!*" She has spotted one of the muskgrasses (actually, a multicellular macroalga), easily identified by their skunk-like odor. An older couple on their pontoon is curious about our excitement. We paddle over to them, share our Secchi data, and explain that *Chara* help keep the water clear by holding sediments in place on the lakebed and consume nutrients, which would otherwise be feeding blue-green algae. The couple has been enjoying Lake Amelia for many years and told us that twenty-five years ago, you could see twenty feet down into the lake. "We noticed the difference in water clarity when our neighbors started using lawn services and a farmer was spreading manure on the field just across the road. It's no wonder the lake isn't as healthy as it used to be." They said that they had a natural buffer strip on their shoreline to reduce erosion and were disgusted at fellow residents who put rock along the shore. These people truly love their lake and understand how to protect it.

Not far from Amelia is Lake Minnewaska, one of the largest lakes in the entire Minnesota River Basin at just over eight thousand acres. Clearly, this is a major recreation site. On each side of the lake, in the towns of Glenwood and Starbuck, there are municipal swimming beaches and public access sites for boaters. We arrive at the one in Glenwood and are stunned by the huge marina with cars and boats everywhere. It reminds us of the popular recreational lakes up north. As we walk along the boardwalk, we find Eurasian water milfoil in dense patches and many zebra mussels. We decide not to put the canoe in this lake for fear of spreading the invasive species to the next lake on our journey. Not to mention, we're more than a little wary about launching our light Kevlar canoe out into the fray of speeding boats and Jet Skis zipping every which way.

Our next stop, just a few miles south of Minnewaska, is Signalness Lake (also called Mountain Lake) in Glacial Lakes State Park. From the moment we arrive, we're enthralled. The park has a spectacular landscape of glacial features: hills and valleys, native prairie, wetlands, and several lakes. In our fifty years of marriage, Geri and I have visited many and varied beautiful places in Minnesota; this gem immediately gets added to our list of favorites.

After a quick drive through the park, we launch onto Signalness and are struck by its crystal-clear water. We paddle past patches of the odoriferous *Chara,* pond lilies, and native milfoil—no invasive species in sight. Some kids are in the water on paddleboards and canoes (available for rental), others are at the swimming beach, and a few more with their parents dangle lines hopefully from the fishing pier. Geri points out "baby" lily pads as she calls them; these stems will soon be flowering. Secchi depth is 3.5 meters (11.5 feet). We wish we had brought our snorkeling gear.

As we return to shore, we meet a man from Fargo who has come here for the last five years. His kids are playing in the water. He sees we are about to lift our canoe onto the car and offers to help—I must look older than I feel. I thank him for the offer. Geri and I explore the campground and vow to bring our kids and grandkids here for a vacation next summer.

We leave Pope County and enter Swift to check out Hassel Lake. We get the impression we're the only ones who have used the boat launch lately. The map tells us that there are several Minnesota Wildlife Management Areas (WMAs) and US Fish and Wildlife Service Waterfowl Production Areas (WPAs) nearby, but the land immediately surrounding the lake is all cornfields. Secchi depth is thirty-five centimeters (about one foot). A cormorant flies over the lake, and we are eyewitnesses to the fact that pelican pee is brown (or maybe it's that pelicans poop runny brown poop). At least one species of *Potamogeton,* commonly known as *pondweed,* is abundant. (There are dozens of species, and distinguishing them is difficult even for aquatic biologists.) *Potamogeton* provides important habitat and spawning sites for fish, and it is also one of the most important waterfowl food plants on the continent. A mix of algae and several other dense masses of aquatic vegetation are also present.

On a sticky, hot July day, we stop in Benson for gas and much-needed ice cream cones and then head east about twenty miles to Monson Lake State Park. There is only one other car in the parking lot. Out on the dock, we see clusters of brownish aquatic plants. Not enticing. Monson is a relatively small lake, just 208 acres. We find lots of snails of different species and many beautiful damselflies and dragonflies. A thin line of trees borders part of the lake, while a cornfield abuts about a quarter of the shoreline. We note that the farmer has established a fifty-foot buffer, and from the look of it, he has been maintaining that buffer for years. We paddle to mid-lake and discover Secchi depth of one meter, about three feet (slightly below the average reported on LakeFinder), in water 6.7 meters (twenty-two feet) deep. Two cormorants wing by overhead as we munch on peanut butter and jelly sandwiches.

We leave Swift County and enter Yellow Medicine to explore Wood Lake.[23] We walk the shore and find not only dense clusters of stringy algae but also blue-green scum on the shore. We launch the canoe and paddle out into the 485-acre lake to record a Secchi depth. The lake is choppy, making Geri's task difficult. It finally calms enough for her to get the number: only twenty-five centimeters (less than ten inches)—about half the average reported on LakeFinder. Choppy water tends to stir up sediment from a lake bottom, reducing clarity significantly.

We leave Wood Lake and drive alongside cornfields on both sides of the road en route to Lyon County's School Grove Lake, a stone's throw south of Lady Slipper Lake. We find it at the edge of a gravel road and note an overgrown parking area. Water at the edge of the shore is surprisingly clear around patches of stringy algae. Flocks of swallows dive for insects off the calm surface of the lake. We find bulrushes, genus *Scirpus,* a welcome contributor to the health of a lake. A guy towing a small motorboat pulls into the lot but pulls right back out, apparently disappointed to discover he's not alone. A deer runs along a cornfield and ducks in. We paddle along the western shore and find a beautiful beach, then notice blue-green algal scum. I hope no farmer's dog wades in to lap up water here. Geri finds this lake has a Secchi depth of 1.6 meters (just over 5 feet) in water 2 meters (6.5 feet) deep. As we load our gear into the car, a man walks toward me from a

---

23. The misnamed Battle of Wood Lake was the final armed conflict in the US–Dakota War. The battle actually took place across the river several miles south, at Battle Lake, a.k.a. Lone Tree Lake.

farm building across the road, seemingly curious about our presence. I ask if it was okay to be on the lake, and he assures me it was. I get the impression he is pleased to see some intrepid paddlers there. Six pelicans glide out over the water.

With canoe roped to the roof of the car, we cross over to Lincoln County and Lake Benton. We find the public landing at the end of a long beach, thick with mats of green algae along the shore. We see only two motorboats off in the distance. The water is dead calm. Thanks to the scholarship of geologists, we know that this seven-mile-long lake was formed in a tunnel valley beneath glacial ice. We paddle out onto a greenish, shallow lake. Water clarity is 90 centimeters (just over 35 inches), and depth is 2.25 meters (about 7.4 feet). I doubt we'll be returning here for a family vacation.

Voices for the River:
Del Wehrspann

Improving the quality and reducing the quantity of water reaching the Minnesota River via drainage systems is an essential step in making the river fishable and swimmable.

—"WORKING TOGETHER: A PLAN TO RESTORE THE
MINNESOTA RIVER" (MINNESOTA RIVER CITIZENS'
ADVISORY COMMITTEE)

Del Wehrspann has lived with his wife, Shirley, along the river outside of Montevideo for many years. Their house is a two-minute walk to the flow, and their property includes a spring-fed stream and backwater. As an avid hunter and fisherman, Del has come to know the river and its quirks and character intimately. He grew up an Iowa farm kid and has been a cattle buyer in the region for half a century, so he is intimately familiar with farmers and the business of farming. Del is also a river rat. His knowledge of the river is legendary, and people from all walks of life come to him for advice. The US Fish and Wildlife Service has formed a working group investigating the ecology of catfish in several backwaters, including Del's, where they found over twenty species of fish. People who visit Del and Shirley, Geri and me included, often get a pontoon ride on the river and a fine catfish meal.

Del was one of the first people in the Upper Minnesota River Basin to advocate for sound environmental practices to clean up the Minnesota River. For many years, he received scant support for his advocacy and much opposition, some overt and some subtle.

In Del's words:

In the 1970s, the city of Montevideo chose to expand to the east side of town. For this expansion, it was necessary to facilitate storm water drainage. City and county officials collaborated with local farmers to dig a drainage ditch through some of the last privately held wetlands in Chippewa County. The Clean Water Act of 1972 exempted agriculture, so draining these wetlands and passing polluted water and sediment into the Minnesota River was an easy sell. The farmers would get a free drainage ditch. My pointing out the negative consequences to water quality was not appreciated, and the science was ignored.

A granite outcrop a mile from the Minnesota River had contained these wetlands through the centuries. "There's one hundred feet of fall in the one mile between the outcrop and the Minnesota River [a relatively steep drop over that distance]," Del explained. "An independent engineer estimated that as a result of breaching this granite outcropping with the ditch, an additional 2,300 tons of sediment would be deposited in the Minnesota River every year. Yet nobody but me cared about that." County Ditch 69A was built.

* * *

Disappointment about the ditch and a cold shoulder from many of his neighbors did not deter Del. "In the 1990s, I was a part of a committee that was given an assessment by the scientists as to what was causing the pollution and flooding on the Minnesota. The evidence was clear. Agricultural drainage and channel straightening had started the problem."

The scientists Del refers to conducted the Minnesota River Assessment Project, a comprehensive four-year study of the river by a broad collaboration of agency and academic experts led by Wayne Anderson of the Minnesota Pollution Control Agency. Their work produced the scientific data on which the Minnesota River Citizens' Advisory Committee based its own research and recommendations. The committee's final report, "Working Together: A Plan to Restore the Minnesota River," has been an influential resource in the cleanup effort. He is too humble to have told Geri and me, but other members of the Citizens' Advisory Committee have related to us that Del was regarded as the conscience of the group.

Back home, though, Del was still catching flak from farmers and others in the community. They often made life difficult for him and his family as he continued to speak out on behalf of the river.

> At a livestock auction in western Minnesota, two influential farmers approached me before the auction began. One sat on each side of me. I had been speaking out about a project they were involved in which would straighten the west branch of the Lac qui Parle River and drain wetlands. It was an incremental project. In itself, it would not make a big difference in what was happening to the increased pollution and flooding to the Minnesota River. But, to my mind, this assault for additional crop production had to, at some point, stop. One of the farmers said, "Now, Del, we know people in high places. You either forget about challenging this little drainage project, or you can kiss any hope you have for cleaning up the Minnesota River good-bye." I did not take this threat lightly. I brought the issue to CURE, a new group in Monte with a mission to Clean Up the River Environment. With their help, the issue was brought before an administrative law judge, and the project was not allowed.

In another incident, the City of Montevideo was fined for dumping thirty thousand gallons of raw sewage into the Minnesota River. A new resident, Patrick Moore, wrote a letter to the editor of the local paper decrying this state of affairs. Del tracked down Patrick, introduced himself, and told him, "Thank you for writing that letter!" Del had been pressing authorities on the sewage treatment plant for some time; finally, he had an ally.

About that same time, Del learned of another voice for the river downstream in New Ulm. Fishing guide Scott Sparlin planned to convene a large gathering of people concerned about the conditions of the river. Del and Patrick attended Scott's first Riverblast, and they determined to recruit many more people from the upper part of the basin for the next one. Del and Shirley set about creating a database of people they could contact. They understood the importance of spreading the word to everybody they knew. Patrick later told us that he and Scott followed Del's lead as they organized their communities to advocate for the river.

Del played important roles helping various other environmental groups concerned about the Minnesota River, including the Sustainable Farming Association and a Montevideo office for the Land Stewardship Project. The goal of both groups was to develop farmer-to-farmer learning around transitioning away from chemically intensive, water-polluting methods of growing food. Del also served on a committee to help folks understand the nature of the regional community.

Today, unfortunately, Del sees agricultural assaults to the environment continuing and efforts to reverse the trend challenging. "The price one must pay for exposing the hypocrisy of these assaults is sometimes subtle, but it is real. The farmers as individuals are good, caring people, but they have become slaves to a corporate and political system they must agree to, or they, too, will 'pay the price.'"

As Geri and I continue our canoe trip on a river that cuts through farm country, we will be reflecting on what Del told us and thanking him for his lifelong commitment to a clean Minnesota River.

Underwater Drummers

The face of the water in time became a wonderful book . . . which told its mind to me without reserve, delivering its most cherished secrets as clearly as if it had uttered them with a voice. And it was not a book to be read once and thrown aside, for it had a new story to tell every day.

—MARK TWAIN

Lac qui Parle behind us, the next stretch of the river will take us from the foot of Lac qui Parle's Churchill Dam to the bustling community of Montevideo. It has been about two months since we have dipped our paddles in the Minnesota River. Autumn has descended, and we look forward to experiencing the river in a different season, a refreshing change from the ninety-degree days at the beginning of our episodic journey.

Montevideo is situated where the Chippewa River, one of the Minnesota River's largest tributaries, flows into the main stem.[24] In the early days of the community, a Mr. Peterson owned a large Indian dugout canoe and ferried travelers back and forth across the two rivers.

A landmark on Main Street in downtown Monte, as the locals call their town, is the canoe adorning the facade of the headquarters of CURE (Clean Up the River Environment). Founded in 1992, CURE is a highly effective nonprofit with a focus on building community as a means of improving water quality. Its emphasis on inclusivity based on a mutual love of

---

24. At 2,080 square miles (1.3 million acres), the Chippewa River basin comprises about 10 percent of the Minnesota River basin. The Dakota name for the Chippewa is *Maya Waka wapan,* meaning "remarkable river with steep places."

the river has been credited not only with improvements to the area's habitat and water quality but (along with the opening of the Java River Café) with a resurgence in the vitality of the community of Montevideo itself.

We call CURE to inquire about logistical help on our journey. Dixie Tilden, CURE's veteran office manager, answers amiably and says she would be delighted to shuttle us upriver to our launch point. We drive into town midafternoon and meet Dixie. Rich conversations ensue, and we gain another kindred-spirit friend. We agree to rendezvous at the riverside city park at eight o'clock the next morning.

To our surprise, we discover that every motel in town is full except one that's in the middle of remodeling. Given our circumstances, the congenial manager there agrees to let us stay in a not-quite-completed unit. The accommodations are more than adequate for a couple of paddlers who have considerable experience pitching a tent in inhospitable places and inclement conditions.

* * *

It is a cold, gray morning, and the wind blows out of the north—downriver. At breakfast, Geri and I strike up a conversation with two men in the next booth. They tell us, "We're from Bemidji.[25] Come here for a little pheasant hunting." Aha! That explains why there was almost no room in the inns; 'tis the season, and pheasant hunting is big business in this part of the state.

We meet up with Dixie after breakfast, and she rides with us the seven miles north to the dam. When we've unloaded the canoe and gear, she takes off in our car and will have it waiting for us back at the city park.

Steep banks along the river below the dam require us to carry canoe and gear the length of a football field to the launch site. Five pelicans float off the far bank, which rises seven feet above the water's surface today.

Paddling in autumn reveals a different river, a different floodplain forest, a different riparian zone. Falling leaves sashay slowly, back and forth, back and forth, lowering themselves closer and closer to the water, becoming tiny boats as they join the flotilla of their kin. Watching those leaf-boats

---

25. Bemidji is some two hundred miles northeast of Montevideo, not far from the headwaters of the Mississippi in Minnesota's North Woods.

float at the whim of the flow, I think of Yellow Ducky Number 91 from the kids' race at Browns Valley. We are all yellow duckies at times, going where momentum takes us, but perhaps canoeists are a little duckier than most.

Around a bend, an eagle nest rests high in a tree across the river, supported by three large branches. No birds are home this time of year.

On the inside edge of the next bend, a sandbar offers an opportunity to pull to shore and explore the floodplain. I want to ascertain how high the water had risen in spring's flow. I climb up the bank and find the land surface festooned with flotsam washed up by high water and stranded when the floodwaters receded. There are downed trees of all sizes and shapes, in all stages of rot.

To better understand the impact of the river on the surroundings, I decide to walk west, away from the river. As Geri, an avid reader, dives into John Sandford's mystery *Shock Wave,* set in the Minnesota River Valley, I start thrashing my way through twenty-five yards of vegetation, some places thick, others thin, before reaching open space. The land spreads out before me, maybe a mile into the distance, before it meets the bluff formed by the glacial River Warren thousands of years ago. How high did the water encroach onto the land this spring? Strewn here and there are tree branches of notable heft. It would have taken a formidable force to move them to where they lie. The water had to have been a good eight feet above today's flow.

A short distance away, rows of soybeans lie, stems flattened to the ground. None of the plants made it to maturity. I see the farmstead in the distance. Fertilizer, seed, and tractor fuel—not to mention the farmer's hard labor—washed away by a late spring or summer flood. Farming in the floodplain is a risky proposition. Wiser, I think, to farm on higher ground and let the floodplain serve its natural purpose.

Farther west and slightly downslope, I find a small wetland, rich in plant species that thrive in conditions such as this. I suspect this floodplain marsh slurped up a goodly amount of the river's water this spring.

Far off to the west at the base of the bluff, another part of the farmer's field has long, robust rows of corn awaiting harvest. A slightly higher elevation saved it from a flooded fate. I make my way back to the river to find Geri still engrossed in her book. We fuel up with a Clif Bar and head back out on the river.

* * *

We are sharing the river with a double-crested cormorant. Its rich, glossy black coat is easy to spot a quarter mile downriver as it perches on a log leaning out over the water. As we near, the bird gets skittish and flies off downriver to another overhanging branch. The behavior repeats itself several times, the bird burning energy to keep us at a safe distance. As we near the next bend, the bird flies over us back upriver and alights about where we first met. I suspect when he's not avoiding us, he's fishing—which, in his case, involves diving and swimming underwater. Cormorants usually fish alone, bring their catch to the surface, maneuver it into the gullet, and swallow it whole.

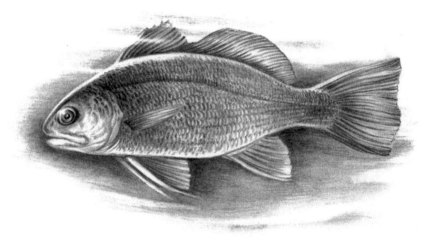

Freshwater drum, a.k.a. sheepshead, thrive in slow-moving, cloudy water.

The river curves and we ride the current to midstream, where Geri notices a cluster of small silvery fish floating dead in the water just off the bow. I pull hard on the paddle, close the distance to the cluster, and see there are five of them, all about six inches long and two wide. At first glance, I do not recognize the species. I scoop three into the canoe for a closer look, and their identity is revealed. All species of fish have a visible, thread-like structure called the *lateral line* that runs from base of head to base of tail. It's a sensory structure enabling fish to detect vibrations and currents as well as predators and food sources. The lateral line on the fish I hold in my hand carries past the base of the tail into the tail itself. That feature identifies this fish as a freshwater drum. The moniker *drum* comes from the grunting, drumming noise it produces by rubbing a unique set of muscles against its swim bladder. The sound is most often heard during breeding season.

Drum are native across the Americas from Hudson Bay drainages to the Mississippi Basin to streams in Mexico and Central America. Here in Minnesota, freshwater drum are often called *sheepshead,* while Louisianans and other southerners call them *gaspergou.* The drum's slight humpback reminds one of a bass. It is a sluggish fish that prefers muddy waters. Its mouth structure, aided by its ability to use its forehead to move small stones aside, allows it to eat a wide variety of foods, including small fish, aquatic insects, crayfish, and mussels. The average weight caught by hook and line currently runs around two to three pounds. A hundred years ago, biologists found them to grow to fifty to sixty pounds; the Minnesota state record is a tad over thirty-five pounds. The size of the specimens I'm looking at indicates they are this year's young.

Historically, drum have been recorded as carrying incredible numbers of larval mussels. A type of mollusk, mussels have a fascinating relationship with fish. They reproduce by producing larvae that must attach themselves to a fish's gills to mature, then release themselves from the fish and go on to complete their development. So, drum eat mussels but also play a vital role in their development. Given the drastic drop in mussel populations in the Minnesota River decades ago, drum have been forced to shift their dietary habits. Mussel populations have shown a slight increase recently, to the benefit of drum.

Archaeological studies reveal that Stone Age people ate drum. While I have never caught or eaten drum, Tom Dickson, author of *The Great Minnesota Fish Book,* says, "Containing delicious, white, bone-free fillets, the drum is a superb food fish."

* * *

We notice the charcoal remains of a fire on a gravel bar surrounded by four-wheeler tracks that disappear into the woods. I expect local farmers and their kids enjoy the river as much as we do.

We begin to see scattered clusters of plants, with stems up to four feet tall, clinging to the riparian edge. The plants are beautifully arrayed in bright red and yellow, in sharp contrast with the brown and gray of our surroundings. I'm a little chagrined that I cannot identify them. I jot down a description and Geri snaps a couple of photos. We will do some research back home.

Finally, we encounter a fellow human being, the first we have seen since launching at the dam. It's a man in camouflage standing on the bank beside a bright yellow four-wheeler. Our greetings carry clearly across the river, and I quickly sense a kindred spirit. He is bow-hunting for deer. I speculate he'll be successful, as Geri and I have been seeing deer tracks whenever we've explored onshore. He is surprised that we are paddling all the way to Montevideo in this late season.

We hear our first guttural call of a pheasant in the distance. Perhaps the hunters we met at breakfast will be successful as well. We have been seeing many kingfishers and great blue herons and ongoing flights of cormorants up and down the river. Now we see our second eagle nest.

We pull to the west shore at a trickling stream by a boat launch named Camp Release, where the Dakota–US War of 1862 finally ended with the release of 269 white prisoners and the surrender of about 1,200 Dakota. Adjoining the boat launch is Camp Release State Monument, which was dedicated in 1894 and features a fifty-one-foot-tall obelisk. The site today includes interpretive signage about the war.

To this point, the river has followed a relatively straight line from northwest to southeast, with the northerly wind nudging our canoe downstream. But here the river changes, taking on a series of sinuous loops. Now we paddle north in the face of the wind, now we loop back south, now north, now south loop after loopity-loop. This section of the river resembles the teeth of a carpenter's ripsaw. The car ride from the city park in Monte to our launch site was about seven miles; by river, the distance is more like fifteen.

A short distance down the beach, I see a densely packed collection of tiny mollusk shells, an indication that water quality here is at least tolerable. Each shell is about the size of my fingernail, and in fact, their common name is *fingernail clams*. What a feast they might make for a freshwater drum.

Geri spots a mink with its blackish-brown fur bounding along a fallen tree on the other side of the river. Aside from raccoons and deer (and the deer hunter), this mink is the first mammal we have seen. At an agricultural drainage conference in Willmar earlier in the year, we had met a young man who works for the public works department there and traps several days each year. When we described how few mammals we had been seeing in our early paddling, he laughed. "There are so many! I can trap a hundred mink per week in a good year and the same number of raccoon and muskrats." He explained that when the market for pelts is good, there are twenty to thirty professional trappers plying their trade in the basin.

Mink are proficient hunters both in water and on land. They are the major predators of Minnesota's leading furbearer, the muskrat. Under most conditions, the interaction of the two species is well balanced, and both can be harvested on a sustained-yield basis. When mink dive, they swim like fish, catching minnows and other aquatic animals. On land, they catch small birds and rodents. They are most common where downed trees or rocks provide shelter along lakeshores, marshes, streams, and drainage ditches. Mink are found broadly across the entire Minnesota River Basin, although wetland drainage and stream channelization have reduced their numbers.

When I was a sixth grader in Morton, my friend Wayne invited me to join him in setting up a trap line at the base of the bluff not far from our house. Approval came from both dads and the landowner, and we were off. As I observed the operation, it seemed to me that Wayne really knew what he was doing. At seven the next morning, we anxiously ran to the traps, and found nothing. Day two, no luck. Day three, bad luck: a skunk, dead. Not knowing what to do next, two eleven-year-olds ran home and alerted the adults. The landowner graciously removed the carcass for us. My trapping days were over.

* * *

As we pull to shore for lunch, we notice behind us several huge piles of sand or gravel that resemble ancient Egyptian pyramids. I would guess the largest to be at least thirty-five feet high. Commercial operators have apparently found a sand-and-gravel bar or terrace from River Warren and piled it into the pyramids we're looking at now.

We navigate yet another of the river's loops and spot the mouth of the Chippewa River. The 130-mile-long river drains a large watershed—2,085 square miles—and delivers a significant amount of water to the Minnesota. We paddle hard to get through the confluence, then make our way upstream into a tired, sluggish river for a quarter mile. The heavily eroded banks say, "A torrent of water during spring thaw will flow out of bank in its headlong race to the Minnesota. Paddlers beware."

We float back down to the Minnesota, hearing the hustle and bustle of Montevideo, reach the landing and our car, and drive to the CURE office. We express our thanks to Dixie and assure her all went well. She has paddled this stretch of river many times herself and is happy to have been able to help a couple of out-of-towners experience this beautiful place.

Ascending above the bluffs as we drive out of town, a strong north wind greets us and almost separates canoe from car. My mind was still on the river, apparently, not on making sure all the ropes were snug. Ropes redone, we set off into the prairie wind and a landscape of corn that looks ready to be harvested. We are grateful to have experienced a beautiful river and generous, passionate people in a vibrant little town in the upper Minnesota River Basin.

Voices for the River:
Patrick Moore

Do unto those downstream as you would have those
upstream do unto you.

—WENDELL BERRY

For years, water quality at the upper stretches of the Minnesota River had been getting worse and worse. One particularly obnoxious problem was that the City of Montevideo's sewage treatment plant had been dumping large amounts of its effluent directly into the Minnesota River. Finally, citizens began to complain and get organized. A major player was Patrick Moore, a relative newcomer to the area, who decried the sewage problem in a letter to the editor of the *Montevideo American-News*. This was welcome relief to longtime Montevideo resident Del Wehrspann, who, as explained in his "Voices for the River" chapter, had for many years been a lone voice for stewardship of the river. Patrick, Del, and six others formed an ad hoc committee to pressure city hall. The Montevideo Rod and Gun Club contributed money to support creation of an organization to advocate on behalf of the river. Inspired by Scott Sparlin's Riverblast event in 1991 in New Ulm (Scott has his own "Voices for the River" chapter), Patrick worked with others to create a nonprofit, grassroots organization they called CURE (Clean Up the River Environment). The group saw themselves as a regional organization for the Upper Minnesota watershed, and they soon reached out to collaborate with like-minded organizations downstream, including

Sparlin's Coalition for a Clean Minnesota River and the Twin Cities–based Friends of the Minnesota Valley (see "Voices for the River: Ed Crozier and Elaine Mellott"). Patrick soon assumed leadership of the organization.

Patrick was intimately familiar with the Minnesota River. His father was a federal employee who worked and actually lived at Fort Snelling at the mouth of the river. The young Patrick spent countless hours exploring the oak savannas and river bottoms there, sometimes pulling his little red wagon behind him, the better to collect . . . you know, *things.* "So, my strong imagination," recounted Patrick, "I would have to say it was really influenced by spending time alone in nature in the Minnesota River Valley. And so that connection is strong and ever present to this day."

Early activities with CURE included field trips to identify problem areas on the river, an annual River Revival event to draw more people into river stewardship, a spring canoe trip to evaluate river changes and conditions, and a Cub Scout–led effort to remove one ton of trash from the banks of the Chippewa River, which joins the Minnesota in Montevideo.

And that's not all. CURE worked with a high school Eco Club (and gave a seat on its board of directors to a high school student), engaged with the Upper Sioux Indian Community (Phežíhutazizi Oyáte) on river protection projects, arranged a National Guard river cleanup effort, and helped educate individual local residents about how to reduce their own contributions to river pollution. CURE also intervened in an ill-advised plan for channeling part of the Lac qui Parle River. The Minnesota Court of Appeals, siding with CURE, upheld the decision to deny the permit for the Lac qui Parle Floodways Project.

In 1994, CURE received the Conservation Award given by the Minnesota Chapter of the Wildlife Society and the Minnesota Fish and Wildlife Employees Association to "an organization or institution that has shown an outstanding commitment to Minnesota's natural resources."

Year after year, CURE continued its missions of river education and recruiting more people to the cleanup effort. Patrick has considerable promotional skills, and he helped produce a program on Pioneer Public Television, *Working for a Cleaner Minnesota River,* that expanded the knowledge of Minnesota River issues across a wider area of the Upper Minnesota River Basin. He also worked with CURE, staff from the Minnesota Historical Society, and photojournalist Anne Queenan to produce an oral history project about the movement to clean up the Minnesota River.

Ever the promoter and community organizer, Patrick lamented the lack of a gathering spot for Montevideo residents, so in 1998, he took a hiatus from CURE and, with his wife, Mary, opened the Java River Café. People flocked to it for the great coffee, delicious food (Geri and I can attest to that!), musical performances, and camaraderie. Java River is still going strong more than two decades later.

Patrick left CURE in 2013 to continue his efforts at community building and environmental stewardship as communications director at Pioneer Public Television, now based in Granite Falls.

Patrick is particularly proud of working with Scott Sparlin and Lori Nelson in the formation of the Minnesota River Watershed Alliance in 2006. Their task was to create a basin-wide citizen alliance that included farmers, elected officials, agency professionals, Dakota people, and others, all coming together not as official representatives of their respective organizations but simply as concerned citizens, each with an equally valid point of view. Today, that collaborative spirit is continuing under the auspices of the Minnesota River Congress.

In 2008, Patrick became aware of a new group of river activists in the Lake Pepin area, the Lake Pepin Legacy Alliance. The lake is actually a wide spot in the Mississippi River fifty miles or so south of where the Minnesota River joins the Mississippi. Sediment, mostly from the Minnesota, gets deposited in the relatively still waters of the river lake, not only threatening the environment and recreational opportunities there but even shortening the life of the lake.[26] Meanwhile, another new organization, the Minnesota Agricultural Water Resources Coalition (now called Minnesota Agricultural Water Resource Center), had formed to research and respond to water-quality challenges from a farmer's perspective. Patrick's imagination and community-organizing skills kicked into high gear. He organized an upstream-downstream "friendship tour," which brought upstream farmers

---

26. Scientists estimate that under the natural conditions that existed before Euro American settlement, it would have taken three thousand years for Lake Pepin to fill in. Now, the estimate is more like three hundred years.

to Lake Pepin to learn about the concerns of residents there, followed by a visit to the upper Minnesota River Basin, where downstreamers could learn about the challenges faced by the agricultural community there.

Thanks to a grant from the Changemakers organization's InCommons initiative in collaboration with the Bush Foundation, the Friendship Tour concept spread throughout the basin and helped forge permanent, positive relationships between individuals in the agricultural and environmental communities. The grant application Patrick wrote is a brilliant summation of the challenges society faces in efforts to restore a river—and the solutions achievable through collaboration.

Patrick's great strength is the building of relationships. For Patrick, in his words, "it's the build-the-road-by-walking, serve-what-seeks-to-emerge philosophy, that good things will come if you get people in the room talking, trusting, laughing, thinking together—that ideas pop in those situations that you can work with and put legs under." He sums it up like this: "Let's find out what we agree on, and work on *that*."

I asked Patrick, "What is at the heart of the issue for you when it comes to all these efforts to restore the river?"

He replied, "To me, it's about community, it's about collaboration and about love, really, that's what it is. So, you have to do something somewhere, and the river is a great connecting force, the river is a place of solace and a great place of wisdom."

Patrick, we love you.

Granite Dams and
Redwood Falls

turgid,

turbulent,

tumultuous,

tumbling,

rumbling,

stumbling,

mumbling

grumbling,

rambling,

roiling,

rocking,

rushing,

roaring,

. . . .

—ELIZABETH SCHULTZ

Geri and I have been looking forward to this leg of our journey for quite some time. For one thing, the destination of this three-day adventure is North Redwood, a mere eight river miles from my beloved Morton. Also, veteran paddlers have been telling us that this is one of the most beautiful stretches of the Minnesota River. And to top it off, our shuttle driver will be our old friend Loran Kaardal.

Loran, an insurance agent by trade, is passionate about the river and its valley. A consummate citizen activist, he was instrumental in founding the Green River Initiative of the Tatanka Bluffs Corridor.[27] "What we have along the Minnesota River," Loran explains, "is a section of land that is pretty much the same as it was centuries ago. The steep bluffs and annual flooding have kept development away. This gives us a wonderful opportunity to create a conservation-recreational area with horseback riding, biking, and hiking along with fishing, canoeing, camping, and birding." Phenomenal recreational opportunities that community activists like Loran are working to enhance will result in significant economic benefit.

Geri and I meet Loran at his office in North Redwood and drive the thirty-nine miles upriver to Montevideo with time enough for good conversation. (Our canoe trip will be about sixty-five miles on the meandering river.) At the public access just out of town, we unload our gear and give the car keys to Loran as he wishes us bon voyage. He will have our car waiting for us when we arrive three days hence. We eat lunch, load the canoe, and nudge the bow into the chocolate-brown river. With a bright blue sky overhead and a tailwind helping the current push us along, we glide onto the smooth, flowing river, examining its banks as we warm up our paddling arms for the miles ahead.

A few miles out, we come upon a picturesque reddish outcrop of rock, about 150 meters long, that constricts the river and bends it to the west. We pull to shore to get a better look, and as I expected, it is the ancient granite bedrock so prevalent in the middle Minnesota Valley. Although most of the river cuts through saprolite (the weathered remnants of granite that evolved over hundreds of millions of years as the rock dissolved), in a few places, the beautifully smoothed bedrock of the chemical weathering front and its corestones are revealed. The paddlers we've talked with were correct: the fifteen river miles from Montevideo to Granite Falls that we're on now offer stunning scenery.

The Minnesota DNR's Water Trails program has published a series of four maps to aid Minnesota River paddlers. The maps identify a total of

---

27. *Tatanka* is the Dakota word for *bison*. The Tatanka Bluffs Corridor comprises twenty-six communities working together to promote tourism and recreation in the Middle Minnesota. I helped secure funding for the corridor in 2010 in my role as a member of the Lessard-Sams Outdoor Heritage Council. The LSOHC recommends to the legislature projects to be funded from money raised by the Clean Water, Land and Legacy Amendment.

six Class I rapids and one, Carver Rapids (located in the Minnesota Valley National Wildlife Refuge in the southwestern metropolitan area), that is Class II or III depending on water levels.[28] We're in Map #1 territory, and it shows that soon we will encounter a Class I rapids. On this balmy July day, though, the water is high enough that it covers any rapids-producing rocks; for us, the Minnesota is a placid river.

* * *

Paddling downstream, we notice a black plastic pipe about two inches in diameter emerging from the ground and opening onto the riverbank. It is a conduit for runoff, a drain tile. It discharges rainwater and snowmelt directly to the river, speeding water off the land instead of allowing the moisture to soak in slowly and replenish the river over the seasons through groundwater flow.

Several miles downstream, I try fishing in an eddy with spinner bait and get two strikes. Neither fish gets hooked. Par for the course—I have inherited the fishing jinx from my dad.

Wild grape seems ever present. Some vines hang over the edge of the riverbank. Others have climbed to the tops of tall trees.

Not far downstream, I catch a glimpse of railcars on a steep slope above the river. I cannot resist. I have been attracted to trains since boyhood and am anxious to see what these idle cars may contain. Geri has no interest in clambering up the slope and is happy to stay with the canoe to make sure our tethers tied to branches at the water's edge do not slip loose. I push through the vegetation and look up at a seemingly endless line of huge, slumbering gray train cars. I look around like a kid who's not supposed to be in the candy store, then carefully climb the rungs to the top of a car. All the cars are empty, and all around me is silence. Corn harvest will be here soon, and the cars will carry the corn away.

The advent of rail in the Minnesota Valley in the 1870s marked the end of the steamboat era and greatly reduced the need for watercraft to

---

28. The International Scale of River Difficulty, created by the American Whitewater Association, defines six classes of rapids. Class I is "Easy"; Class VI is "Extreme and Exploratory Rapids."

transport people and commodities. The DNR map shows railroad tracks entering at the bottom corner of the map, passing through Granite Falls, and extending all the way to Appleton. I realize it must be the same rail line that Geri and I paddled under as we approached the dam at Marsh Lake.

* * *

Just upriver of the city of Granite Falls, where we'll need to portage around a major dam, we find a section of riverbank that looks to be a good place to end the day. We swing to shore and set up camp with just enough light to complete our chores. A rather Spartan dinner—too bad I couldn't catch those fish—and then into our sleeping bags we roll. The sound of traffic in Granite Falls blends with the burble of the river, and we wonder what sights and sounds we may experience tomorrow at the portage and beyond. We have covered eleven miles for the day, pretty good for a couple of senior citizens, especially considering we didn't get out on the water until after lunch. Sweet dreams!

* * *

In the morning, we shove off toward the Granite Falls Dam, and immediately a river otter swims upstream to welcome us. We have often encountered otters on river trips, though this is the first one we've seen on the Minnesota. They were reintroduced here in the 1970s[29] and are doing quite well. Mostly fish eaters, river otters also eat a variety of aquatic life from salamanders and crayfish to frogs.

At the top of the bank, I see a sign indicating the floodplain here is enrolled in the Conservation Reserve Program. CRP, run by the US Department of Agriculture, encourages farmers to convert highly erodible cropland or other environmentally sensitive land to vegetative cover such as riparian buffers and native grasses. CRP contracts typically last ten or fifteen years and provide a government subsidy in exchange for the landowners' sacrifice of cropland and the time it takes them to establish and maintain the land for conservation.

---

29. Otter restoration was one of the first projects of legendary Minnesota DNR Nongame Wildlife Program supervisor Carrol Henderson.

If you want to catch a really big channel cat, the Minnesota River is the place to be!

A small channel catfish swims lazily at the surface and, wouldn't you know it, slips from my fingers and submerges when I try to bring it into the canoe. Catfish are a favorite target of Minnesota River anglers. They have barbels that look like long whiskers (thus the name *catfish*) and function as feelers, enabling the fish to find food. Their bodies are shaped like torpedoes that speed through the water with thrust from their sharply forked tailfin. Insects make up roughly half their diet; channel cats eat more mollusks and snails than flatheads, the other catfish species found in the Minnesota River. Females deposit eggs in sheltered places, and the males guard the nests for several weeks until the sac fry have hatched. In the heat of summer, they seek out deep pools or riffles, then at night move to shallows and rocky substrates to eat.

According to fish expert Tom Dickson, "The traditional way to fish for catfish is to build a fire along a riverbank at sundown, toss out a baited line, and wait for a take while watching sparks rise up into the dark summer sky. Anglers bored by that are better off working a quarter-ounce lead-head jig tipped with a black twister tail and bouncing the lure along deep riffles or in seams between fast and slow water."

* * *

Power lines appear ahead, and the dam comes into view. Unlike dams designed to hold back water, such as the ones we encountered on the Upper Minnesota River, the purpose of the Granite Falls Dam is to harness the power of moving water to generate electrical power. In operation for more than one hundred years, the dam produces about 70 percent of Granite Falls' electricity. The trade-offs are that the dam was constructed over a beautiful eighteen-foot waterfall over granite bedrock, and it blocks the upriver movement of fish. Creative citizens and city officials have recently wondered if it might be possible to achieve the best of both worlds; they are studying the feasibility of removing a section of the dam to create a whitewater park that they hope would be a magnet for kayaking enthusiasts and provide a passageway for fish. In an interview with *West Central Tribune* reporter Tom Cherveny, Granite Falls economic development director Justin Bentaas says, "I believe the river is being underutilized. Not all small towns have a river running right through downtown." (And I would add that not all small towns with a river running through downtown have a pedestrian bridge that affords fantastic views of the river and the power-generating dam. It's definitely worth a visit.)

We pull to the west shore and carry our belongings to the edge of the highway. Courteous drivers allow us to portage across the road, and we trek down to a riverside park overlooking the turbulence below the dam. Ah, a place to fill our four one-gallon water jugs. Geri and I learned years ago that one gallon of water per person per day is essential and two is preferable.

Dozens of pelicans float close to the base of the dam in their typical coordinated teams—a spectacular display of nature right here in downtown Granite Falls. We watch as the ungainly yet elegant birds bob and dive and gulp fish into their gular pouches. Then they float off individually and ride the current downstream to digest and rest.

A steep slope drops off from the edge of the park to the river, making it a bit dicey to carry the canoe down to the water. But we're wearing sensible shoes, and all goes well. As we load the canoe on a strand of sand, I see a huge mass of fingernail clams, apparently brought together by currents. I suspect catfish must be frequent visitors to this site.

The roiling current below the dam splays itself broadly across the river, revealing rock-studded places that call for caution. Geri, in the bow, can spot danger ahead, while I in the stern am responsible for steering. A rapid dialogue ensues as we snake our way through the hazards. Geri is very skilled at her task, and over the years, I've become proficient at following instructions. We zip through to calmer water.

We are seeing at least one eagle every day, not surprising given the abundance of fish in the river; carp are jumping and splashing all around us. Eagles are actually one of the more common avian sightings on the river, yet they command one's attention every time.

Less than a mile downstream, we run into our first real rapids—actually what we call a *rock garden*—with rocks scattered hither and yon at or just below the surface. The current isn't particularly strong, but the obstacles are ubiquitous, and, despite our best efforts, the canoe gets wedged sideways between two boulders. We are able to stand on them and free the canoe with no problem aside from getting our sensible shoes soaked.

* * *

Three miles downstream, we encounter the Minnesota Falls Dam. It was built in 1905 over a ten-foot drop in the river to create a pool of water for cooling the Minnesota Valley Generating Plant. The plant closed in 1961, so the dam has served no useful purpose for half a century. A power company sign on the left bank warns "Not a Portage." We eventually spot a DNR sign on the opposite side of the river and maneuver our way to the downstream side of the dam.

We let the gentle current carry us downstream while we contemplate what we have seen and learned. The seat of a canoe floating down a placid river is a wonderful place for reflection.

* * *

Geri and I paddled this stretch of the river in 2009, and I am delighted to report that the dam was removed in 2013 by Xcel Energy. The dam had been a barrier not just to paddlers but to the natural movement of fish. The pool of water above the dam covered a rocky substrate, which is excellent spawning habitat for fish and produces a series of rapids coveted by adventuresome paddlers. As reported in the *Minnesota Conservation Volunteer* (May–June 2017): "In the short period since removal, 12 fish species have returned upstream, including shovelnose sturgeon, sauger, flathead catfish, state threatened species paddlefish and black buffalo, and species of special concern[30] lake sturgeon and blue sucker." Not to mention walleye. People are now catching walleye in downtown Granite Falls.

The Minnesota DNR has recognized that, in many places, the Minnesota River and its tributaries are better off without dams. For example, in 1998, the DNR removed the dam on the Pomme de Terre River in downtown Appleton. The project included restoring the original, meandering nature of the river there, and the result was the creation of a delightful attraction for paddlers and the natural reintroduction of fish to the upper stretches of the river. More recently, the DNR has proposed removing three dams on the Cottonwood River in Redwood County.

* * *

A short distance downstream from the Minnesota Falls Dam, we come upon a most gorgeous change in the scenery, reminiscent of the Boundary Waters Canoe Area (BWCA). We are paddling among outcrops of chemically rounded granite domes. Eastern red cedar trees saturate the air with an aroma likewise evocative of the BWCA.

We pull to shore and climb up the rounded knobs. This site is designated as the Gneiss Outcrops Scientific and Natural Area. It is one of 159 SNAs in Minnesota, more than a dozen of which are in the Minnesota River Basin. The SNA program preserves natural features and rare resources of exceptional scientific and educational value, including plant communities, habitat for birds, and natural geological formations and features. Small parking lots tend to be the only amenities at SNAs; as stated on the DNR's website: "Enjoy the undisturbed natural quality of these sites. However, most Natural Areas do not have trails, and none have restrooms or drinking water, so you will need to come prepared."

---

30. From the Minnesota Department of Natural Resources Rare Species Guide (available online): "A species is considered a species of **special concern** if, although the species is not endangered or threatened, it is extremely uncommon in Minnesota, or has unique or highly specific habitat requirements and deserves careful monitoring of its status."

Geri and Darby about to launch from Le Sueur. Destination: confluence.

Home sweet home away from home.

You've heard of
Minnesota Nice.
This is Morton Gneiss.

Morton Outcrops
Scientific and Natural
Area. Darby played
here as a kid, before
it was designated
as an SNA.
credit: Ron Bolduan

The Highway 71 bridge
just west of Morton,
with a railroad bridge
in background.
credit: John Hickman

Highway 28 in Browns Valley at the Minnesota–South Dakota border.
credit: Ron Bolduan

Big Stone Lake near Ortonville, looking across to South Dakota.
credit: Ron Bolduan

Minnesota River backwaters at Big Stone National Wildlife Refuge.
credit: John G. White Photography

Taking time to contemplate where we've been and what we've learned.

A giant cottonwood at the Treaty Site History Center in St. Peter.

One of Darby's many precarious climbs up the riverbank to see what he can see.

The Le Sueur River got just a little too shallow for paddling.

Gneiss Outcrops Scientific and Natural Area near Granite Falls.

credit: Ron Bolduan

Minnesota River at New Ulm—the land where the water reflects the sky.
credit: Beth Dale

Minneopa Falls—water falling twice—at Minneopa State Park near Mankato.
credit: John Hickman

The meandering Minnesota. When you're paddling, it's headwind, tailwind, headwind, tailwind….
credit: *Mankato Free Press*

Scott Sparlin sharing his love of music and the river at the Riverside History and Nature Learning Center in New Ulm.
credit: Ron Bolduan

Confluence of the Minnesota and Mississippi rivers on
Pike Island at Fort Snelling at Bdoté State Park.

The "Minnissippi River" from the Pine Bend Bluffs Scientific
and Natural Area in Inver Grove Heights.

credit: John Hickman

Prepared we are, and enjoy we do. My first discovery is of prickly pear cactus. These plants tend to grow in clusters, often in slight depressions in the bedrock, snuggled into the thinnest of soil. I continue my walk upward and reach the top of the granite dome where I sit and marvel at the great valley below. Simultaneously, I am grateful for the solitude and hopeful that more and more people will discover the beauty and opportunities for adventure along our state's namesake river. Returning my attention to my immediate surroundings, I notice that Geri is hunched over, engrossed in examining the flora and fauna at her feet, and I'm grateful for nearly five decades of companionship with a kindred spirit.

* * *

We walk back down to our canoe and get on the river. A crow flies over us, screeching more than cawing, as though we had interrupted his plans for the day. House wrens chatter from seemingly everywhere along the shore. A long-legged shorebird stands on a sandbar downstream and flies off as we approach.

We come upon a narrow sandbar island some hundred meters long. Fast water flows on both sides, and we pull onto the fine sand to have a snack and give paddling arms and backs a rest. Sandbars come and go on this ever-meandering, often-flooding river, and we're happy to be able to take advantage of this particular sandbar at this particular time.

A mile later, we see our first motorboat on the river. We are surprised it has taken this long to meet fellow recreationists. Aside from Big Stone Lake, the river has been all ours.

We arrive at Upper Sioux Agency State Park at noon, pull the canoe up on the mud bank, rope both ends to exposed elm roots, set up camp, and set out on foot. We hike past many hackberry trees, some basswood, elm, oak and ash, and one ironwood tree. Buckthorn, an aggressive invasive species, is thriving in the floodplain but peters out as we approach the top of the bluff. We walk to the high point where we see great views not only of the Minnesota River valley but also the valley of the Yellow Medicine River as it flows into the Minnesota. We return to our campsite to enjoy the sunset and a good night's sleep.

In the morning, we investigate the mouth of the Yellow Medicine and discover it is not canoe-able. Paddling enthusiasts have told me the Yellow Medicine is one of their favorite waterways in the spring and early summer. The water is quite clear, in contrast with the brown water of the Minnesota. Today, it's not so much a river as a series of shallow pools and dribbles over pebbles. We have company in the campground, and it seems everyone except for us has come here to fish. Some have fished all night. A woman caught a seven-pound walleye and plans to have it mounted. Others show us that they have filled coolers with live catfish to keep for fresh eating at home.

As we launch the canoe, two immature bald eagles fly low right over us. I try fishing at the mouth of the Yellow Medicine, but no bites. Geri spots Black Angus cattle at the unfenced shore. The map shows this land to be part of the state park. Is the park leasing that property to a farmer? The cattle are eating wild plants, and several munch on wild grapevines.

Several miles downstream, we see another black pipe sticking out of the riverbank, much larger than the one we had seen near Montevideo. This one has a hinged cover that appears designed to allow water to flow out and prevent animals from getting in. Originating in a farm field, it removes water from the soil and dumps it in the river, exacerbating erosion downstream.

We cross the river to the east bank, where Hawk Creek flows through Skalbekken County Park before it enters the Minnesota. (The upper stretch of Hawk Creek is visible as it flows under Highway 212 a few miles east of Granite Falls.) Its volume exceeds that of the Yellow Medicine this day. We pull ashore and discover water as clear as can be. The contrast with the river is stark. I roll up my pant legs and begin walking upstream in fine sand. Tiny minnows dart for cover as I approach. Continuing upstream, the sand disappears, and I find myself walking on pebbles and well-rounded stones worn down after eons of time. This is midsummer. In spring flow in a normal year, water must inundate the park and rush pell-mell, twisting and turning at breakneck speed in a race to the river—a kayaker's delight. A picnic table and DNR canoe sign stand at the mouth of the creek. Time for lunch and journal writing.

Like most Minnesota River tributaries, Hawk Creek has two origin stories. The first relates to slope. Most of southwestern Minnesota is flat land, once native prairie and now farm fields. The creek begins its journey in that flat farming country and eventually encounters downward slope as it nears the Minnesota River Valley.[31] The structure of the stream changes from babbling to the rapid, twisting nature so enjoyed by paddlers.

The second story relates to till, the unsorted, unstratified mix of all sizes of rock material deposited directly by melting glacial ice with little or no reworking by water. The composition of till varies with depth, representing the many different glaciers that passed this way over the last two million years. Hawk Creek till exposes a sandy clay loam that varies from pink to reddish-brown. Its color and rock types give a clue that this ice lobe's origin was in the Lake Superior region. It was an advance of ice that much predated the one that spread gray, clayey till on the surface. The evidence of it is reduced to a thin seam exposed on the banks of this river, and distinctive pebbles washed out of it and concentrated on point bars.

Because of the complex pattern of multiple glacial advances and subsequent erosion, multiple till layers are exposed in the vicinity of Granite Falls and New Ulm. Each type of till has a different mix of minerals and rock types that describe its path, ultimately producing slightly different layers of glacial sediment stacked beneath the surface till. Glacial geologists have canoed the tributaries, piecing together the evidence to reconstruct the full history of glaciation over the last two million years.

Skalbekken Park is a great place to camp; were it not midday, we would do so. We are only eight miles from Joe Slough, seven from a Renville County park, and have plenty of daylight. We somehow miss the county park but pass by Joe Slough still with daylight to spare. Two red hash marks on the DNR map indicate rapids ahead. Geri goes on alert in the bow. We sense an increase in velocity of the river's flow, and shoals show more rocks and less mud. We are approaching a section of river known as Patterson Rapids.

Charles Patterson was an Irishman who established a trading post at the rapids in the late 1700s when white folks were few and far between in the Minnesota River Basin. Legend has it that he wore a bearskin hat.

---

31. Until about thirteen thousand years ago, the Minnesota was a small river in a shallow valley into which the river's tributaries gently flowed. But then glacial River Warren carved out the deep Minnesota River Valley, and ever since the tributaries have been cutting into the bluffs. They create deep ravines or, where they encounter bedrock, impressive waterfalls. That process continues today, helping explain why the Minnesota River carries so much sediment.

Dakota consider the bear sacred, and they called Patterson Sacred Hat. The moniker stuck, sort of. Redwood County named one of its townships Sacred Heart.

We pass the mouth of Boiling Springs Creek, which adds significant flow to the river. Unlike Hawk Creek with its endless zigzagging turns, Boiling Springs Creek gathers a notable amount of water from numerous straight-lined drainage ditches. Now the river takes a turn northeast, and our map shows three bright red hash marks. We quickly understand why. Dead ahead, it looks like almost all rocks and almost no water.

The river narrows, and Geri begins yelling out steering commands to me, but with water only a foot and a half deep, the rock garden wins the day. We hop out of the canoe and lead it along as best we can. After scraping bottom several times, we reach deeper water and hop back in. But the challenges continue, and we realize we're just now coming upon the actual Patterson Rapids; the stretch we had just come through was merely an introduction to the real deal. The river is too shallow for navigation, so we pull in and walk the shore looking for a place to portage. We finally find a slot between two boulders through which we can negotiate the canoe. We unload our heaviest packs from the canoe and complete the short portage.

Though the water is now notably deeper than it was just upstream, large stones in the middle of the river and many more at the shore still make it difficult to get back on the water without damage, and the bottom of the canoe gets scraped up a bit. Kevlar, the material our canoe is made of, is great for minimizing weight but not so great at handling close encounters of the lithic kind. Luckily, the damage to our craft is cosmetic, not structural. We are on the river in late July; earlier in the summer, water levels would have been more accommodating. These rapids are significant, dropping in elevation about five feet in a third of a mile. Finally, we reach a calmer stretch. We've had more than enough excitement for one day and find a nice spot, high and dry, to spend the night.

* * *

Three miles or so downstream from Patterson Rapids, we paddle past Cedar Rock Wildlife Management Area (WMA) and Whispering Ridge

Aquatic Management Area (AMA). I am delighted. These places are familiar to me and are among the most picturesque sites along the river.

* * *

Two weeks earlier, Loran Kaardal, our shuttle driver, had organized a daylong tour of sites in Redwood and Renville Counties. I left home at five thirty in the morning and headed for Olivia to join a group of twenty-one people concerned about the river, its surroundings, its future. My route took me past cornfields as flat as land can be. I arrived early, walked around town, and paid a visit to the fifty-foot-tall statue of an ear of corn that declares Olivia "Corn Capital of the World."[32] Our group included a planner from the National Park Service, a Soil and Water Conservation District representative, the DNR's Area Fisheries manager and Water Trails supervisor, two county commissioners, a county historical society representative, and members of several citizen groups.

In the late 1890s, the Minnesota Valley Historical Society established the first tourist trail in Redwood and Renville Counties that travelers by the hundreds would take to Spring Lake on hot summer weekends to picnic and take a dip in the spring-fed lake. The lake's name was later changed to Gold Mine Lake when rumors spread that there was gold in the area, but it didn't pan out. Loran kept us moving from one site to the next all day. We admired the river from the top of Whispering Ridge and visited several scenic places where the public can enjoy hunting and other forms of recreation. I learned much about this corner of the basin that day, but driving home that evening, I came to realize that it was the people I met that inspired me. These people truly love this place, this river, this Green Corridor, and they are of a mind to protect and enhance it. Amen.

* * *

The river narrows as Geri and I approach Whispering Ridge. My heart quickens. I can't wait to see what this stretch of the river looks like from

32. The appellation was given by the Minnesota Senate in 1973, and deservedly so, not only because so much corn is grown in the area but also because Olivia is home to nine seed-research facilities.

the water. We enter a canyon strewn with massive stones. We merely steer with paddles and allow the current to carry us through this magical stretch of the river. Ahead, a long, broad sandbar offers an easy landing spot. Out of the canoe and onto the floodplain. A thin curtain of trees separates the shore from a farm field that looks like it could produce a bountiful crop one year and get inundated the next. A vacant deer stand overlooks a wooded corner of the field.

A path guides us to the granite apex of the ridge. Silently, we admire a panorama of valley, river, and the boulders forming the gate through which we had floated. A picnic table and fire ring beckon. A second table rests a dozen yards downslope from the peak. We will gratefully camp here tonight. Five-star accommodations for a couple of itinerant canoeists.

We return to the beach, take off our boat shoes, and wade into surprisingly clear river water. Geri makes a discovery: an animal bone I can't identify, broken at a joint. What stands out is its deep black color. I suspect it is very old. What fascinating stories might it hold?[33]

Working my way along the sand, I discover something even more exciting, at least to me: the trail of a live, freshwater mussel. "Geri!" I yell. She has never before seen the watery trail of one of these creatures. Historical records reveal that mussels were once numerous in the Minnesota River, but in recent times, many species have become extirpated—that is, locally extinct. Their comparative abundance here is an indicator of relatively good water quality and a heartwarming sight for an aquatic biologist and his paddling companion for life.

Mussels are most numerous in larger rivers such as the Minnesota and play a significant role in river ecology. They filter water through their gills, straining algae, zooplankton, phytoplankton, and miscellaneous organic detritus from the water. Each has a foot that thrusts it forward by muscular contractions. Some species are reported to be able to travel several feet per hour, leaving a trough-like track like the one I've just found. The internal color of the shells can range from silvery white through pink to

---

33. In 2016, the giant leg bone of a woolly mammoth was unearthed in nearby Sibley County. It's now on display at the Joseph R. Brown Minnesota River Center in the river town of Henderson.

Many of the fifty species of freshwater mussels in the Minnesota River Basin have been extirpated, but the populations of about half are holding steady or increasing.

dark purple. In the early twentieth century, there was a significant industry that made buttons out of the lustrous, colorful shells. Historically, there were forty-two species of mussels in the Minnesota River. By 2011, there were only twenty-three species, but in the wake of floodplain restoration and other cleanup efforts, the populations are showing significant signs of recovery. Some names bestowed on these creatures are *purple wartyback, pink heelsplitter,* and *deer toe.* Mussel taxonomists have a sense of humor.

I wade along the mussel's trail until the water is too deep for safety. Time to set up the tent and help Geri with supper. We've paddled nineteen miles this day and are a mere six miles from North Redwood, our car, and the falls of the Redwood River. We get into our tent and fall asleep to the sweet, soft sounds of a contented river.

* * *

Breakfast today is thin; we ran out of granola yesterday and have to make do with what Geri calls *IB*: Instant Breakfast, a concoction of powdered milk, chocolate, and sweetener that we carry for just this circumstance. We are on the water at 8:48 a.m.

We soon come upon a sizable backwater and paddle in. Its tired flow today contributes little water to the river. Advancing deeper, around a sharp bend, we come face-to-face with a huge, thirty-foot-high pile of downed trees. We are looking at the remnants of a full rush of water in the spring surge. What a sight it would have been to see the river when it was making that pile.

Back on the main stem, the paddling is easy. We navigate around one lazy bend after another and soon enough spot our landing just downstream. The banks there are well trodden by fishermen and boaters. When we arrive, Geri begins packing up our gear, and I set out jogging to our car half a mile away at Loran's property. This leg of our journey has ended—almost.

We drive into downtown Redwood Falls. On State Highway 19, the main drag through town, there's a short walkway leading to an overlook of the Redwood River Dam. Originally constructed to generate hydropower, the dam remains in place today to maintain recreational Redwood Lake. A pedestrian bridge affords an up-close-and-personal view. The fall of the water over the dam is impressive, but to see a truly spectacular waterfall, one need only descend from the main highway down the bluff into Alexander Ramsey Park[34] where Ramsey Creek plummets more than twenty feet over granitic bedrock.

Old memories begin to stir. When I was nine, I tried to organize boyhood friends to walk the bluff line from Morton to North Redwood but had to give up the outing because only one mother approved—mine. Now I have new memories of the area, and they surpass even the wildest dreams of my childhood.

---

34. From the Explore Minnesota website: "At 219 acres in size, Alexander Ramsey Park is the largest municipal park in the State of Minnesota. Termed as the 'Little Yellowstone of Minnesota,' the park is enhanced by 1930's Civilian Conservation Corps shelters and bridges and picturesque Ramsey Falls."

A Day at Lower Sioux

The power of the Dakotas had always dwelt in the land, from the great forest to the open prairies. Long before the white man ever dreamed of our existence, the Dakota roamed this land.

—LOOKING EAGLE (WAŊBDÍ WAKITA)

It is an early, chilly November morning as Geri and I drive west into corn and soybean country. I am delighted that our destination is right across the river from Morton. We depart before daybreak to allow plenty of extra time for me to wander my boyhood haunts. Geri knows me well and understands when the power of place lures me home. We get out of the car where Morton Creek passes under Highway 19 and discover that the creek is dry. Come spring, it will be roaring toward the Minnesota River a few blocks away. I find a few worn pieces of gneiss.

Our destination is the Lower Sioux Agency Visitor Center, where we are to attend a "Lunch and Learn" program in the morning and other activities in late afternoon at nearby Jackpot Junction Casino. The Lower Sioux Agency was established in 1853 by the federal government to be the administrative center of the Lower Sioux Indian Reservation that was created by the treaty signed in 1851 at Mendota. I am thrilled that we have a couple of hours to explore the grounds of this historic site before the program begins. The Dakota call this place Čháŋšayapi, "where they marked the trees red," which explains half the name of the nearby white settlement that arose: Redwood Falls.

In my wanderings as a boy along the bluffs above Morton, I could see the Indian lands across the river, but I never went there. It strikes me as odd now, but as a kid, I never questioned why nobody from Morton ever seemed to visit their neighbors across the river. Today, I will visit. I am delighted that I will finally see where Peewee lived. His Dakota ancestors lived where prairie and woodlands met. The lands were rich in game, fish, waterfowl, and edible roots, and the fertile soil enabled the cultivation of maize and other crops. Wild rice flourished in the wet lowlands. The people moved from river's edge to bluff top and other environs to take advantage of seasonal changes in the landscape. And then suddenly they were confined to this little reservation.

We drive west through Morton and turn south to cross the Minnesota River on Highway 71. Just before the steep ascent out of the valley to the city of Redwood Falls, we turn east to climb out of the valley on Highway 2. Soon we see the reservation's water tower and Jackpot Junction Casino. We find ourselves on a flat landscape of prairie and farm fields, where several small houses are scattered. Corn shocks cover the land amid tracts of brown wild grass. A strand of trees parallels the highway.

We arrive at the Lower Sioux Agency Visitor Center way too early for the program but right on time for a little exploring. It's a short walk to the edge of the woods, where Geri and I pause to take in a spectacular view of the valley below. An interpretive sign stands at the top of a hiking trail, and down we go into a series of steep ravines that leads to the water's edge. The river here swings toward our shore, creating an inside eroding bank that soon slips away into a sandbank downstream. The life of a river: ever eroding, ever accumulating.

A break in the trees affords us a grand view of Morton on the opposite shore. I look more closely and realize that this must have been where steamboats hauled supplies and trade goods to and from the river. This is the farthest point upriver that steamboats were able to reach. A Minnesota Historical Society sign confirms that this was indeed the site of the Redwood Ferry. Atop the bluff sat the Lower Sioux Agency, where the Dakota received their treaty-prescribed annuity payments from the federal government and where one of the first battles of the Dakota–US

War took place. When we paddled this section of the river, we had looked in vain for this site; now we are standing on it.

In 1861, Henry David Thoreau and his traveling companion, Horace Mann Jr., climbed up to the ridge above the river here and were able to see much of the Lower Sioux reservation. Suddenly, my toes are tingling. Is it possible I am standing on the exact same ground where my hero once stood? Thoreau wrote, "Redwood [Lower Sioux Agency] is a mere locality, scarcely an Indian Village—where there is a store and some houses have been built for them. We were now fairly on the Great Plains, and looking south, and after walking that way three miles, could see no trees in the horizon. The buffalo was said to be feeding within twenty-five or thirty miles." He also noted that the Indians looked "hungry, not sleek and round-faced." One year later, some desperately hungry Indians started a war, and the Lower Sioux Agency was one of the first places they attacked.

Two paths connect river to bluff top. The way we came down is a series of switchbacks, considerably longer but not nearly as steep as the way we are returning. As we huff and puff our way to the top of the bluff, it occurs to me that when the ferry landing was active, all the trade goods, food, and other supplies would have had to have been lugged up these steep slopes to get to the settlement above. Transporting supplies by steamboat was one thing; getting it all up the hill was another matter.

Back on flat ground, Geri heads off to check in at the visitor center while I head over to an old stone building of great historical significance. Built in 1861, this secure warehouse served as the distribution center of food, trade goods, and money owed to the Dakota people. It was here that agency storekeeper Andrew Myrick's words—*Let them eat grass*—so enflamed the starving Dakota people. Within a fortnight, there was war.

Turning my gaze to the panoramic valley before me, it seems I am overlooking a spot where the rampaging glacial River Warren must have carved out a large chunk of land in its rush to reach the Mississippi and points south.

Heading back to the visitor center to join Geri for Lunch and Learn, I notice that the historic stone warehouse sits only thirty feet or so back from the ravine. Ravines are conduits for water to run downhill, carrying away silt, sand, and sediment from the uplands and the bluff itself. I hope the surrounding land that sheds its water into the ravine is well cared-for so the warehouse remains safe from erosion.

* * *

Some thirty people are in the visitor center, where there are displays depicting Dakota life and a gift shop focused on books by and about Indians. The Lower Sioux Agency historic site sits within the Lower Sioux Indian Community tribal lands. The community manages the site through a cooperative agreement with the Minnesota Historical Society.

Since 2015, the Minnesota Valley History Learning Center (headquartered in Morton!) has sponsored the Lunch and Learn series, organized by Loran Kaardal. The program is funded by citizens who support the Lower Sioux Interpretive Center, the Dakota Wicohan, the Renville and Redwood County Historical Societies, and the Minnesota DNR and Historical Society. Topics include ecology, geology, history, and culture. Geri and I have enjoyed several of these learning sessions, which are fund raisers for the Renville and Redwood County Historical Societies' summer day camps for kids.

Bison herds have been re-established in Blue Mounds State Park (outside the Minnesota River Basin) and in Minneopa State Park near Mankato.

American bison, the largest land mammals in North America, are the subject of this morning's talk, presented by Minnesota DNR naturalist (and paddler par excellence) Scott Kudelka. We learn from Scott that an estimated sixty million bison (also called *buffalo,* or *thatháŋka* in Dakota) roamed across North America in the early 1800s. By the late 1880s, there were at most one thousand. The massive extermination was partly for commercial harvest and sport, but it was also an effort to deprive Native Americans of one of their most important natural resources. In the early 1900s, President Teddy Roosevelt played a significant role in saving them from extinction; one place buffalo now roam is Theodore Roosevelt National Park in western North Dakota.

Bison were an integral part not only of Native Americans' way of life but also of prairie ecology generally. As a boy, I recall watching two bison in a paddock in the Bemidji zoo just a few blocks from my two grandmothers' homes. The animals sometimes made shallow depressions by clawing their hooves in the ground. This behavior spreads prairie seeds, which contributes to prairie diversity. Bison dung fertilizes the soil. Both male and female bison have horns that do not shed. During winter, they use their enormous, horned heads to plow the snow to uncover food.

There are now some 150,000 American bison, but unfortunately, most are hybrids carrying cattle genes. As bison numbers declined, cattle began cross-breeding with them such that most of the bison living today are of mixed genetic heritage. Cattle are less adapted to extreme temperatures and drought than bison. The bison herd in Blue Mounds State Park in southwestern Minnesota is one of two or three herds in the country (Yellowstone Park is another) whose genes remain 99.8 percent pure. In 2015, a genetically pure bison herd was released on 331 acres of fenced prairie in Minneopa State Park in Mankato. Eleven females comprised the initial herd. Scott informs the lunch-and-learners that the Minneopa enclosure can support up to thirty individuals and that it will take about five hundred animals statewide to maintain long-term viability. As many as three hundred vehicles drive through the enclosure on a good day. Stay in your car! Bison may appear docile, but they can become aggressive when disturbed.

Cheyanne St. John, site manager at the agency, takes over the program and describes the causes that led to the demise of bison: overhunting, increased settlement, more sophisticated firearms, expansion of railroads, and the cruel-beyond-words US government policy of exterminating bison as a means to eradicate Indians.

To the Dakota and other native peoples, bison were much more than a source of protein. Every part of the animal was used: dried dung for fuel; bones for such tools as scrapers, knives, and hoes; hair to make rope; the stomach to store and carry drinking water; the horns for headdresses, cups, and spoons; the skull for religious ceremonies; hides for clothing as well as tipi covers. It takes about a dozen poles, fourteen to sixteen hides, and six to eight people to set up a tipi. I marvel at the tipi frame on display outside the visitor center.

Learning accomplished, it is time for lunch. Our meal is delicious fry bread, pulled bison meat with barbecue sauce, and ice cream. We continue conversation with the program attendees and leaders. Cheyenne shares information about other events at the visitor center.

We then drive to Jackpot Junction Casino for the last event of the day: a powwow. Many cars occupy the large parking lot. Geri and I have never been inside a casino. We walk through the doors and enter into a cavernous, darkened space filled with cigarette smoke, flashing colored lights, and a cacophony of clanging. About half of the slot machines are occupied with players staring intently at their screens. Geri and I know the odds and walk through into a large arena.

People trickle in and take seats in the bleachers. Many are dressed in brightly colored, traditional clothing. We understand that powwows can have different purposes: social interaction, congresses, and ceremonies of one kind or another. The purpose of this one is to honor tribal members who have served in the US military. A parade of dancing adults and children in costume enters to the beat of drums and forms a large, circling group. The veterans form a large circle of their own, and all ceremoniously shake hands.

We stay until all the vets have been honored, and we depart glowing about the day. I feel grounded, with a new sense of connection to my home. After all these years, I have finally come across the river from Morton to tread the ground of one of the most important historic sites in Minnesota.

Power of Place

A place is not a thing; it is a relationship. A location becomes a place only in the context of time, of history.

—PAUL GRUCHOW

It's a bright, sunny day in the river city of New Ulm, founded by German immigrants in 1854. We'd love to visit the picturesque grounds of Schell's Brewery (in continuous operation by the same family since 1860) or ascend the immense statue of Hermann the German for a panoramic view of the valley, but we're on a mission. We're here to meet Marj Frederickson, who has graciously agreed to shuttle us to the landing at North Redwood, where we ended the last leg of our river odyssey and will begin the next. Though we have never met Marj, I've known her husband, Dennis Frederickson, since we both served in the Minnesota legislature in the 1980s. A farmer by profession, he was a state senator from the New Ulm area for a remarkable thirty years; I was in the House for six of those years. He had no sooner retired from the Senate in 2010 than he was tapped to become director of the Minnesota DNR's southern region, in which capacity he served until his retirement in 2018. Throughout his life, Denny has been a champion of wise stewardship of the Minnesota River.

We check in at the police station to get their advice on a safe place for Marj to leave our car and are pleased when they recommend the parking lot just outside their station. Then we meet Marj at the iconic Glockenspiel

Clock Tower and head to North Redwood, some forty highway miles (and sixty river miles) downstream. Time flies; it's apparent Marj shares her husband's passion for the river.

An unoccupied pickup truck greets us as at the boat landing. The owner must be up the shore fishing. We unload our gear and hand Marj the car keys. As we wave a thank-you, she sets out for the parking lot back in New Ulm, and we set out for the same destination in our trusty Bell canoe.

We allow the gentle current to nudge us along. The river is little more than a hundred feet wide here, and occasionally a tree leans out over the water. A river of this size feels intimate. We spot our first backwater with a seven-foot pile of logs and branches at its outlet, much like the one we had encountered upriver.

Soft maple dominates the floodplain forest. The damp ground is covered with seedlings one to two inches high, as though adult trees had simply dropped their seeds all at once as soon as spring floodwaters had receded and germination began immediately. Up from a mud bank is a terrace of invasive, pervasive reed canary grass. Eight feet above the water, there's a flat, dry place ideal for camping, but it's way too early to end the day. A brilliant blue damselfly lands on my leg, perhaps grateful to have found a perch in the middle of the river. I, too, am grateful.

Along the bank, I see alternating layers of mud and sand, indicative of changing water levels over time. This is a dynamic place. *Instability* is the watchword. Nothing is permanent. Mud layers tell of quiet times, when the river's flow lacked the energy to push along even the tiny particles of silt and clay. Sand layers tell of more robust times when the river's flow had enough energy to suspend the silt and clay and bounce sand along the bed of the stream.

I think back to my early years of paddling, when my marker of accomplishment was the number of miles covered for the day. Nowadays, I am more attuned to intellectual and spiritual accomplishments. How much can I see and learn in a day? How often do I find myself in reverie?

Beaver Creek, one of the larger feeder creeks we've seen, flows in from the north. It's in the Hawk Creek watershed, which drains an extensive acreage of farmland from Renville to Olivia and beyond. We go up the creek (with paddles) and get a Secchi reading: sixty-five centimeters (about twenty-five inches), reasonably clear water. We paddle back to the main stem and record a depth of a mere eighteen centimeters (about seven inches). The sediment load carried by the creek is notably less than I expected, but I remind myself that a single Secchi reading is just a snapshot. Researchers interested in the whole story do frequent sampling by hand or deploy electronic equipment that gathers a continuous data stream.

I hear the unmistakable, strident call of the killdeer: *kill-deer kill-deer kill-deer.* I am not surprised to find them here. A shorebird, they nest on the ground and are commonly found in prairie and farmlands as well as along shorelines. I am delighted to hear one today, even though I'm not able to catch sight of it.

Now a gaggle of geese comes swimming round the bend, sees us, and takes flight, honking in earnest. When they're out of earshot, all is quiet save the murmur of the gently flowing water. The river has its own soundtrack.

We approach a sandbar a quarter mile long. It's six o'clock, and we decide to camp for the night. I explore our overnight home and discover another live mussel, the second one we have seen so far. The beach begins with an upward-sloping stretch of sand varying in width from twenty to thirty feet. As it tapers at the downstream end, the sandbar becomes what I'd have to call a *mudbar*—rich, thick, black mud—that deer have obviously slogged through. I imagine their feet turned the same deep, rich color that my boat shoes are now.

Geri calls out to tell me our little camp stove is acting up. I prefer cooking over dry sticks lit by a single match, just like Peewee taught me all those years ago in Morton, but Geri is the cook, and I'm happy to get the stove going for her.

Two curious cows show themselves on flat land above the river's bank, their hides a rich brown. A panoply of goose footprints makes a path down our sandbar. Still no mosquitoes as we enter the tent for the night. There's no place I'd rather be right now.

* * *

Years ago, Geri and I were about to paddle a lengthy segment of the Yukon River in Alaska. Just as we were prepared to launch, a local man, sensing our naïveté, came over to give us some advice. "Know this," he said, "rain events can happen suddenly far upstream that can produce notable, unexpected increases in a river's water level overnight that could wash away your gear." Such events are highly unusual on the Minnesota River, but they have been known to happen.[35] I end each day of paddling by shoving a stick into the edge of the river to mark its elevation. This morning, I learn that the river has dropped two and a half inches overnight.

Stagnant backwaters indicate we are approaching Morton, where the river hits a wall of gneiss and makes a sharp turn to the southeast. We spot the boat landing, pull to shore, and rope our canoe to a small tree. The gravel parking area has three cars, and several families are fishing along the edge of a backwater. Fishing is slow today, they tell us. I find a handgun, of all things, half buried in the gravel at the landing. What to do? I feel uncomfortable even touching it but certainly don't want some other unsuspecting soul to stumble upon it. We decide to bring it to the police in New Ulm.

Two teenage boys stand atop an old bridge, thirty feet above the backwater, their baited lines submerged in the placid water below. They're not having any more luck than the people we met onshore and are happy to engage us in conversation. They're Morton kids and know family names familiar to me. Every time I visit Morton, I feel a sense of gratitude for having grown up with the river as my playground, and right now, this feeling is especially poignant. As the boys reel in their lines and head for home, I see myself doing the same thing sixty years ago.

Moving on, we pass by another backwater where I recall townsfolk used to dump their trash. Garbage disposal circa 1953: put it in the river and pass it on. I went with Dad on a garbage run one Saturday, and as I recall, it was the last such run he made. I think he and other townspeople finally recognized that they were disrespecting the river and their downstream neighbors.

---

35. In August 2017 and again in July 2018, the Redwood Falls area was deluged with a downpour of eight-plus inches of rain. Yow! That's exactly the type of event that triggers flooding far downstream. In this area, a rainfall of that amount is supposed to be a once-in-a-thousand-years event but has happened several times in the past ten years. No one who lives in the Minnesota River Basin (or anywhere else, for that matter) should doubt that climate change is happening.

Mostly hidden by floodplain forest, we see railcars on tracks just at the edge of town. Like the ones we saw on our previous outing, I surmise these cars are marking time until needed to take grain to market, or perhaps until the quarry is ready to ship off another load of Rainbow granite. For many years, Morton served as an important rail hub, moving grain and supplies up and down the Minnesota River Valley. The Morton Hotel was a very busy place; nowadays, visitors can stay at a chain motel on the outskirts of town or at the casino at the Lower Sioux Indian Community.

Morton is a skeleton of its former self. In the mid-1950s, the town's population stood at 596 souls, and businesses abounded. The town had the Farmer State Bank where I once saw a cornstalk fifteen feet high brought in by a proud farmer. There was a bakery, blacksmith/welder, barber shop, pharmacy, lumberyard, and three grocery stores, although one grocer saw the handwriting on the wall and shuttered his business soon after we moved to town. The *Morton Enterprise,* the town's weekly newspaper, enabled people to keep up on local news, and the *Minneapolis Star* dropped off daily newspapers to be distributed by paper boys like me. Now only about 400 people call Morton home, all those businesses are gone, and the local newspaper is out of print.

We beach the canoe at a spot at once familiar and peculiar. Dense vegetation has covered the many paths and gravelly spaces that attracted me and kids from town and the reservation as well as fishermen from Iowa. An old bridge spanned the river. Today, I see no evidence of kids or Iowans, and all that is left of the bridge are the two pillars that supported the deck.

Morton Creek receives its water from rivulets trickling off the bluffs. Although the creek is dry most summers, as a kid, I discovered a rich variety of small fish swimming in the rock-channelized stream no more than five to six inches deep. Though I did not have names for these fascinating fishes then, I suspect they were mainly creek chubs and river darters.

Downstream, the river takes on a different character: fewer sandbars, more floodplain forest, and much more mud. We pull into a small backwater filled with the black goo, and I scramble up the seven-foot bank to flat land—a farmer's field. No crop this year; it looks like the river flooded this field. Crop insurance from the federal government can partially compensate a farmer for such setbacks, but farming in the floodplain is a gamble. Some years you get a bumper crop, some years you're underwater, and most years you don't know going in how things will turn out. Many farmers in the Minnesota River Basin have taken a conservative approach, enrolling their floodplain land in temporary set-aside programs such as the federal Conservation Reserve Program (CRP) and the state's Reinvest in Minnesota (RIM), or the Conservation Reserve Enhancement Program (CREP), which is a combination of CRP and RIM that protects land in perpetuity. Landowners who enroll some of their property in one of these programs benefit by creating beautiful wildlife habitat on their own land, and their downstream neighbors benefit by receiving cleaner water.

At the east end of town, along the bluff, two stone monuments stand high above the valley floor. One obelisk honors the soldiers who fought at the Battle of Birch Coulee in the Dakota–US War, and the other commemorates the six Dakota who saved the lives of whites during the conflict.

A short distance downstream, we arrive at Birch Coulee Creek. Its flow delivers a mere trickle into the river today. We tie the canoe to a log sticking out of the muddy bank, and I maneuver myself precariously across the downed tree limbs lying on the slippery surface. Once up on flat land, I discover this creek is better called a drainage ditch—the streambed has been dug out and straightened to move runoff to the main flow as quickly as possible. I walk into the floodplain forest to explore. Deer tracks are everywhere, so I'm not surprised to see deer stands here and there up in the trees. I envy the hunters who seek venison here.

Back on the river, I tell Geri that we are in the vicinity of the site of the old Redwood Ferry. Not known to have been a native village site, it became one in the 1850s when the Lower Sioux Reservation was created as part of the 1851 treaties of Traverse des Sioux and Mendota, and the Lower Sioux Agency was created atop the bluff there. Because food and other supplies were stored here, it was one of the first places attacked by the Dakota in the war of 1862. A year before that, Henry David Thoreau visited the site.

* * *

Henry David Thoreau had a fascination with the American West. His health had been deteriorating for some time, and his doctor advised that traveling to a different climate, specifically Minnesota's, might cure his ills. Henry, then forty-four, set out with Horace Mann Jr., a teenager deeply interested in science, as his traveling companion and assistant. On May 11, 1861, Henry and his young companion left Concord on the Fitchburg railway and continued west on a series of railroads to Chicago, then took the steamship *Itasca* onto the Mississippi River to St. Paul, a journey of sixteen days. For the next three weeks, the two explored Minneapolis, St. Anthony, and St. Paul. One thing they happened upon was a promotional flyer for a "Grand Pleasure Excursion" up the Minnesota River to the Lower Sioux Agency at the Redwood Ferry aboard the steamboat *Frank Steele*. Fortuitously, the steamboat would be arriving upriver to coincide with the annual distribution of annuity payments to the Dakota. (The payments were compensation—extremely meager compensation—for the Dakota surrendering almost all of their land in the Minnesota River Basin.) The flyer claimed that passengers would see five thousand Indians or more. Although Thoreau had had few interactions with Indians, he was intrigued by them and had written a series of eleven journals that he called the *Indian Notebooks*. He must have been ecstatic when he learned of the *Frank Steele* excursion.

In a letter to his friend Franklin B. Sanborn, Thoreau wrote this:

> This is eminently *the* river of Minnesota (for she shares the Mississippi with Wisconsin) and it is of incalculable value to her. It flows through a very fertile country, destined to be famous for its wheat; but it is a remarkably winding stream, so that Redwood is only half as far from its mouth by land as by water. There was not a straight reach a mile in length as far as we went. . . . In making a short turn, we repeatedly and designedly ran square into the steep and soft bank, taking in a cart load of earth, — this being more effectual than the rudder to fetch us about again; or the deeper water was so narrow and close to the shore, that we were obliged to run into and break down at least fifty trees which overhung the water, when we did not cut them off, repeatedly losing a part of our outworks. . . . I could pluck almost any plant on the bank from the boat.

A journalist on the expedition reported, "The river . . . is distressingly crooked. Sometimes we go six to fifteen miles to achieve one; and so frequent and aggravated are the ox-bows that we pass every house on four sides at least."

En route to the Redwood Ferry, the *Frank Steele* stopped for the night at Fort Ridgely, then still under construction. Despite a growing discord between settlers and the Dakota, the fort was undermanned because so many Minnesotans were off fighting in the Civil War.

The *Frank Steele* docked the next morning at the Redwood Landing. During the festivities, the boat's deck cannon burst when it was ceremoniously fired, and the heavy breach was propelled into the cabin, barely missing some passengers. Then it was learned that the annuity would not be handed out to the Indians at this time. Instead, there was to be a program of speeches by the superintendent of regional Indian affairs, the Indian agent Joseph R. Brown, Governor Alexander Ramsey, and Red Owl, spokesperson for the Indians. Typical of Thoreau, he and Horace found time before the speeches to hike to the top of the bluff and look for new kinds of plants.

On the way back to St. Paul, Thoreau wrote:

> We once ran fairly onto a concealed rock, with a shock that aroused all the passengers, and rested there, and the mate went below with a lamp expecting to find a hole, but he did not. Snags and sawyers [uprooted trees] were so common that I forgot to mention them. The sound of the boat rumbling over one was the ordinary music. However, as long as the boiler did not burst, we knew that no serious accident was likely to happen.

I'll take a canoe any day.

Thoreau and Mann left St. Paul on the steamship *War Eagle* en route to Prairie du Chien, Wisconsin, then by steamer on Lakes Michigan and Huron, and finally by rail back to Boston. Thoreau died May 6, 1862. The Dakota–US War began some three months later.

The Thoreau Society recognizes areas visited by Thoreau as "Thoreau Country," and this includes Minnesota. There is an ongoing, informal effort to establish interpretive signage and promote events at locales such as the St. Anthony Falls area in Minneapolis and the Ney Nature Center in the Minnesota River town of Henderson.

* * *

After flowing through Morton, the river twists and turns in a series of loops all the way to the town of Franklin, ten river miles away. If you drive, it's about half that distance. We pull into the landing at the Highway 5 bridge and are pleased to see it has a large picnic area. I settle in for some time alone with my journal, while Geri, ever considerate of my need to write, goes up the hill to fill our jugs with water. The elementary school has an open door, and the custodian there is happy to fill the jugs and regale Geri with stories about Franklin's annual Catfish Derby Days, coming up in just a couple of weeks. It sounds like an event not to be missed.

* * *

And miss it we don't! On the last weekend in July, we drive to Franklin with our daughter and her family. Our first stop is the Highway 5 landing, where a gaggle of spectators is watching a woman wielding one of her twelve fillet knives. She is, of course, cleaning catfish. She dispatches each fish with alacrity and precision. There will be plenty of fish all winter in her household. A lively discussion ensues about the taste of various fish. The consensus is catfish tastes better than walleye.

Anglers are obliged to use stout tackle if they want to have a fighting chance of reeling in a big cat. The boats at the landing have flat bottoms for navigation in shallow water. They are well stocked with hefty rods and reels, big landing nets, and coolers.

Back in town, we check out the huge tank of writhing catfish, where the DNR fisheries expert is taking in and weighing them for the contest as well as making sure they stay well hydrated until they can be returned to the river. Our daughter's reaction? "They sure aren't the cutest of fish." The grandkids'? "Can we pet them???" (Yes, under the watchful eye of the DNR expert.) The biggest cat so far this year, caught by a guy from nearby Sleepy Eye, weighs thirty-one pounds. The biggest one caught since the contest debuted in 1976 was fifty-two pounds, five ounces. Minnesota fisherfolk are justified in boasting that this river is home to world-class cats.

This hometown festival has something for everyone: softball, volleyball, and beanbag tournaments; a 5K race; music and street dances; games for kids; a queen contest and variety show; crafts; food; even a football-player auction. To my eternal regret, we're informed that we've missed the Kiss the Catfish contest. I would have liked to have been a judge for that event.

* * *

Back to our river journey: when Geri returns with the filled water jugs, we explore our surroundings and discover what I assume is Franklin Creek. The tiny stream, just a few inches deep, carries sand particles to the river. In contrast to the river and some of its larger tributaries, nearly all the small feeder streams we've seen have had remarkably clear water and a delicate alluvial fan. Seeing these little streams running clear gives me a glimmer of hope that through persistent effort we can someday see clear water at the mouths of the larger tributaries as well.

We get back on the water and paddle a ways. We seem to have over-looked the Renville County Park and boat landing, so as evening descends, we set up camp on a narrow strand of shore with a twelve-foot mudflat behind us and enough firm sand for laying out the tarp to keep mud and sand at bay. In the waning light, two men motor upstream in a johnboat. I suspect they are putting out catfish bait for a night of fishing fun.

Flathead catfish will lie in wait for any prey swimming by and snatch them up with their big mouth.

Setting out next morning, we come upon the "overlooked" camp-ground less than a mile downstream. Five campsites are occupied, and license plates indicate there's a party from Iowa. A pair of anglers sits on lawn chairs at the edge of the river. We paddle over to chat. He is a machinist from New Ulm, and she is a banker. I ask them which catfish species tastes best. He prefers flathead cats; she prefers the oilier channel cats. We wish our new friends good luck and head off downstream. It occurs to me that I don't recall which kind Geri and I enjoyed at Del and Shirley Wehr-spann's—I just remember it was deep-fried and delicious.

The sky today is the deepest blue imaginable. A magnificent adult bald eagle sits in the upper branch of a tree and appears to be keeping an eye on an immature eagle on a neighboring tree. I look for a nest—the huge, twiggy structures aren't hard to spot—but don't see one. At the end of the day, we see two flocks of cedar waxwings with their distinctive crests and gorgeous, delicate brown-and-yellow plumage. Waxwings are berry eaters. Given the abundance of wild grapes in these riverine forests, it is not surprising to find them here. We also watch a group of three belted kingfishers. I have never seen so many at one time. They are usually solitary; I suspect we're blessed to be observing a mated pair with their offspring.

So many times it looks like the river comes to an abrupt end up ahead, then it surprises us with a new direction. Often at these points there is a massive pile of trees dropped every which way. In many respects, Geri and I are experiencing a Minnesota River very much like the one Henry David Thoreau described.

In other respects, though, the river is very different from the one Thoreau traveled. Geri, as navigator, has occasionally been frustrated with the map, trying to determine precisely where we are. I remind her that the river is constantly changing; a bend in the river when the map was made, or when Thoreau was here, may now be a backwater or oxbow. With such a vast floodplain left behind by glacial River Warren, there is much flat land over which the river can meander. The current today is sluggish. It hasn't rained much lately, and the river is dropping.

We meet the outflow of Fort Ridgely Creek and beach the canoe. The water is exceptionally clear, and I walk beside the creek the length of a football field, stopping to watch countless groups of minnows and other tiny fish darting this way and that. I'm as happy as I imagine a hungry heron would be, seeing such an abundance of fish in such wonderfully clean water.

We stop paddling a little early because we've come upon a high-and-dry sandbar and because we are fascinated by the ecology of a logjam on the other side of the river. Logjams happen when one tree trunk or other big log gets hung up, and over time other woody debris piles on until a literal logjam develops. This one is now five feet high. Beneath the log-bound surface is open water, and we hear the *pucker-smack* sounds of carp. It hosts a rich collection of plants—masses of duckweed and what must be at least twenty other species, including several kinds of moss. This micro-cosm provides food for a great variety of aquatic creatures that enrich the biological diversity of the river. At our campsite's beach, we find a signifi-cant number of mollusk shells in fresh condition. Apparently, raccoons or river otters recently enjoyed a feast here. Logjams can present obstacles for navigation, but I've heard river ecologists say that the best thing a tree can do is to fall into a river.

* * *

Marj Frederickson had urged us to visit Harkin Store, about a dozen miles upriver from New Ulm. The original, nineteenth-century store and several modern buildings at the site are visible from the river, but getting up the steep bank is a challenge. We crawl up leaning logs, grasping at limbs to get to the top of the bank, only to encounter the most obnox-ious thorn bushes we have ever faced. (The more conventional access to Harkin Store is via Nicollet County Highway 21, part of the beautiful Minnesota River Scenic Byway.)

We are fortunate to arrive when the building is open and Minnesota Historical Society staff is present. Ruth tells us that the store opened in 1871 in what was then the town of West Newton, halfway between Fort Ridgely and New Ulm. Back then, there was a much more user-friendly landing, and steamboats frequently stopped here.

Early in the 1800s, the only way to move goods from place to place was in canoes. The first steamboat to make it up the Minnesota River past Carv-er Rapids (at the southwest end of today's Twin Cities metropolitan area) was the *Anthony Wayne* in 1850. By 1856, at least five steamers, sometimes towing heavily laden barges, plied the river as far as Fort Ridgely to convey passengers and cargo, leaving the canoe to history. Goods being moved included flour, flaxseed, oats, lumber, shingles, bricks, furs, and hides.

West Newton and the Harkin Store thrived for just a few years, until railroads came to the Minnesota Valley and relegated the steamboat to obscurity. The railroad was routed through New Ulm, bypassing West Newton, and businesses started leaving. The Harkin family continued to serve local farmers until 1901, when the store closed, leaving all the remaining stock intact. The Minnesota Historical Society established it as a museum in 1938.

* * *

Half a mile downstream, we come upon a beautiful campsite and stop for lunch. Immediately across from our sandbar burbles a stream maybe four feet wide, sharply incising the woods behind and ultimately the bluff itself. These streams are still responding to the legacy of glacial River Warren, cutting through glacial till layers, bringing their gradients into equilibrium with the deep valley and, in the process, conveying sediment to the river. That is a major reason why the river carries so much sediment.[36] The incising is slowed considerably where streams encounter bedrock, and that is why there are so many waterfalls on Minnesota River tributaries. The waterfalls are nick points—that is, steps in a river's profile—that will take much longer to wear away than do layers of till. Every rapids is also a nick point in the river's profile. They lower the waterway into the landscape bit by bit, millennium by millennium.

Two pelicans fly over us heading upstream, the first we've seen in many miles and a nice reminder of the flocks we saw at the Granite Falls Dam and elsewhere upriver. Pelicans have become something of a talisman on our journey. Seeing them always brings a smile and a sense of gratitude that the river is clean enough to support these magnificent, fish-eating creatures.

---

36. The other major reasons are not natural. Sedimentation of the river has been significantly exacerbated by human changes to the landscape, including draining of wetlands, replacing prairie with row crops, constructing drainage ditches, and installing subsurface drain tile on farm fields.

According to the DNR, the Marsh Lake colony of American white pelicans
is the largest such colony in North America.

We cross over to the west side of the river where several carp are working their way up a tiny stream less than eight inches deep, the tips of their
dorsal fins poking out of the water. Downstream a bit, we come to an even
smaller stream and watch two carp wriggle up it with their dorsal fins completely exposed and their bellies scraping bottom, putting them at high
risk of being caught by a predator. Reproduction is a powerful instinct.
Carp wriggling their way into backwaters and silty streams stir up mud and
make the water cloudy—not good for ecosystems that rely on clear water.

Soaking up the sun on a fallen log protruding out of the water at river's edge is a softshell turtle. These reptiles are skittish, and this one slips
back into the river before we can get close enough to tell whether it's a
spiny softshell or a smooth softshell. The spiny softshell is fairly common
on the Minnesota, while the smooth is a species of special concern. Mud,
sand, sandbars, and beaches are their preferred habitat. Unlike the seven
hard-shelled species of turtles found in Minnesota, softshells have leathery

shells that lack bony plates, with light and dark splotches that produce an element of camouflage. The carapace (top side of the shell) of the spiny has many small projections. Females can grow up to eighteen inches long and are roughly twice the size of males. These turtles are carnivorous: they eat crayfish and aquatic insects, as well as frogs, earthworms, fish, tadpoles, and even carrion.

We have not seen many campsites. We pass one that we deem too narrow, with scant space between the water and the woods. We decide to go on. We have learned that one can always find a campsite on this river, though some may not be as commodious as one would like.

With darkness imminent, we find a boat landing that will suffice. The concrete is plastered with a thick, slippery layer of mud, so getting up the slope is precarious. Rocks mushed into the mud serve as stepping-stones. At the far end of the idle field above sits a well-maintained farmstead. State law dictates that the land from a river's shore to the high-water mark is public domain. Although we have the right to camp on this spot, we feel obliged to check in with the landowner and explain our situation. Geri trudges toward the farmhouse up the hill while I begin organizing camp.

After thirty minutes, I begin to worry. Where is Geri? I jog to the farm-house to find her in animated conversation with the landowner, Beth Dale. Beth is an accomplished photographer whose pictures are stunning: sun-rise and sunset on the river and views of past floodwaters that almost reach her shed. She tells us she feels privileged to have hosted the Dakota Trail of Tears contingent on their journey to commemorate the 150th anniver-sary of their ancestors' forced march to the Fort Snelling internment camp in the winter of 1862. All too often on our journey, Geri and I encounter reminders of the often brutal story of the Euro American conquest of the Minnesota River Valley.

Ominous rain clouds are building out of the south. We must leave our new friend and scamper back to camp. We finish supper and retreat to our tent just ahead of a monster downpour.

The next morning, we break camp under a beautiful blue sky. It's not even noon when we come around yet another bend in the river and see our destination: New Ulm's boat ramp. There is a clatter of commerce: the banging of railcars and sounds emanating from industrial buildings up from

Unlike most turtles, softshells have a leathery, flexible carapace. In Minnesota,
the spiny softshell (shown here) is relatively common,
while the smooth softshell is a species of special concern.

the bank of the river. There's no competition at the landing at the moment.
We wade the canoe among small rocks, then lower it onto a gravelly strand
beside the concrete. How different this scene would have looked from the
1850s to the 1870s with steamboats and barges vying for dock space.

The car is soon loaded with all but one of our possessions: the handgun
we found in Morton needs to be turned in to the police. I am nervous about
carrying it at all, let alone toting it into a police station. I slip it into my fanny
pack, enter the station, and explain the odd circumstance to the officer behind the glass window. She directs me to slide it to her. She thanks me and I
thank her. As we drive away from New Ulm, Geri and I reflect on the twists
and turns of this journey and wonder what we may discover on the next leg,
from New Ulm to Le Sueur. There's never a dull moment on this river, and we
look forward to new adventures as we make our way toward the confluence.

Lakes of the Middle Minnesota River Basin

He leads me beside the still waters, he refreshes my soul.

—PSALMS 23: 2B-3A NIV

We are in Minnesota, in the Minnesota River Basin, so we figure we should at least take a look at Minnesota Lake. It's about thirty miles south of Mankato on State Highway 22. The lake is thick with algae and devoid of boaters. There's a canoe launch in a residential area on the east side and another on the northwest side, but otherwise the lake is surrounded by corn and bean fields and has a cattail fringe ninety meters wide. On the other side of the highway, though, is Stokman Wildlife Management Area (WMA), managed by the Minnesota DNR, and just southwest of the lake is Minnesota Lake Waterfowl Production Area (WPA), managed by the US Fish and Wildlife Service. Buffer zones are beneficial for water quality and wildlife habitat at least as much around lakes as they are along streams and rivers. Converting another bit or two of adjoining farmland to a WMA or WPA would be much appreciated by all concerned, human beings included.

Driving west just a few miles we come to Lura Lake, where we find a nice campground, playground, fishing dock, picnic shelter, and boat landing at Daly Park on the east side of the lake. No people are around, but we're greeted by several pelicans passing overhead. Parts of the shore are smothered in bright green algae. There are patches of blue-green algae scum along the shore and at the dock. Some species of blue-greens, technically a type of bacteria, can be poisonous to dogs and can sicken people. We launch and paddle past lots of houses and cottages, most with boat docks, spread along the shore. As we watch two fishing boats launch, I ponder the attraction people have for this lake. How powerful is the pull to a lake, even one whose water is chunky and pungent.

Another short jaunt west and we're at Eagle Lake, not far from Mankato Airport. It has some of the greenest water I have ever seen. A narrow fringe of cattails and line of willows do not protect the badly eroding shore. At the trailer launch, I watch a man climb into a high-powered motorboat and roar over to the opposite shore. He takes a couple swings up and down the lake, makes his way back to the trailer launch, and abruptly leaves. Sadly, I empathize. Eagle Lake is a disaster, with a Secchi depth of only twenty-eight centimeters (about eleven inches) in pea-green water. We return to shore among tiny balls of green algae, and I decide to investigate the surrounding area to see if I can figure out why the lake is in such poor condition.

I walk back from the shore and discover a large culvert directed at the lake. As I approach it, I see a second culvert. The land across the road is farmland with a gentle slope toward a highway ditch with standing water in it. Now I find a third culvert that goes under the road delivering nutrient-laden water directly to the lake. Aha. Runoff containing nitrogen and phosphorus from farm fields has degraded the lake and its resource value. It's a common situation in the Minnesota River Basin: shallow, temporary wetlands are turned into farmland by draining them via ditches to deeper, permanent lakes. And the lakes suffer.

* * *

Mills Lake is in Blue Earth County near the town of Lake Crystal right off US Highway 169. We pull into a gravel landing and launch the canoe under blue sky. And we are not alone; another couple in a canoe is enjoying the quiet morning. They live twelve minutes away and are playing hooky, they say. He tells us he has paddled the whole Minnesota River and is delighted when we tell him we're doing so too. They are curious about what we are doing on the lake. Geri shows them the Secchi disk, and I explain that I am writing a biography of the Minnesota River and its basin. Our new friends have to get to work, so Geri and I paddle out to mid-lake and find, again, less-than-clear water. Curly leaf pondweed has invaded the lake. Long strands of algae float on the surface.

In the town of Lake Crystal, a culvert large enough for a powerboat connects Loon Lake and Crystal Lake. Houses line the shores of both lakes, though there are lengthy stretches of natural shoreline. In places, we see pea-green water with no discernible aquatic plants. I wonder if they sprayed chemicals on the lake, eliminating aquatic vegetation to facilitate powerboat traffic. Loon Lake has a Secchi depth well within hypereutrophication status.

We drive into the town of Lake Crystal, population 2,549, and stop at the city park on the west side of Crystal Lake to eat lunch under shade trees. Adults watch kids splash along the shore. The community obviously loves its lake. We paddle to mid-lake and record a Secchi reading of seventy centimeters (27.5 inches): eutrophic but not hypereutrophic. Not bad! Clumps of algae line the shore, and we spot the invasive curly leaf pondweed and clusters of native duck weed. We then explore a peninsula by a cemetery where the shore is quite natural. I draw the canoe into a leaning tree branch, tie our canoe rope to it, and think about where we are. Crystal Lake. When it got that name, the water had to have been crystal-clear. How different is its reality today. But despite the brownish water and algal blooms, people who have lake homes along the shores of these basin lakes and recreate there find it worthwhile. The not-bad Secchi measurement suggests that the citizens here are working to reestablish a lake worthy of its name.

* * *

The next day, we head to Swan Lake in Nicollet County. At approximately ten thousand acres (fourteen square miles), it is the largest prairie-pothole lake in North America. Even so, the lake today is half the size it once was, having been drained for agriculture in the late nineteenth and early twentieth centuries. Swan Lake (Bde Maġataŋka) is highly significant for its natural history, cultural history, and conservation efforts. There is archeological evidence of people living here as far back as eight thousand years ago. In the 1800s, it was the summer home of the Sisseton branch of Dakota, led by Ištáȟba, Chief Sleepy Eye.

Like all prairie-pothole lakes, Swan Lake is landlocked. Historically, the depth of the lake varied dramatically, depending on annual precipitation and runoff. This natural phenomenon was problematic to settlers, especially as more and more of the surrounding watershed was plowed up for agriculture. Nutrient runoff from the farmland caused eutrophication, greatly diminishing the lake's value to fish and wildlife. Various conservation efforts, beginning in the 1950s, have alleviated the problems through creation of Nicollet Creek (a man-made drainage ditch connecting the lake to the Minnesota River) and a control structure that allows watershed professionals to adjust when and how much water drains from the lake. It was once a seasonal home to trumpeter swans and a migration resting spot for tundra swans. As part of its enormously successful reintroduction program led by Nongame Wildlife coordinator Carrol Henderson, in 1988, the Minnesota DNR released five trumpeter swans into Swan Lake. Today, no fewer than thirty DNR Wildlife Management Areas are scattered around the greater Swan Lake area, and the lake is again a magnet for anglers and waterfowl hunters. The Nicollet Conservation Club, one of the largest such organizations in the state, maintains a lodge there whose rooftop sports an observation deck.

Geri and I glide into Swan Lake among a rich diversity of aquatic plants and very clear water. A flock of black terns soars overhead. We launch at the southwest corner at a landing by a control dam and start paddling against a sluggish current in the labyrinthine cattail side channels. Extensive stands of *Vallisneria americana* (wild celery) and a number of other native species indicate a healthy lake. The lake lies from north to southwest on a scrambled line of about ten miles with a seemingly endless series of waterways headed off in many directions, broken up by patches of cattails. As we meander through the wetland, we realize how easy it would be to get lost in this vast watery world and begin noting landmarks to guide us on our return. I might advise fellow paddlers to bring a GPS to Swan Lake.

A solitary yellow-headed blackbird flies overhead. I'm delighted by how much native milfoil and other aquatic plants are visible in this clear water. Gardens of water lilies enrich the scene. Microcrustaceans and leeches abound. The lake depth is 1.3 meters (about four feet), and we can see the Secchi disk all the way to the bottom. It's refreshing to spend time on a shallow lake that is in such good health.

Just to the east of Swan Lake is Middle Lake, around which are three of the Swan Lake WMA units. Middle Lake is more wetland than lake and is managed as a hunters' paradise. We follow a long, dusty road to the parking lot. The boat ramp extends twenty-five feet onto the shore, leading me to think the water level must be quite variable. Cattails extend far out into the lake. Behind us, rich green cornstalks stand at least ten feet high.

Heading east on Highway 99, we soon arrive at Oak Leaf Lake, with Swan Lake WMAs on the north and west sides. We flip the canoe off the roof of the car and notice the logo sign of the Clean Water Land and Legacy Amendment,[37] which provided the funds to create the public access here. Cattails line the shore except for a 20-meter-long corridor from the landing out into the lake of 139 acres. We are pleasantly surprised to find a Secchi depth of 1.8 meters (nearly six feet); the DNR LakeFinder website shows that most years this lake is hypereutrophic. Shallow lakes' clarity can vary dramatically with changing conditions; a sustained, strong wind can agitate the water and bring sediment and nutrients up from the bed. We find only native aquatic plants here: *Elodea,* a water plant common in biology classes, native milfoil, and one of the *Potamogetons.* Multitudinous minnows swim by in schools. As we steer the canoe back up the water corridor to land, we spot numerous tiny leeches. We're in the heart of corn and soybean country, but for the second time on our lakes tour I find myself wishing we had brought our snorkeling gear.

* * *

Our first visit to Bass Lake, just south of Lura Lake in Faribault County, had found the DNR finishing up some roadwork and maintenance on the dock and boat ramp. Today, the work is complete, and Geri and I are on

---

37. The amendment was passed by Minnesota voters in 2008. It raised the state sales tax by three-eighths of a cent and, according to the website, provides funding to "protect drinking water sources; to protect, enhance, and restore wetlands, prairies, forests, and fish, game, and wildlife habitat; to preserve arts and cultural heritage; to support parks and trails; and to protect, enhance, and restore lakes, rivers, streams, and groundwater." The tax increase expires in the year 2034.

Bass Lake. Thanks, DNR! Schools of minnows zip along the shore in relatively clear water. We paddle slowly and see *Elodea* and one of the large *Potamogeton* plants. This one is *P. foliosus,* one of the few species in this large family that I can identify. I am pleased to see it here, as it provides waterfowl food and fish habitat. Common bur reed grows in a marshy bay and along edges of the lake. Like many aquatic plants, bur reed produces fruits valued as food for ducks, geese, and swans as well as muskrats and other mammals. The plants mature to form clusters of prickly spheres with diameters the size of a quarter.

We leave the littoral zone, head out to mid-lake, and measure a Secchi depth of 1.5 meters (almost five feet). Excellent! The greater water clarity may be due in part to the Smith Wildlife Management Area that occupies much of the land between Lura and Bass. Several long stretches of undeveloped land abut the shore. There are also groups of lake homes with docks and motorboats. Some houses look quite new. The weather is cool, and a light mist begins to dampen our day if not our enthusiasm. Minnows escort our canoe back to the landing. Snug in the cozy car, Geri makes an important observation: Habitat restoration projects like the one we've just seen are vital to the restoration of the Minnesota River itself. The river can be clean only when the water it receives from the land is clean.

We next visit two of about eighteen lakes in Martin County with an unusual north-south alignment. We reach for geologist Richard Ojakangas' *Roadside Geology of Minnesota* to find out how these lakes, including Hall and Budd Lakes, were formed. An old glacial channel, thirty to forty feet deep, up to a mile wide, and twenty-five miles long, cut into till deposited by the retreating Des Moines Lobe. A tunnel-valley formed beneath the ice sheet, ultimately creating all these small lakes north and south of the city of Fairmont. Both Hall and Budd Lakes have similar littoral vegetation to our last few lakes and identical sixty-centimeter Secchi depths. The channel between the two lakes is armored with big chunks of Sioux quartzite.

We had been told by an aquatic researcher that Bean Lake, in Cottonwood County near the small town of Storden, was his favorite lake in the basin, a real gem. Geri and I get out the map and realize it's quite a distance away. Though our day has been long, there is still enough daylight and we decide to go now. We arrive at the parking lot and see a Walleye Club sign, which seems incongruous given the dense algal bloom and windrows of blue-green algae at the lake's edge. Bean is no gem this day, it appears. But suddenly my disappointment is disrupted by a ruckus in the water not far from the landing: eight enormous pelicans taking flight from our intrusion. Out over a patch of bulrushes, I now see dazzling blue damselflies flitting over the water and hundreds of whirligig beetles zipping wildly around one another in their seemingly silly swimming games. As we paddle to mid-lake, I expect a low Secchi measure based on all the algae at the shore, but Geri can see the disk a full one meter (just over three feet) down. I'm not so skeptical about the Walleye Club anymore. The heat of midsummer and lower-than-usual water levels are possible reasons for the muck on the shoreline.

In the deepening twilight with a rising moon as our guide, we drive forty miles east to a motel in St. James. The next morning, we find the crescent-shaped St. James Lake in a beautiful park obviously valued by the community. People are walking around the lake, gathering in the picnic area, playing disc golf, fishing from the docks, even renting canoes and kayaks. The lakeshore is mostly lined with large, hauled-in rocks and stately box elder trees. The invasive curly leaf pondweed is well established, making for cloudy water in the littoral zone. We put our canoe in the water and paddle to the middle of the lake. The Secchi disk reads one meter (just over three feet), relatively clear water. The more I dip my paddle into these lakes of the Minnesota River Basin and talk with the people who live here, the more I appreciate that these prairie-pothole lakes are treasured resources.

We hop in the car, cross the Cottonwood River and continue north to Sleepy Eye, where I had my very first memory of a lake. Dad taught and coached at Sleepy Eye High School for two years when I was a toddler. One warm fall day, Mother, who loved lakes more than anyone I have ever known, attached me to her bike for a jaunt to Sleepy Eye Lake. As soon as she started pedaling, though, my foot caught in her spokes. I still remember that pain.

As we're eating lunch at the park along the lake, a large van pulls up to the soybean field across the road and a gaggle of teenagers piles out. Curious, I go talk to the adult supervisor. Monsanto has hired the kids to pull corn plants from the soybean field to prevent cross-pollination of the experimental corn plants in the adjoining field.

Sleepy Eye Lake is about 240 acres, with shoreline plants—curly leaf, milfoil, duckweed, several lily pads, and patches of rushes—extending almost to the middle. We paddle out into the small area of open water and record one-meter Secchi visibility.

Clear Lake is five miles southwest of New Ulm. About the same size as Sleepy Eye Lake, the average depth is a mere five feet, and it is so dominated by cattails that virtually the entire lake is a littoral zone. We record thirty centimeters (nearly one foot) of Secchi depth. As we paddle back toward the landing, something big and white swimming along the edge of the cattail fringe grabs our attention. Drawing closer, we see that a man is out swimming with his two dogs—one of them pure white. We glide up and hear his story. A gregarious sort, he relates a legend that during the war with the Dakota, army payroll was sunk in the lake. He feels strongly about protecting this small lake and the environment that surrounds it and thanks us for stopping by.

The proprietor at the motel in St. James had told us that, in addition to the lake in town, the locals like to fish on Fox and Hanska Lakes. Neither had been on our itinerary, but looking at the map, we see we're close to Hanska and decide to check it out. Geri drives while I do a little research. At nearly 1,800 acres, Hanska is the largest lake in Brown County and home to a county park complete with modern campground. Archeological evidence indicates people lived around the lake at least 2,500 years ago; Norwegian immigrants settled here in the 1850s. People say it's one of the best walleye lakes in the area.

Ten pickups with empty boat trailers are at the landing. We can see four fishing boats on the water; the rest must be farther down the long, skinny lake. This end of the lake has mostly undeveloped shore, and the water looks as clear as any we've seen on our trip so far. We amble over to a sand beach, where two gents are fishing off the dock and two more in hip waders are in the water. They are catching mostly crappies and perch, they say, and while we're talking, one of the anglers reels in a bullhead.

Hanska, a Norwegian-sounding variation of the word for *long* in the Dakota language, has an inspiring story. An interpretive sign in the picnic area tells about Ole Synsteby, an immigrant from Norway who acquired land here in 1879. Ole was greatly disturbed by talk that Lake Hanska might be turned into a slough, as monster Hubbard ditching machines made it possible to drain almost anything and the appetite for farmland was insatiable. He lobbied for public access to the lake and a dam to regulate the water level. People say Ole guarded a gate to make sure cows could not get into the lake. In his later years, he said, "I do not know why but some used to call this the Synsteby Dam, for to ridicule me or to honor me, I do not know, and I did not care a snap. I got what I worked for and these same people who opposed me are giving me thanks today for what I did." Ole was an ecologist and environmental activist long before the Sigurd Olsons and Aldo Leopolds came along. Geri and I join in giving thanks for what he did.

Voices for the River:
Scott Sparlin

It's time we all understand

It's what we do on land

That makes our water what it is today

This simple fact is true

It's controlled by me and you

It's time to fix the mistakes of yesterday

—SCOTT SPARLIN

Explorer-naturalist George William Featherstonhaugh traveled the Minnesota River in 1835 and recorded in his journal that "the water was beautifully transparent, and the clams stuck in countless numbers in the clean white sand." One hundred years later, Dakota elder Carrie Schommer was five years old and living in a small village on the river near Granite Falls. "Growing up along the Minnesota River," Carrie explains, "the water was clear and, you know, you could see the bottom." But things changed, and not for the better.

One day in the early 1980s, a relative newcomer to New Ulm named Scott Sparlin took his young son to the river to fish. They set up on the river's bank, dangling bait into the water. Scott was taken by the particularly brown color of the water that day. It began to trouble him, and by the end of the day, he vowed, "I can't leave my son a river that looks like this." Scott became an activist, a voice for the river.

His first step was to gather fishermen friends to form an organization, the Sportsmen's Coalition for a Clean Minnesota River (SCCMR). The first task of his fledgling group was to inform others about the river's condition and to recruit them to join the cause to improve water quality. As leader of the musical group the Bockfest Boys, Scott had the instincts of a promoter. He convinced his organization to hold a weekend event to draw an audience.

A large pink flyer headlined the event with "A clean, useable Minnesota River? Someday is now! Our region's greatest resource needs YOU! How do we start?" The flyer describes the event as an invitation to join forces with sportsmen's groups, farmers, environmental groups, and concerned citizens throughout southern Minnesota in a long-term effort. Scott and the other organizers managed to draw ten state and federal agencies as well as people from seven colleges and universities and all thirty-seven counties in the basin. Governor Arne Carlson gave welcoming remarks, and a number of local politicians spoke. The editor of *Sports Illustrated* gave the keynote address. The gathering was covered in a documentary for public television. Events included a hog roast, the nation's number-one male chorus, and lots of seminars and workshops. As the event drew to a close on Sunday, people were already gathering ideas for the next year's conference, and "Riverblast" became a mainstay on the New Ulm events calendar, providing fun and learning by day and musical performances in the evenings. Teachers from around the area began to ask Scott to give talks to their students and to bring his guitar; he had written several songs about the river and cleanup efforts, including the one cited at the top of this chapter.

SCCMR's next initiative was a storm drain awareness project. The flyer urged, "Join us and help improve our rivers and ground waters." Citizens were encouraged to spread the word that storm sewers are not trash cans. Whatever gets dumped into storm drains ends up in rivers, lakes, and wetlands. Groups formed to press the New Ulm City Council to allow volunteers to paint signs at storm sewer drains that say, "Please don't pollute. Drains to the river."

Scott's group continually got newspaper coverage and established a presence at Farmfest to share information about the river and its circumstances, drawing additional attention from a key constituency. Employees at the New Ulm 3M facility adopted a section of river near New Ulm to reduce debris. The Izaak Walton League added support.

In the 1990s, Congress began considering a new program that would induce farmers to set aside marginal lands, particularly near waterways. The idea was to combine the existing federal Conservation Reserve Program (CRP) with similar state-run programs, thus providing sufficient incentive to persuade farmers to establish permanent conservation easements. The proposal was controversial, but soon enough, environmental activists and the agricultural community alike saw the program as a way to protect rivers and other vulnerable lands without imposing a financial burden on those who owned the land.

Scott became a leader in the effort to see that the legislation got passed. He organized others in Minnesota and went to the US Capitol to lobby for the bill. The legislation passed, and CREP, the Conservation Reserve Enhancement Program, was established. The Minnesota River Citizens' Advisory Committee, of which Scott was a key member, had recommended that the entire floodplain, some two hundred thousand acres, be restored to its natural purpose. CREP, with about $250 million in state and federal funds, acquired one hundred thousand acres. Half a loaf is far better than none.

Scott and his organization received numerous awards for their efforts to promote environmental causes, including commendations from the Minnesota Board of Water and Soil Resources, US Department of the Interior, Izaak Walton League of America, and many others.

Following Scott's example, other organizations emerged to join in the work to protect the Minnesota River movement. In 2006, a group of river advocates determined that protecting the river could best be accomplished by joining ranks, and they formed a group called the Minnesota River Watershed Alliance. It met quarterly in Hutchinson to make it convenient for people from throughout the watershed to participate. I attended most of those meetings as a silent observer. Scott, I would bet, attended virtually all of those meetings as an active participant. Everyone was welcome: farmers, newspaper writers, elected officials, representatives of the US Army Corps of Engineers and other agencies, and often up to a dozen volunteer groups. I recall that at one meeting a man sitting next to me noted, "Not all the groups have the same interest and ideas. Trying to gather them together is like herding fish." Challenging, but it can be done, as Scott and other voices for the river have demonstrated.

A few months after the alliance's first meeting, Willmar's *West Central Tribune* reported on a survey that had been conducted the previous summer. The article stated, "Residents in the Minnesota River Basin are well aware of the pollution problems the river faces, and they want to see them addressed at a faster pace than they believe is currently the case." Polling by the Friends of the Minnesota Valley and the alliance revealed that 48 percent of those surveyed said they would pay something toward the river cleanup.

When the county boards of the basin disbanded the Minnesota River Board in 2014, the river suddenly had no basin-wide governmental entity to oversee and coordinate cleanup efforts. Scott and others felt a need for action and conducted listening sessions around the basin. Consensus was reached that a new basin-wide group was needed. The next step was to determine what the group would look like and what its goals would be. Scott, the community organizer, brought to life the Minnesota River Congress in 2014 to advance goals shared by farmers, recreationalists, educators, agency professionals, elected officials, conservationists, and quality-of-life advocates. It has proven a worthy successor to the Minnesota River Watershed Alliance.

Scott has been at this effort to protect and enhance the Minnesota River Basin for some thirty years and counting. His contributions are legendary, but he is by no means resting on his laurels. Speaking of one of his more significant accomplishments, Scott says, "CREP was huge. We did a nice job on that, but we've got a lot of work to do yet."

A River Bends

Sense of place is the sixth sense, an internal compass and map made by memory and spatial perception together.

—REBECCA SOLNIT

Scott Sparlin meets us at Riverside Park in the heart of New Ulm, our starting point for this leg of our adventure. With a population of 13,342, this city founded by German immigrants is the largest town we have encountered so far. Scott in his pickup and Geri in our Saturn take off for Le Sueur, our destination in five days. It's forty miles or so on the road, more like sixty-five miles on the meandering river. I stay back organizing our gear, listening to the sounds of a bustling city, and watching the river roll by.

The drivers return sooner than I had expected. I hand Scott a modest check in thanks for his help, which he accepts as a contribution to the Coalition for a Clean Minnesota River.

We launch midmorning. Within minutes, we encounter a recreational presence greater than we've seen thus far: Minnecon Park. There are folks basking in lawn chairs, small boats drawn up onshore—often with a rod and reel dangling over the transom—and kids playing at the water's edge. New Ulm has taken advantage of its waterfront property, thanks in part, no doubt, to Scott's longtime efforts to promote appreciation for the river.

Farther downstream, we see a greenish water surface and paddle toward it. It is an algae bloom, and parts of it appear to be blue-green algae, suggesting that there has been a notable flow of nutrients into the river. I stabilize the canoe so Geri can record the Secchi depth. The disk is visible to only nine centimeters (3.5 inches). A mile or so downstream from the algal bloom, we record a Secchi depth of a still-pitiful sixteen centimeters (just over 6 inches). It's apparent that conservation efforts are sorely needed in the adjoining landscape.

A cicada chorus fills the air.

We're still within the city limits when the mouth of the Cottonwood River, a major tributary of the Minnesota, appears around the bend. Had we paddled up it a few twisty miles, we would have found ourselves in Flandrau State Park, another recreational and natural resource in this river town. A delta of broad expanses of sand has formed. We beach the canoe and I walk a distance upstream. The Cottonwood here today is placid. The skeleton of an immense flathead catfish dries partly buried in the sand.

As we leave New Ulm behind us, we find ourselves paddling through a section of fascinating geological history. I spot an erosion bank with several different layers of rock and pull the canoe to shore. Here are Cretaceous deposits of the marine sea finally uncovered by the erosion of the freshwater river. I might have lingered here all day had Geri not reminded me that we had miles to go before we slept. I didn't find any, but I know fossilized leaves and ammonites are here. As much time as we have spent exploring the Minnesota River, we could spend ten times more.

We continue downstream several more miles before stopping to rest our paddling arms and stretch our backs at an extensive bar of sand and mud dotted with a few mollusk shells. As I walk into the riparian zone, I note wood nettle, a native wildflower with broad leaves, growing uniformly about ten feet into the forest, avoiding the sun. Common stinging nettles, by contrast, are a narrow-leafed invasive species that prefer clearings.

Scott Sparlin, professional fishing guide among the hats he wears, had warned us of two potential navigation hazards in this stretch of the river: an abandoned quarry and its pile of sharp, pinkish rocks that could be lurking just beneath the surface, and the area around a bridge a little farther downstream. We avoid problems, as the water level is plenty high. Scott offers his guide service only in the New Ulm area familiar to him because the ever-changing nature of the river makes navigation tricky. It's challenging enough in a canoe with a draft of a few inches; in craft that require deeper water, navigation can be downright perilous.

A green heron, no more than half the size of its great blue cousin, flies swiftly over the river and lands elegantly on the shore. They are shy birds; this one disappears into the foliage as we approach.

We come upon two fishermen in a punt, a flat-bottomed boat with a square bow well suited to rivers. They haven't caught anything yet. Farther downstream, we meet two more anglers just in time to watch them land a beautiful flathead catfish. They tell us a group of kayakers had floated by a few minutes ago. Fisherfolk and paddlers and birdwatchers and those who simply enjoy sitting on a riverbank tend to form a bond, a sense of kinship. Seeing more and more people come to appreciate this marvelous resource we call the Minnesota River fuels my optimism that, working together, we will clean it up.

We're paddling along the sinuous shoreline (Thoreau's description of his journey comes to mind), and Geri spots a green frog with black spots. It's a northern leopard frog, the most numerous species in the state. We have fourteen species of frogs, nearly all of which can be found in the Minnesota River Basin. I relish seeing this critter; they were a common sight in my childhood, but today frog populations have declined significantly worldwide due to climate disruption and other disturbances to their habitats. I remember, sadly, that in 1995, students from the New Country School (then in Le Sueur, now across the river in Henderson) were studying frogs and discovered that about half the frogs they found were deformed. The students' discovery sparked scientific research aimed at identifying the cause(s) of the problem. But funding for the research in Minnesota dried up in the early 2000s, and to date, the causes of the deformations are still not known.[38]

A brief foray up another six-foot bank at the edge of a farmer's field and I see a sign indicating that this is Conservation Reserve Program land. I silently thank the farmer.

---

38. Two books chronicle the discovery and subsequent research: *Peril in the Ponds* (University of Massachusetts Press, 2012) by MPCA biologist Judy Helgen, and *Plague of Frogs* (Hyperion, 2000) by William Souder.

A creek flows into the river—a drainage ditch, actually—and we paddle a short distance upstream to take a Secchi reading. Thirty-five centimeters (not quite fourteen inches). Back out on the river, Secchi says fifteen (six inches). Muddy water.

Midafternoon, we pull over to stretch our legs. In the distance, we hear the bellow of a cow. Minutes later another bellow, and this time, we see it—a large, pure-black animal. Other cattle follow, heading toward us and the river. We get back into the canoe and watch. Like rambunctious kids, the behemoths trample the riverbank, eroding the shoreline. Next the herd begins to wade into the river, farther and farther, out to shoulder height. I count over fifty animals standing in midstream. I think about the bacteria, phosphorus, and nitrogen in their effluent being added to an already overburdened river. The people downstream don't deserve such treatment.

Our next landmark is the boat launch where Nicollet Creek flows from Swan Lake. The creek is sparkling clean; we're not surprised after having seen the healthy Swan Lake surrounded by parcels of land set aside for conservation.

* * *

We are some ten miles from Mankato. Were we in a car right now, we'd choose to be on the Judson Bottom Road on the north side of the river, perhaps our favorite stretch of the Minnesota River Scenic Byway. It features beautiful views of the river as well as a small county park at Minnemishinona Falls, where the water falls some forty-two feet—the longest such drop in the Minnesota Valley—over a nick point composed of a layer of hardened Jordan sandstone. A septuagenarian named Charles Smith has lived in the floodplain below the falls all his life. He has taken photographs over the years documenting how increased runoff from the land above the falls has accelerated erosion of the nick point.

But of course we're not in a car, we're still paddling, and we can now see Minneopa State Park, which hugs the south bank of the river for about eight miles coming into Mankato. Minneopa (Mniópha) has long been famous for its own waterfall, a spectacular double cascade. In recent years, the park has added a 331-acre enclosure for bison, which we had heard about at the Lunch and Learn program at the Lower Sioux Agency. A visit is on our to-do list.

We now encounter a series of natural steps that lead from the river up to the ground above, each step indicating a different water level. A collection of large, weathered mollusk shells lies scattered on the terrace steps.

The next thing we know, the river is captured by a levee overlain by slabs of rock covering the shores. A few minutes downriver, the levee is itself replaced by massive concrete walls. It's all part of Mankato's protection against flooding of the Minnesota River.

* * *

Leader of the Sisseton tribe of Dakota Ištáȟba (Chief Sleepy Eye) recommended Mankato as a townsite to white settlers. But he said to build only on the uplands, as the area adjacent to the river was prone to flooding. Oh, the misery that would have been avoided had the settlers heeded his advice. The settlers established the city of Mankato, in the floodplain, in 1852. It suffered horrendous floods in 1881, 1908, 1916, 1951, and, most recently, in 1965.

No floods have occurred in Mankato since because after that 1965 flood, a decision was finally made to enclose the river. Built by the US Army Corps of Engineers to a level several feet higher than the highest-ever flood there, the flood walls and associated infrastructure have kept Mankato dry, even during the historic 1993 flood that inundated much of the Minnesota and Mississippi River valleys.

There are trade-offs to this protection. Most of Mankato is now cut off from the river that runs through it. Rather than enjoying a spectacular view of the river, residents and visitors see a concrete wall.[39] And the water that would have spread out over Mankato and dissipated gradually now rushes through town and causes problems downstream for the landscape as well as such urban centers as St. Peter, Henderson, and Chaska.

---

39. In 2016, a group of artists led by Julie Johnson-Fahrforth painted a beautiful, 540-foot-long mural on the wall. The mural shows scenes of the bend of the river behind the wall from sunrise to sunset and was created in consultation with the US Army Corps of Engineers, Mankato City Council, and the Dakota community. It shows this stretch of the river as the artists imagine it would have looked before human settlement.

* * *

Throughout our meandering trip down the Minnesota River, we have been heading generally south and southeast. Now, abruptly, the river bends due north, and no one knows why. A yet-to-be-discovered sequence of events somehow caused the powerful glacial River Warren to change course. Over the past two hundred years or so, scientists have learned a lot about the geological history of the Minnesota River Basin, but there is much more to be learned, and what caused the river to bend here remains a perplexing mystery.

According to the DNR water trails map, we have paddled about sixteen miles so far today. It is time to fill our water jugs and eat lunch. We paddle up to the boat landing at Land of Memories (Wókiksuye Makhóčhe) Park at the confluence of the Blue Earth River (Makhátho Wakpá, "the river where blue earth is gathered"), rope the canoe to a tree branch, and walk up to the picnic tables.

We camped here a year ago—it's a large, beautiful park with great significance to the Dakota people. It was here on the day after Christmas 1862, that thirty-eight Dakota men were hanged, having been convicted of killing whites during the Dakota–US War. The largest mass execution in United States history and a dark day indeed in the history of our state and nation.

Across the mouth of the Blue Earth River sits the massive CHS soybean-processing plant. Wild places and industry coexist on the Minnesota River. Most beans brought to this plant are processed into meal to feed livestock, while some are made into edible products, such as vegetable oil and tofu. Minnesota keeps about half of the beans it grows and exports the rest.

We let the current guide us into the heart of a city of just over forty thousand souls. The population of the metropolitan area, which includes the city of North Mankato, is more than ninety thousand, making it the fifth-largest city in the state. Minnesota State University at Mankato is home to the Water Resources Center and its Minnesota River Basin Data Center, an invaluable resource for the region. The data center was established in the mid-1990s in response to a recommendation from Governor Arne Carlson's Minnesota River Citizens' Advisory Committee, which said, "All of the [water-quality] data gathered should be housed in an academic institution and made readily available to the public." In recent years, the center has been seriously underfunded; only the ingenuity and perseverance of the staff have kept it going. Full funding for the center would be of great benefit to scientists, politicians, and citizens throughout the basin working to improve the river.

We float under the US Highway 169 bridge carrying the hustle and bustle of cars and eighteen-wheelers trying to keep out of one another's way. We're finally downstream from the flood wall, and we observe many people out and about by the river today at Riverside Park—picnicking, promenading with strollers, just sitting by the river.

No sooner have we put the Mankato urban center behind us than we enter the East Minnesota River State Game Refuge. It's seven miles long and two miles wide, with ten miles of meandering river frontage characterized by wide, extensive sandbars. It's astonishing; on this leg of the journey in which we have paddled through two large cities, we have also passed by two state parks, several county and municipal parks, and now this refuge.

I see a sedimentary rock formation at the river's edge. The ochre color identifies it as a dolomite from the Prairie du Chien formation. Known by the trade name Kasota stone after the small town near where it is quarried, it's popular as a building material. It supports the interior walls of the Minnesota State Capitol, embellishes the Minnesota Twins' Target Field, and, as Geri and I shall soon see, was used in the construction of the Treaty Site History Center north of St. Peter.

Still within the game refuge, we stop at the Seven Mile Creek landing. It's right on Highway 169, and had we taken the time to cross the road, we would have found ourselves in a charming county park. A sign at river's edge warns of wing dams—man-made piles of rock or concrete that project out into streams, creating a V-shaped formation that forces water away from the bank and increases the current downstream. Depending on water levels, paddlers may easily collide with the submerged structures. The river is relatively high today, so we hadn't even seen the dams.

We call it a day at Riverside Park at the south end of St. Peter, forty-nine river miles from where we started this leg of our journey in New Ulm. It's a beautiful park, with a promontory overlooking the river and an expansive sand beach. Geri's camera battery is just about kaput, so she hikes to town to find a replacement while I survey our surroundings and pick out a campsite. Six parties are already camped here, and kids are having a great time sliding down a soft slope of sand, running back up, sliding back down . . . summertime sledding! Two fishing boats are beached next to our canoe. It's nice to have company on the river.

* * *

As we prepare to break camp next morning, I see a most idyllic spot across the river. On the sandy shore is a folding aluminum chair and two planks leading to a hammock. A hand-painted sign nailed to a tree says simply "65"; perhaps it's a marker for the high-water level of the epic 1965 flood. A sturdy forked stick stands rooted in the sand, ready to prop up a fishing pole. Hannibal, Missouri, Mark Twain, Tom and Huck, and a young Darby flash through my mind.

We paddle under the Highway 99 Bridge and let the river carry us out of town. Three miles downstream, we reach perhaps the most significant site in the history of Euro American settlement of Minnesota: Traverse des Sioux. The Dakota name is Oíyuweğe, "the place of crossing." It was here on July 23, 1851 (and at a similar event two weeks later in Mendota, near Fort Snelling), that the Dakota ceded virtually all their land, twenty-four million acres of what is now southern Minnesota, to the US government. This opened the land to settlement by whites, and their numbers grew exponentially over the next several years. One of the Dakota signatories was Ištáȟba (Chief Sleepy Eye). I wonder if it was here that he warned settlers not to build on the floodplain at Mankato.

Our map indicates that Traverse des Sioux Park lies where the river does a roundabout bend a mile long. Several openings in the trees reveal a path at the water's edge. We paddle across a broad sandy bar over water three to four inches deep and push to shore. We find ourselves on a backwater of the river and discover water notably clearer than out in the main flow. Where sediment settles, clarity improves. We rope the canoe to a tree root, scramble up the bank, and begin walking on a trail through floodplain forest that I presume will lead us to the visitor center.

Kiosks and other signage inform us that the first people to occupy this ground arrived about nine thousand years ago and left evidence of their presence in the form of a large spear point of the type used to kill megafauna, the likes of mastodons and other large mammals now long extinct. When fur traders arrived in the late 1700s, a site across the river, Mayáskadaŋ, was in use by the Dakota; explorer Joseph Nicollet described it as "the rendezvous of all the villages of Sisseton when they left for buffalo hunts or when they went to gather wild rice in the area." Moving to its present location in the 1830s, the site grew as a gathering point for fur traders, missionaries, explorers, and assorted entrepreneurs.

Trade goods were not always transported on the river. For a time, Traverse des Sioux was also a launch point for oxcarts traveling overland to Lac qui Parle and from there north to Pembina on the Red River near the Canadian border. Typically, in times of high water, commerce was moved by dugout canoes or keelboats. At low water, transportation was by oxcart.

Tom Ross, Dakota leader and member of the Upper Sioux Community, wrote the text on one of the kiosks about the treaty signed here. It includes these haunting words from one of the Dakota elders:

Give us something for the children.

The words reverberate in my heart. I can imagine a discussion among elders about the portentous implications of the treaty. *What are we going to do now? How do we prepare for the future?*

Another kiosk tells of the building of a town in 1856: five taverns, two hotels, several churches, and a brewery—seventy buildings in all for a population of three hundred. Investors wagered that Traverse des Sioux would be chosen as the county seat. But St. Peter won that prize, and a little over a decade later, the town at Traverse des Sioux was abandoned.

Continuing on the trail, I come upon the largest tree I have ever seen in Minnesota—a gigantic cottonwood. I reach as far as I can around the trunk and don't make it even halfway. I remember reading about the immense loads canoes once carried. No wonder! A canoe made—that is, dug out—from the trunk of a cottonwood tree would dwarf the typical modern-day canoe built for recreation.

The hiking trail splits, and we enter a restored native prairie in all its splendor. It's late July, and the prairie is in bloom.

The visitor center comes into view. Constructed of Kasota stone, the building opened in 1994. It houses several excellent exhibits about the history of the area and is home to the Nicollet County Historical Society. I have some questions, so I approach the woman at the reception desk. "You're in luck!" she exclaims. "Bob is here today."

"Bob" is Robert Douglas, retired professor of geography at St. Peter's Gustavus Adolphus College. For two hours, this educator with a deep love of history answers my questions, shares additional insights, and prints off copies of material I will find useful. He gives me his business card and tells me to contact him if further questions arise. I thank him profusely, and we return to the canoe and the river. Later, back home, I retrieve my May–June 2010 issue of the *Minnesota Conservation Volunteer* magazine and read "Searching for Waterfalls" by Marc Hequet, in which "a geographer [Bob] scours a river valley [the Minnesota] for streams still plunging after a deluge 10,000 years ago."

* * *

The river has followed a surprisingly straight course for the fifteen miles or so from North Mankato to Traverse des Sioux. A few miles out, the twists and turns resume. West of the river here, on a large stretch of prairie, Indians annually gathered for bison hunts. That stretch of prairie ran from the tiny town of Ottawa to Le Sueur, the end point for this leg of our journey. We pull the canoe onto the sand at the landing and start hauling gear up the steep slope to the parking lot where Geri and Scott Sparlin had left our car.

The penultimate leg of our journey is complete. We will return to this landing a few weeks hence, determined to reach the confluence some seventy-five river miles to the north. I wonder what kind of a river we will encounter as we paddle our way into the Twin Cities metropolis.

Lakes of the Lower Minnesota River Basin

A lake without plankton is like an orchestra without violins.

—DARBY NELSON IN *FOR LOVE OF LAKES*

Scotch Lake is about ten miles south of the Le Sueur county seat of Le Center. The DNR LakeFinder website tells us that Scotch is 598 acres averaging ten feet deep, has a "trailer launch" public access, and is home to fifteen fish species, including black bullhead, common carp, walleye, and yellow perch. We tote the canoe down the concrete launch and paddle slowly along the littoral zone where we find a rich variety of aquatic plants. Duckweed and cattails dominate, and we also note bur reed (a valuable food source for wildlife), floating leafy plants, and copious submerged vegetation. Geri pulls our plankton net through the water to see what tiny creatures she might scoop up and empties the contents into a white sampling pan. The water has a bit of a greenish tinge to it, and it's positively teeming with tiny, squirmy copepods, crustaceans the diameter of pencil lead sometimes referred to as the cattle of lakes and ponds. These creatures, along with water fleas (*Daphnia*), play a major role in the food web of most lakes. Two fish jump close to the cattails. I expect they are common carp, which will eat copepods, *Daphnia,* and just about anything else they can fit in their mouths.

To get a meaningful measure of water clarity, we paddle out to the middle of the lake. Geri, in the bow, lowers the Secchi disk and records a hypereutrophic depth of twenty-five centimeters (just under ten inches).

It starts to rain, so we paddle skedaddle back to the boat launch, scramble to the car, and eat lunch. On return of the sun, we drive to our next lake, Emily, on the other side of the Minnesota River from St. Peter. The rain may have stopped, but the wind has picked up, and big waves make canoeing a risky proposition. So we head into town and find a grocery store with a deli and eat a tasty supper of broasted chicken, potato salad, and baking powder biscuits. Settling into our motel room, we're pleased that our visit to a basin lake has contributed to the commerce of the community.

Bright and early, we return to Lake Emily. Its littoral zone has water lilies, invasive curly leaf pondweed, and at least one species of *Potamogeton*. Thick stands of cattail provide habitat for all manner of creatures—amphibians, insects, birds, and fish. Indeed, buffers of vegetation between lake and lawn at many of the homes show that residents are mindful of the importance of minimizing nutrient runoff. Enjoying the lake with us are a family of geese with half-grown goslings, a great blue heron, a kingfisher, and a dozen or more barn swallows acrobatically capturing insects on the wing. Birds are a balm to the soul.

On to Lake Washington, which straddles Le Sueur and Blue Earth counties east-northeast of Mankato. It's a large lake, about 1,500 acres, with closely spaced homes along the north shore. Seeing very few buffers and heavy boat traffic, I'm concerned about erosion from waves and pollution from nutrients. I spot native duckweed, lots of green algae, native milfoil, and invasive curly leaf pondweed. And then I am delighted to also see the native aquatic plant *Vallisneria americana,* better known as wild celery. This plant is sought by a wide range of wildlife and is a favored food for migrating canvasback ducks and tundra swans.

Next morning, we head for Madison Lake in the town of the same name in Blue Earth County. A multitude of cottonwood seeds drift lazily downward like giant snowflakes as we arrive at Bray Park and Campground, a county facility across the lake from town. Picnic tables, a campground, a trailer launch, and a nice launching shore for canoeists and kayakers indicate that residents here appreciate the recreational value of their lake.

As we explore the littoral zone, we see *Polygonum* with its pink cluster of flowers, but given the degree of public use, it is no wonder that much of the area around the launch site has sparse vegetation. We work our way to a less disturbed littoral zone, where we find broadleaf cattails, both male and female. I suspect it may be one of the invasive hybrids. An alert, head-bobbing shorebird takes flight before we can get close enough to ID it. Dipping our Secchi disk in deeper water, we discover that Madison Lake has slightly better water clarity than many of the other lakes we've visited so far, but it's still hypereutrophic.

At Blue Earth County's 480-acre Perch Lake (one of twenty-four Minnesota lakes of that name, not including First Perch, Second Perch, and Third Perch), mama ducks with their ducklings swim by, and we get a scolding from red-winged blackbirds defending their cattail territories. Perch is very shallow, more marsh than lake. In 2009, the Minnesota Valley Trust[40] acquired and restored three hundred acres of the uplands around the lake. A trust press release quotes Charlie Blair, then manager of the Minnesota Valley National Wildlife Refuge and Wetland Management District: "These lands on Perch Lake had been identified as top priorities by the USFWS for development as a top-producing Waterfowl Production Area. The public will enjoy hunting, wildlife observation, and other wildlife-dependent recreation on these lands well into the future." Hear, hear. We see more ducks and lots of frogs as we paddle back to the landing.

We drive to Gaylord, get a motel, and eat a scrumptious meat loaf dinner of generous proportions at the Prairie House Family Restaurant. Next morning, we introduce ourselves to the 842-acre Lake Titlow (sometimes spelled *Titloe*). I'd guess this lake appealed to the settlers who established the town of Gaylord, but it's not particularly appealing today. I wade along the pea-green shore in both directions, then look out over the lake and see more of the same. A flock of eighteen pelicans glides over the lake low and

---

40. Established in 2001, the Minnesota Valley Trust is a nonprofit that manages funds provided by the Metropolitan Airports Commission to mitigate the effects of noise pollution on the Minnesota Valley National Wildlife Refuge across from MSP International Airport in Bloomington. The trust uses most of the funds to acquire critical habitat from willing landowners in the Minnesota River Basin and turns over ownership of the land to the US Fish and Wildlife Service. To date, the trust has acquired and restored more than 5,600 acres.

slows and settles on the surface a safe distance from us. Magnificent! Despite murky water and lots of algae, fish must be plentiful in this lake; most are probably black bullheads, fathead minnows, and carp—easy pickings for pelicans.

A flock of kids has gathered for swimming lessons in the city pool, which shares its parking lot with public access to the lake. I think back to the shallow gravel pit in Morton where my classmates and I were taught to swim, sometimes joined by kids bused in from Winthrop, Gibbon, Fairfax, and Franklin. I could hold my breath in the five-foot-deep water and watch all kinds of aquatic insects and tiny fish dart about in front of me. The Gaylord pool is a valuable resource for the community, but I thank my lucky stars I learned to swim in a more natural setting.

Several decades ago, Lake Titlow was a magnet for duck hunters. Over the years, though, a significant amount of pollution has been coming from both town and farm. The city has upgraded its stormwater system so that runoff no longer flows directly into the lake, but effluent still seeps in from failing septic systems. In the surrounding agricultural area, two streams have been converted to drainage ditches that speed nutrient-rich water and sediment into the lake. Scientists and students from nearby Minnesota State University Mankato have been working with the community to study the problem, and I dearly hope they are able to devise a solution. Healthy lakes make for healthy communities. Kids who fall in love with lakes sometimes grow up to be aquatic ecologists who help preserve lakes for the next generation.

Voices for the River:
Ed Crozier and Elaine Mellott

Just think, just over the lip of that airport, with the highways
going by, and yet—a tremendous, tremendous wildlife area.

—WALTER MONDALE

As we paddled into the Twin Cities metropolitan area, Geri checked the map. It showed that between state and city recreation areas and the Minnesota Valley National Wildlife Refuge, fifty of the fifty-five miles from Belle Plaine to the mouth of the river at Fort Snelling are bordered by public land. (There is a stretch of industrialized floodplain in Savage and Burnsville.) These public lands enable paddlers and hikers to experience both the terrestrial and aquatic life of the river. Who were the voices for the river and its valley who enabled this to happen? Why was this stretch of the river never "developed"?

Theodore Wirth, superintendent of the Minneapolis Park System from 1904 to 1935, was one of the earliest voices pushing for public access to this part of the Minnesota River Basin. He recommended that the Lower Minnesota Valley be established as a metropolitan park from Shakopee to Fort Snelling, where the Minnesota joins the Mississippi. The powers that be declined to act on Wirth's recommendation. Most of the valley remained unprotected, although Fort Snelling State Park was established in 1961.

Forty years after Wirth advocated preserving the Minnesota Valley in the metropolitan area, two inspired individuals made it happen. Ed

Crozier, Bloomington resident and veteran manager in the US Fish and Wildlife Service, joined his city's Natural Resources Commission, which had been established to examine the impact of development and land-use decisions on the city's natural resources—including the Minnesota River, which forms its entire southern boundary. The chair of the commission at the time was Elaine Mellott. Mellott had been advocating on behalf of the Minnesota River since at least 1964, when she participated in meetings led by fellow Voice for the River Clyde Ryberg about creating the Minnesota River Valley Trail. Ed's decision to join the Natural Resources Commission—thereby meeting Elaine—was to play a critical role in the creation of a national wildlife refuge in the Lower Minnesota Valley.

When Ed and his family moved across the river to Burnsville in 1970, he met Dick Duerre, a kindred spirit who chaired a citizens' group called the Burnsville Environmental Council. Freeway Landfill, on the west side of the river at Interstate 35W, was asking for renewal of their permit to continue operations in the floodplain. The Burnsville Environmental Council opposed it, but the Burnsville City Council renewed the permit regardless. Today, the landfill is an EPA Superfund site, and the cost to prevent it from polluting groundwater and the river with illegally dumped hazardous wastes is estimated at $47 million.[41]

They were losing individual battles to protect the river bottoms, so Duerre and Crozier decided they needed a more comprehensive approach. Crozier devised a cunning plan: he anonymously wrote a proposal for a national wildlife recreation area in the lower Minnesota River Valley. Duerre signed the proposal and sent it to the Minnesota congressional delegation and the president. In response, Congressman Bill Frenzel asked the US Fish and Wildlife Service to assess the proposal's feasibility. Fortuitously (though not unexpectedly), the assignment was given to the chief of the Regional Wildlife Refuge Planning Office, who just so happened to

---

41. Recently, the Burnsville City Council expressed support for a plan to dig up the landfill and transfer its contents to a new, expanded location just downriver. Actually, *landfill* isn't quite the right term; the plan is to, literally, build a mountain of garbage that would be the tallest structure for miles around. Ed has been a vocal opponent of the plan.

be none other than Ed Crozier. As you might guess, the planning office concluded that the proposal was indeed feasible.

But bureaucrats at the Department of the Interior in Washington, who had the ultimate say-so, had zero interest in what they considered an outlandish idea to establish a refuge in the middle of a major metropolitan area. Being well familiar with federal bureaucracy, Ed knew that their plan would never become reality unless they could bypass the bureaucrats and appeal directly to Congress. As a federal employee, however, Ed was prevented from making such an appeal himself. Only citizens could lobby Congress.

So Ed quietly, strategically reached back across the river to Elaine Mellott and asked her to chair a citizen committee to promote the plan. She agreed with great enthusiasm. Her friend Marialice Seal joined her, and together they organized and cochaired the Lower Minnesota River Valley Citizens Committee. They made presentations to service clubs, sportsmen's organizations, units of government, and other local groups. With the okay from his superiors, Ed accompanied Elaine and Marialice as a technical advisor. In this way, forty organizations from Carver to Fort Snelling became aware of the project, press coverage proliferated, and the idea to create a refuge along the river gathered steam.

The citizens committee engaged TRC Productions to produce a program using two slide projectors and a synchronized audiotape—the 1970s version of a fancy PowerPoint presentation. Ed writes, "The media production equipment was so heavy, it became difficult to use and we were ready to abandon it." But, as Ed puts it, "the river spirit was looking out for the refuge. One night hauling all this weight back to the office, we found a two-wheeled cart lying in the middle of the road, apparently having fallen off a truck." The campaign continued.

Even so, it became clear that to succeed, people in high places would have to be brought into the effort. Elaine was a senior consultant for public affairs at the prestigious Control Data Corporation (CDC), which enabled her to put on presentations for bigwigs at the CDC boardroom overlooking the river valley.

And CDC executives were more than happy to host meetings attended by influential individuals such as Senator Walter Mondale. Ed writes that after one such meeting, executives spoke informally with the senator and explicitly supported the idea. Similar expressions of support were voiced at a public hearing Mondale convened, and that convinced him to sponsor legislation establishing the refuge. He assigned one of his staff people, Gail Harrison, to work on the project. One of her most effective strategies was to keep river-dependent barge and grain interests and Northern States Power (now Xcel Energy, which has a power plant on the river) in the loop to make sure their concerns were addressed.

On July 11, 1975, Senators Mondale and Hubert Humphrey introduced Public Law 94–466: "Be it enacted by the Senate and House of Representatives of the United States of America in Congress assembled, That this Act may be cited as the 'Minnesota Valley National Wildlife Refuge Act.'" Mondale recruited Senator Wendell Ford of Kentucky as cosponsor, who, as chair of the Senate Environment and Public Works Committee, added extra gravitas. Meanwhile, Minnesota congressman James Oberstar provided the necessary leadership in the House of Representatives. The subcommittee he chaired couldn't propose a wildlife recreation area as Ed had originally envisioned, but it could propose a national wildlife refuge.

A further impetus came unexpectedly on August 29, 1976, when President Gerald Ford released an announcement that thrilled the environmental community across the nation. He called for Congress to pass a bicentennial Land Heritage Act, a ten-year, $1.5 billion program that would double both the existing funds and the acreage of recreation areas and wildlife sanctuaries, giving a huge boost for funding the Lower Minnesota River Valley efforts.

Between Ed's proposal, citizens' strong advocacy, and congressional and presidential support, the Minnesota Valley National Wildlife Refuge became a reality in 1976. At the time, it was one of only four urban wildlife refuges in the nation. And the establishment of the Minnesota Valley refuge was distinctive in two other ways. First, almost all national wildlife refuges are created through an appropriation in the budget of the US Department of the Interior, not through a discrete act of Congress. Second, Ed made sure that a focus on public education be mandated in the legislation; most wildlife refuges have a singular emphasis on protection and enhancement of wildlife.

Many people and organizations made passage of the Minnesota Valley National Wildlife Refuge Act possible, but Ed writes that the real heroes were Elaine Mellott and Marialice Seal, who persevered and faced the toughest battles in the effort. The act of Congress that created the refuge provided funds to acquire only some of the originally authorized nine thousand acres, so Mellott, Seal, and their allies kept up their efforts for many years, advocating for the federal funding required to purchase all the authorized land. Without them and Gail Harrison from Mondale's staff, there would be no refuge. In subsequent years, Senator David Durenberger was supportive. It helped that Elaine was a good friend of Durenberger's environmental aide, Shirley Hunt Alexander. Thanks to Elaine, Marialice, Shirley, and those who have followed in their footsteps, the endeavor has been so successful that the refuge today has grown to more than 14,500 acres, all of it purchased from willing landowners and all of it freely available to the public.

In 1982, the original citizens group started a 501(c)(3) nonprofit called Friends of the Minnesota Valley that is still going strong today. Its original purposes were to advocate for federal funding for land acquisition and, in general, support the refuge. A highlight was securing funds for a beautiful visitor center, which opened in 1989 with the help of Congressman Martin Olav Sabo. Beginning in the early 1990s, with a grant from the McKnight Foundation, the Friends expanded its environmental efforts into the entire basin, with an emphasis on the Lower Minnesota watershed. Friends of the Minnesota Valley was the very first refuge "Friends" group; today there are hundreds across the nation.

Ed received the Department of Interior's top two awards primarily for his work to establish the Minnesota Valley National Wildlife Refuge. He retired in 1994 but has never stopped advocating on behalf of the river. Elaine is no longer with us, but her passion, powers of persuasion, and love of the Minnesota River continue to inspire those who were fortunate enough to have known her.

Were it not for Ed and Elaine, there's no telling what Geri and I would have seen as we paddled through the metropolitan area. We are grateful to have paddled through a national wildlife refuge.

Confluence

The abundance of state parks, the national wildlife refuge[s],
fishing and hunting opportunities, river canoeing, historic sites,
hiking and camping—all close to home along our heritage of ma-
jestic river and valley—offers us enormous recreational opportu-
nity. Use it, take care of it, and enjoy.

—THOMAS F. WATERS

At the landing in Le Sueur, our daughter and granddaughter help us prepare to embark on the final leg of our journey. If all goes well, we will have
paddled every meandering mile of the Minnesota River, from Big Stone
Lake at the western boundary of the state to the confluence with the Mississippi River in the Twin Cities. On paved highways, this leg of the trip
would be a little over fifty miles; on our riverine road, it will be more like
seventy-five. The four of us carry gear down to the water, with breaks for
eating some ripe wild grapes. Our daughter will have our car waiting for us
at Fort Snelling State Park in five days.

Two fishermen across the river watch us ease our craft into the water.
We wave and shout, "Good fishing!" One returns the wave; the other sits
stone quiet. In all the time we've spent on the river so far, we have seen relatively few fellow travelers. What draws a person to come to the river? Do
they only come to catch fish? I wonder for how many people, like me, the
song of the river is the lure—the flow, and the silence.

Downstream from town, much of the right bank has been hardened with
stones. Geri lowers the Secchi tube just before we reach the Rush River outlet
and records a visibility of twenty-one centimeters (just over eight inches).

We pull to shore for lunch just upstream of the Highway 169 Bridge. It's only three miles since we launched, but apparently the wild grapes whetted our appetites. This site is visible from the road, and we've always been curious about the pilings here. A line of rotting wooden posts juts from the shoreline—vestiges of an old steamboat landing, perhaps. Well back from the river, wooden posts support huge planks. Receding into the woods, the weathered structure looks like an abandoned railroad trestle and, as I eat lunch, I am also taking in the aroma of creosote. A family of three is fishing under the highway bridge. Deer tracks are plentiful, and I notice that those who left them have nipped off the tips of willow saplings like a lawn mower with the blade set eight inches high. Common cocklebur covers the ground; it's a native species that can invade disturbed areas and is considered a noxious weed by the Minnesota Department of Agriculture.

Eight miles downstream, we approach the old river town of Henderson, which sits at the base of the bluff on the west side of the river. We see high-water marks that bespeak of a river in various levels of flood. The town wards off high water with a system of levees along the river and floodgates across its two major roads. But it's not enough, not anymore. There is more high water more often than when the protections were put in place, and seven of the past eight years the town has been inundated. Roads leading east, north, and south of town go underwater. The city does not have the financial wherewithal to rebuild them, and requests for support from county or state government have yet to bear fruit.

Henderson was founded in 1852 by Joseph R. Brown, a pioneering Minnesota soldier, fur trader, statesman, Indian agent, and entrepreneur who also established the townsites of Stillwater and Browns Valley. Brown recognized that the land where Henderson sits could be a hub for both river and overland transportation. Steamboats often had a hard time navigating farther upstream, and there was potential for a road there to connect the river with Fort Ridgely, a military outpost then in the planning stages. The Fort Ridgely Road that Brown and other residents of Henderson built was one of the first constructed in Minnesota Territory. Today, Henderson is home to the Sibley County Historical Museum, the Joseph R. Brown Minnesota River Center, and, atop the bluff on the east side of the river, the Ney Nature Center. Civic-minded citizens are revitalizing the community through events such as Sauerkraut Days, Hummingbird Hurrah!, and weekly summertime classic-car roll-ins.

We see a fisherman under the bridge just out of town. He has been casting for walleyes.

I ask, "Any size to them?"

"Good size for eating," he replies.

I'm seeing more and more evidence that the capacity for walleye fishing on the Minnesota River is underappreciated by those who live outside the watershed.

A web of feeder streams and ditches about fifty miles to the west joins to form High Island Creek, which, in turn, empties into the Minnesota about five miles north of Henderson. From tiny rivulets come tremendous rivers. We set up camp on High Island Creek's broad, sandy delta. The flow is five inches deep, but the streambed is very sinuous and has eight-foot-high banks. Spring runoff could bring a wild canoe or kayak ride. At its mouth, the creek is forty feet wide. I hike up it a little ways and discover logging on one side.

* * *

Twenty-five miles or so up from its confluence with the Minnesota, High Island Creek runs through High Island Lake in the town of New Auburn. A prairie-pothole lake in the middle of farm country, this lake had become pea soup over the years, choked with nutrients from runoff from both farm and city. Where most residents saw a lost cause, local cattle farmers Deb and Kerry Wuetherich saw opportunity. With help from Scott Sparlin and his Coalition for a Clean Minnesota River as well as the Friends of the Minnesota Valley, they recruited a dedicated group of volunteers and engaged the fisheries people at the regional office of the Minnesota DNR. After years of cleanup efforts, including the installation of rain gardens in New Auburn's storm water system and a new control structure at the lake's outlet, water quality has improved to the point that the DNR started using High Island Lake as a hatchery for walleye. A small group of thoughtful, committed citizens *can* make a difference.

* * *

Geri has found liverworts in the sand and she is ecstatic. She became intrigued by these rare plants in high school biology class and can now tell you, in detail, about each time she has seen them since. Unlike typical plants, they do not have tubes to transport water or nutrients internally. They make no seeds, flowers, or fruit; instead, they produce spores for reproduction. Their flat, lobed bodies sprawl over moist soil and rocks.

Meanwhile, across the river, I spot the iconic bird of rivers, lakes, and wetlands—the great blue heron. Standing more than four feet tall and with

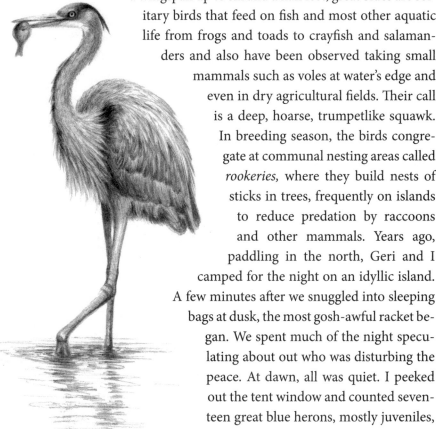

a wingspan up to six and a half feet, great blues are solitary birds that feed on fish and most other aquatic life from frogs and toads to crayfish and salamanders and also have been observed taking small mammals such as voles at water's edge and even in dry agricultural fields. Their call is a deep, hoarse, trumpetlike squawk. In breeding season, the birds congregate at communal nesting areas called *rookeries,* where they build nests of sticks in trees, frequently on islands to reduce predation by raccoons and other mammals. Years ago, paddling in the north, Geri and I camped for the night on an idyllic island. A few minutes after we snuggled into sleeping bags at dusk, the most gosh-awful racket began. We spent much of the night speculating about out who was disturbing the peace. At dawn, all was quiet. I peeked out the tent window and counted seventeen great blue herons, mostly juveniles, quietly standing around in our little bay.

Next day, we meet two fishermen in an aluminum boat, a small motor attached. A four-wheeler with boat trailer is parked at the water's edge. One of the

In flight, the great blue heron folds its neck into an S-curve and trails its legs straight back.

men lives just up the hill. His partner has a fish that is giving him a workout, and the fish slips off the hook. They are after, wouldn't you know it, walleye. Like other walleye fishermen we have met, they keep pan-sized fish but throw the occasional lunker back into the river—good conservation behavior. We are seeing more and more anglers the farther downstream we go. That stands to reason, as the lower end of the basin is much more densely populated. But it's also reasonable to conclude that water quality here must be good enough to support a healthy fishery; people wouldn't be fishing here if there weren't fish to catch.

An odd, round rock pillar stands in the middle of the river. My guess is that this served as a roundabout to enable trains to shift from one track to another. We round the bend and see what looks like the pilings of an old bridge.

Downriver, a young man is standing on a rocky shore staring at the ground, and we paddle over to chat. Surprisingly to me, he's not toting a fishing pole. Geri asks about the old bridge, and he confirms that it was one of those turntable bridges now long abandoned.

"What are you doing here?" we ask.

"Looking for rocks. Agates and stuff."

I try to hide my incredulity; surely, all good Minnesotans know that the only place to find agates is along the north shore of Lake Superior. I wonder if he might actually be an antique collector taking advantage of the low water levels, looking for artifacts from the days of steamboats, when cargo landed on the river bottom following a capsize. I had found such an artifact myself several miles back, a vintage glass bottle that gives a glimmer of insight into the history of the Minnesota River. Back home a few days later, though, just to be sure, I consulted a geologist friend about the young man's claim. She informed me that there is indeed "Superior-provenance till, including agates" in the subsurface of the area and that they have even been found exposed along the Rush River near Henderson. Will glacially induced wonders never cease?

Now the river widens, leaving a broad strand of sand from the water's edge and extending a good quarter mile downstream. It is a great spot to have lunch. We find a comfortable log and eat our sandwiches. For the first time on our travels, we find evidence of others camping on the river: two fire pits and foot traffic to the edge of the woods. Three tall, forked

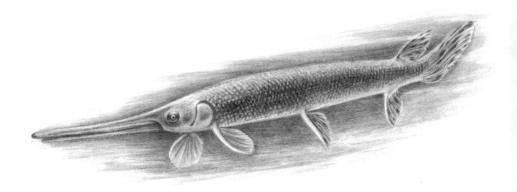

Gar are known for their sharp teeth and aggressive nature. Handle with care!

sticks stand at the water's edge, each one having one or more fish heads impaled on its branches. Most of them are gar heads.

I suppress for a moment my queasy feeling about seeing fish heads on sticks and review what I know about gar. Some fish experts call them a living fossil. The shortnose gar and longnose gar are both found in large rivers and tributaries in central Minnesota. The scales of these fish are interlocked, diamond-shaped plates. They are as hard as tooth enamel and were used by Native Americans to tip arrows. A gar can survive more than twenty-four hours out of water, breathing air by using its swim bladder as a lung.

Now I return my attention to the present situation and notice that there are also several impaled turtle heads. Did we stumble on a cult of some sort? Were the people who did it simply hungry for turtle soup? Based on the amount of charcoal scattered around, it appears this sandbar is a popular spot for bonfires.

Lunch digested and paddling resumed, we pass under a bridge by the tiny hamlet of Blakely on the eastern shore. A young man fishing there is not in a particularly talkative mood, but he does allow that he's after catfish and walleye.

A couple miles downstream, we come upon another big logjam, another opportunity to see what may be growing and swimming on and under this miniature ecological system. Duckweed dominates here in the water out of the current, along with myriad tiny algae. The word *algae* has many negative connotations. Too much algae can create pea-soup lakes and green scum on rivers. But algae also are an important part of an aquatic ecosystem, providing food at the base of the food web. I count ten species of aquatic plants here. Moreover, several species of terrestrial plants find a foothold and thrive atop the organic pile protruding from the surface of the river.

We poke the canoe into a small, unnamed creek and discover a fresh logging operation. No one is here. Is the plan to clear more land for crops or to harvest logs? I remember as a kid a Morton man who made a living logging commercial-value floodplain cottonwood, soft maple, and, in places, even oak, up and down the Minnesota River Valley. Years later, as a college student, I learned that prior to European American settlement, this area was once part of what was known as the Big Woods (a translation of the name *Grand Bois* given by early French explorers). The forest was dominated by American elm, basswood, sugar maple, and ironwood. Originally extending over two million acres from western Wisconsin to south-central Minnesota, today only tiny fragments remain, most notably at Nerstrand Big Woods State Park near Northfield, Minnesota. Settlers systematically chopped down the Big Woods to create land for agriculture and lumber for building.

We finally spot our first great egret. This thin, long-winged, pure-white bird is a little shorter than its cousin, the great blue heron. Both birds feed primarily on aquatic critters. The great egret has the distinction of having been driven almost to extinction in the era of plume hunters in the millinery fashion trade in the late 1800s and early 1900s. The slaughter of great egrets ultimately aroused the public and led to the birth of the conservation movement in general and the National Audubon Society in particular.

The river is widening, and the map says we're approaching Belle Plaine. With a population of seven thousand, it is one of the larger Minnesota River towns. French for *beautiful prairie,* Belle Plaine was once an oasis of open space in the Big Woods. The miles pass, and we still do not see evidence of the town except for two motorboats with fishermen. We are puzzled. I consult our map again and discern that the town is built facing US Highway 169, rather than the river. When steamboats plied the river, the orientation of the town would most certainly have been reversed.

We're about fifty river miles from the confluence, and the DNR water trails map shows that most of the way, the river will be flowing through public land: first the Minnesota Valley State Recreation Area, and, a little farther downstream, the Minnesota Valley National Wildlife Refuge. I am giddy the rest of the day knowing that, even though we are paddling ever deeper into the metropolitan area, we will still find a campsite for the night on public property.[42] I silently thank Ed Crozier and Elaine Mellott.

* * *

We're resting at the Thompson Ferry Public Landing, near the town of Jordan. A young woman and her three-year-old daughter are sitting watching the river—on their daily outing while big sister is in school. Mom is interested in our trip. They settled in Jordan last December after moving nine times in two years. She has been free of alcohol and drugs for eight years—still a struggle, but she is buoyed by the joys and responsibilities of motherhood. After suffering a pulmonary embolism two years ago, she went on disability, but she is grateful to be able to be with her girls. She left us with, "May the river smile on you." Given all her life challenges, she has chosen to come to the river. She, like Geri and me, apparently finds peace here. Water is healing.

* * *

We leave Thompson Ferry and approach Carver Rapids, in the Rapids Lake unit of the Minnesota Valley National Wildlife Refuge. An annotation on the DNR map advises us of the possibility of large boulders at the upper rapids and turbulence at the lower rapids, and it cautions that some maneuvering may be necessary. Depending on the water level, Carver Rapids can be anything from a Class III rapids (low water) down to no rapids at all (high water). Today, I would rate what confronts us as Class III: "Rapids with moderate, irregular waves which may be difficult to avoid and which can swamp an open canoe." I didn't know it at the time, but I learned later

42. Camping is allowed on all public property in the Minnesota River Valley—that is, except for the national wildlife refuges at the source and mouth of the river. NWRs are dedicated to wildlife.

that we were experiencing a rare phenomenon. It's only in times of serious drought that the river is low enough for the rocks to be exposed.

We beach the canoe to ponder our alternatives. I look at the roiling water and number of exposed rocks, trying to identify a spot for safe navigation. No steamboat could have made the run this day. With our canoe's three-inch draft, we have more options, and we decide to conduct an up-close-and-personal assessment. Back in the canoe, we dither to and fro across the edge of the rapids. Ultimately, if a bit reluctantly (a vestige of my youthful, risk-taking days), our "safety first" rule wins the day. We paddle back to shore for a portage.

It's a bit of a challenge, but we manage to elevate ourselves and our canoe up and out of a ten-foot-high ravine to flat land above. Fortuitously, a refuge ranger is driving by on the service road in his pickup and asks if he can help. A rich and enlightening conversation ensues. He has many things to tell of the importance of this place for Indians, fur traders, explorers, and the namesake of the rapids, Jonathan Carver. He tells us of the many Indian mounds at this site, that a trading post was once on the opposite side of the rapids, and that, for about a hundred years, it was the homesite of a prosperous farming family until the refuge acquired the land in the 1990s.[43] He wonders why we are portaging. We explain our decision. "Too bad," he replies. "I ran the rapids with some kids a couple of days ago." *Oh well, perhaps the water was a little higher then,* I say to myself. At any rate, Geri and I are still comfortable with our decision to portage and thankful for the serendipitous history lesson.

* * *

Jonathan Carver, a New Englander and military man, joined an expedition in early 1766 whose mission was to find a Northwest Passage. He was a draftsman and mapmaker and kept an extensive journal of his experiences and observations.

---

43. The Carver Rapids unit of the refuge now is home to a visitor center with classroom space and interpretive exhibits. The old brick farmhouse still stands, and there are remnants of the farm's outbuildings, including an outhouse, whose hole is situated above the river itself.

Carver arrived in the Minnesota River Valley in December 1766. He tells of proceeding up the frozen river, chopping ice with axes, and estimated he had traveled sixty-seven miles from the mouth of the Minnesota River to his destination. Actually, it was half that. A few days later, he found himself at the grand encampment of five bands of Dakota, who he called Naudowessies and wrote they "came to hunt among their brethren of the plains." Carver spent six months among the Indians near the present-day town bearing his name and developed a relationship with the chief, describing him as "my very good friend."

Carver was enthralled with the richness of the soil and wild vines full of heavy, hanging clusters of grapes, writing that the "juice of these grapes was very rich and imagin' t'would make the best of wines." He was also taken by the vast number of waterfowl that graced the endless wetlands. He notes the plains above the wetlands and the "groves of maple suitable for the sugar manufacture and plums of a very good taste." He goes on, "For a space all the way when I was on this river between the meadows and the plains is thousands of acres of marshy land where grows vast quantities of Indian [wild] rice where the Naudowessie gather the hundredth part."

As we'll see when we paddle downriver, much of those thousands of acres of marshy land exist to this day. Unfortunately, however, those rich rice beds of Carver's time have faded into history in this part of Minnesota—or so I had thought. A biological surveyor I spoke with recently reported that she had come upon a stand of it in the floodplain in Bloomington. Another small indication that the river is recovering.

Geri and I are avid wild ricers but do our ricing in northern Minnesota. I am delighted with a conversation I had with a woman from the Lower Sioux Indian Community who is a descendent of Little Crow. She told me the Dakota people of the area have decided to attempt to reestablish wild rice in their part of the basin.

Back home in New England in 1768, Carver was unable to secure funding to publish his journals, so he left his family and sought a benefactor in England. He was ultimately successful there and in 1778 published *Travels through the Interior Parts of North America: 1766, 1767, 1768.* The book commanded a large audience in England, America, and Europe. The accuracy of his accounts has been questioned by some and lauded by others.

Whatever one's opinion, Carver's book gives us a peek at the Minnesota River and part of its watershed some seventy-five years before most settlers began to arrive.

* * *

We now encounter a peculiar concrete slope the width of a baseball diamond that ends at vegetation well above the river. A series of blocks the size of gravestones are situated in rows across the cement base. Curiosity demands that I climb this odd formation. On my way up, I leap across a watery bed of marshy vegetation and land in soupy mud up to my belt buckle. Yikes! By lunging, I manage to extract myself, crawl to the edge of the cement, and continue my climb, dripping with mud. From the top of the slope, I see an extensive wetland in the distance. I surmise the configuration of the alternating "gravestones" is designed to slow down the water and perhaps trap debris during runoff events.

I finish my inspection and gingerly work my way along the edge of the concrete and back down to the riverbank. Geri sees me covered in thick mud and can't quite decide whether my condition is hilarious or horrendous. I reassure her with a little mud-eating grin. Thankfully, no one is in sight. Geri digs out my extra set of clothes while I strip and wash myself and my dirty duds in the river. A hot lunch of pasta with kidney beans and tomato sauce tastes much better than the humble pie I had just ingested.

Not far downstream, the river has cut away a steep bank, leaving a mix of downed trees leaning out over the water. I am curious, as usual, about what lies above. I grasp limb and vine, hand over hand, and finally make it up to flat ground, where I find myself at the edge of a soybean field with plants packed so tightly together it is hard to see where the rows were planted. Unfortunately, no buffer has been established to reduce runoff of water, sediment, and fertilizer into the river. I scan the field stretching into the distance. The farmer's crop looks outstanding. The river? Not so much.

We cross under two bridges—one modern, the other old. We've arrived at the city of Chaska, whose name is derived from the Dakota Šaská or Čhaské (six), a name commonly given to an eldest son. We are about forty miles from our launch point at Le Sueur and about thirty from the confluence with the Mississippi at Fort Snelling. Geri spots an apartment building with an attractive gazebo that allows people to look out over the river. We paddle along a giant levee that protects town from river. Completed the year after the historic 1965 flood that inundated the Minnesota and Mississippi valleys, the levee was constructed by the US Army Corps of Engineers. It is nearly two miles long and forty-one feet high (enough to protect the town from a five-hundred-year flood event) and is supplemented by a series of gates, pumps, relief stations, and diversion channels. Total cost of the system: $43 million. Towns up and down the river have gone to great lengths, at great expense, to protect themselves from excess water from their upstream neighbors. Unfortunately, as in Henderson, yesterday's preventative measures don't always measure up to today's floods, and Chaska suffers. I say it's time for us Minnesotans to invest more resources on infrastructure and land-use practices that will hold more water on the land.

Another four miles of paddling and the river begins to wend its way through Shakopee, a city that takes its name from an eighteenth-century Dakota chief. There's a nice boat landing in Huber City Park, and the river begins to meander along a series of five lakes: Rice, Grass, Blue, Fisher, and a second Rice. The first two lakes adjoin the Upgrala unit of the Minnesota Valley National Wildlife Refuge on the north side of the river, the next two are part of the refuge's Wilkie unit on the south side, and the last is in the Rice Lake unit, also on the south side. All these lakes are magnets for migratory birds, especially waterfowl and wading birds. There is a great blue heron rookery in the floodplain forest of the Wilkie unit. We are traveling for quite a few miles along these wetlands that so impressed Jonathan Carver, and aside from the near disappearance of wild rice beds, much of the valley appears to be relatively unchanged in the 250 years since his visit. Geri and I know we are entering the metropolitan area, but it sure doesn't look like it from a canoe in the middle of the river.

Suddenly, an immense, three-legged structure topped by American flags emerges over the trees on the south side of the river. The huge red sign marks Valley Fair Amusement Park, a favorite of Minnesota kids. Across the river sits a group of large trees, and I wonder if it's a remnant of the Big Woods. Just downstream, I notice a farm field, pull to the bank, and discover a nice fifty-foot buffer between field and river. I tip my hat to a conservation-minded farmer.

We're still within sight of the Valley Fair sign, and I recall that we must be passing the Blue Lake wastewater treatment plant. As the river moves into the heart of the metropolitan area, it receives over sixty million gallons per day of treated wastewater from two large sewage treatment plants: the Blue Lake facility, which adjoins the Wilkie unit of the National Wildlife Refuge, and the Seneca facility, adjoining the Long Meadow Lake unit of the refuge in Eagan. Both plants treat human sewage before discharging it to the Minnesota River. Sludge is dewatered and either pelletized for use as a fertilizer or incinerated with the ash carted off to a landfill.

The river is important to many besides paddlers and fishermen.

Farther downriver, a bright yellow sign warns in large black letters, "Pipeline Crossing. Do Not Anchor or Dredge." Just downstream of the pipeline crossing, the river is covered in white foam emerging from a huge culvert and drifting off downstream. I am puzzled. What is its source? What is the content of the foam? We presume the state Pollution Control Agency responds to situations like this; nevertheless, I feel deeply hurt. This is Minnesota. This is the Minnesota River. This shouldn't be happening. It's a sad way to end a long day. Even though we're just upriver from the heavily industrial section of the river, we're able to find a muddy but tolerable spot to pitch the tent.

* * *

Morning opens under partly cloudy skies, and we set out our homemade granola to soak. Geri, as usual, has planned well: we're on the final day of our trip, and our sacks of granola and powdered milk are almost empty. Before breaking camp, I walk the shore and discover a large mass of mussel shells. We have not seen bivalves like this for over one hundred miles. As we break our last camp, we are in no hurry to reach the mouth of the river and so allow the current to do our work. Partly cloudy is giving way to a uniformly gray and darkening sky.

Around a bend, we encounter a series of large, rusted iron pipes along the river's bank. They must be ten feet tall, and most of them lean out over the water at a 45-degree angle. We conclude that these structures must have been used as places for barges to be tied until a tugboat was ready to move them downriver. Indeed, there's a tug sitting at anchor at the mouth of a backwater, and we paddle over. We are a bit reticent, suspecting that tug captains might not appreciate canoeists getting in their way, but curiosity emboldens our approach. What a pleasant surprise: the tug master is most accommodating. He tells us his job is to move barge loads of sand a short distance downstream where a bright orange Caterpillar with a giant bucket scoops the muck from the barge into a dump truck, which in turn will haul it to a newly constructed basin well back from the river. Periodic dredging by the Lower Minnesota Watershed District maintains a nine-foot-deep navigation channel for barges moving grain and other commodities. But so much sand from upriver is being deposited in the channel that finding places to dump the dredged material has become a major challenge.

* * *

The navigation channel has its origins in World War II. In February 1942, a mere two months after Pearl Harbor, the United States Navy asked Minnesota-based Cargill to build ships to support the war effort. Cargill was already building ships on the East Coast, but the navy wanted a facility in the middle of the country out of fear of an enemy attack on the coasts. Cargill agreed, no doubt out of patriotism, but it also recognized the undertaking as an opportunity. It would be necessary to maintain a shipping channel for the warships, and after the war, Cargill could convert the shipyard to a grain-shipping terminal that could connect to the Mississippi. The company acquired a parcel of land in Savage, just east of Shakopee, and built a shipyard there. Meanwhile, the government dug out the navigation channel from the shipyard about fourteen miles to the confluence with the Mississippi. (Most of the cost of the channel construction was borne by Cargill.) The shipyard built nineteen fuel transport tankers and four tugboats. These vessels were towed through the channel to the Mississippi River and down to New Orleans. When the war was over, Cargill did indeed convert the shipyard to a grain terminal. Commodities grown in the Minnesota River Basin could be transported there by rail or truck instead of being hauled across the metro area to a terminal in St. Paul.

Other companies recognized the strategic location and built facilities nearby. Cargill and CHS are the most prominent of river users here, but as we paddle, we also see Kramer Mining, US Salt Terminal, and, a few miles downriver, the Black Dog Generating Station. Less visible are entities that simply release water into the river, such as Flying Cloud Airport, Minneapolis–St. Paul International Airport, and the Blue Lake and Seneca wastewater treatment plants.

The State Department of Transportation estimates the economic impact of commercial waterways in Minnesota at more than $1 billion a year. A substantial part of that is based on the Minnesota River. When it comes to fuel efficiency, one gallon of diesel fuel moves a ton of freight 576 miles by river barge, 435 miles by railroad, and only 155 miles by truck, as reported by the Texas Transportation Institute. Barges are by far the most efficient way to move freight. But there are trade-offs. Dredging, straightening, and, on the Mississippi River, damming to accommodate barges have fundamentally changed our rivers.

Over the years, the channel began to fill with sediment. The Lower Minnesota River Watershed District (LMRWD) was created by the Minnesota Legislature in 1960 to work with the US Army Corps of Engineers to maintain the navigation channel, with a secondary goal of improving water quality. The LMRWD reports that between 2011 and 2014, a yearly average of 1.4 million tons of sediment accumulated in the channel, stream banks, and floodplain on the forty-mile stretch from Jordan to Fort Snelling. That volume of mud is enough to fill a city block 670 feet high. Ninety percent of this sediment originates upstream of Jordan, well beyond the jurisdictional boundaries of the LMRWD.

* * *

The captain must now move his tug with another load of dredge spoils to the sediment "landfill." We wave good-bye and watch as he navigates into the channel. The river looks too narrow for such a large vessel, but he expertly swings the barge around and heads downriver.

The river here bears little resemblance to the one we left at Carver Rapids. Part of the navigation channel construction involved removal of meanders; from here to the confluence, the river is straight. We drift with the sluggish, placid water. A huge industrial building looms on the south side of the river. Now a giant erector set with pivoting arms leans out well over the bank. Another limb stretches several football fields aimed in another direction. A third set arises out of the woods overlooking a long, sandy strand at the river's edge. The building looks like scaffolding of an urban skyscraper.

We drift slowly toward a barge positioned at the base of an erector scaffold. A tiny cabin sits at its top. Two pipes lean thirty feet down to an opening in the barge. A bright blue tank rests at the side of the scaffold, and a long metal walkway tapers toward other buildings in the distance. I look back upriver and see a string of six groups of large iron pipes much like the ones we saw upriver. Unlike the others, these lean stiffly toward shore, and clearly have the role of holding barges in wait until it's time for them to be loaded and sent off to new adventures. A workman wearing a hard hat and a bright yellow T-shirt sits at the bow of a barge resting on the top of a rusty iron pipe. We exchange smiles and waves. The sides of this barge are riddled with dents. We float toward a long metal-and-cement wall high above the water level. A workman stands higher yet, guiding a large derrick, which is lowering big lids down onto the barges. We look downstream over a river of glass. A long chain of barges fades into the distance. An island appears in the middle of the river built of concrete and planks supporting a movable turret that seems unused. We paddle to shore, beach the canoe, and scramble up a steep bank to two sets of railroad tracks. A No Trespassing sign forbids further exploration.

We pass under the Interstate 35W bridge and can see the Black Dog Generating Station downstream. Built in the 1950s as a coal-powered plant to generate electricity, the plant was recently converted to burn natural gas. The adjacent Black Dog Lake is the receptacle for the millions of gallons of cooling water discharged from the plant. The water is warm, and in winter, the lake is often free of ice and thus attracts hardy waterfowl, such as mallards, Canada geese, and a variety of less common species.

The cloud cover is turning ominously dark. We increase paddling cadence as raindrops start to fall. Suddenly, thunder booms and the sky opens. Rain gear is buried in our big pack. We are in the middle of the channel and quickly head for shore. The hell with raincoats: where there's thunder, there's lightning, and lightning can be deadly, especially to those on the water. Soaking wet and shivering, we paddle hard to shore, hop out, and only then fish out our raincoats. We huddle together on some big concrete slabs until the thunder ceases and the rain lets up.

Before long, all is calm. Our sponges remove most of the water sloshing on the canoe's bottom. We paddle under the Interstate 494 bridge as sunshine returns.

We begin to hear the scream of jets dropping elevation as they head to runways at Minneapolis–St. Paul International Airport. The noise is so intense I must stop paddling and plug my ears. I ache to think of residential families that must endure airplane noise day after day. Ironically, we are paddling past the Long Meadow Lake unit of the Minnesota Valley National Wildlife Refuge. It's astonishing that such a magnificent natural resource exists in the heart of a major metropolitan area, right across from an international airport and the nation's largest shopping mall.

We let the river push us through the refuge into Fort Snelling State Park, and at last we reach the tip of Pike Island. The confluence. We hop out of the canoe and pull it onto the sandbar where the Minnesota releases its flow to the Mississippi. Sixty-odd years after he first conceived it, a young boy's dream of paddling the Minnesota River has been realized. I close my eyes and see myself standing atop the bluffs above Morton, admiring the vast river valley and trying to imagine what adventures might await me beyond where my eyes could see.

A well-worn, giant piece of driftwood, once upon a time a tall tree, provides a natural picnic table for one last meal on the river. I wonder: When and where did this driftwood tree we're sitting on topple into the river? Did it pass through Morton? How many flooding events were required to transport it to the confluence? Will a future flood carry it down the Mississippi? What, indeed, does the future hold for the Minnesota River?

We pack up our gear for the last time on this epic voyage. In a sense, we say good-bye to the river, but we know we will return. We love the Minnesota River, every single twist and turn of it.

The Minnissippi River

Every man should have his own Holy Place where he keeps lonely vigil,
harkens for the Voices, and offers prayer and praise.

—CHIEF WABASHA (LE FEUILLE)

As we're packing up our gear at Fort Snelling State Park—the confluence—I wonder aloud, "Where does the water go? What happens to the Minnesota River after it joins the Mississippi?"

"Well, it's easy enough to find out," teases Geri. I know exactly what she's suggesting and love the idea. We'll be taking a little side trip before heading home. We have a favorite place a short drive away on Highway 52—the Pine Bend Bluffs Scientific and Natural Area—which offers a spectacular view of the Mississippi River as it flows through the southeastern corner of the metropolitan area. It's an ideal spot to see the combined Minnesota-Mississippi, an ideal spot to reflect on what we have learned on our river odyssey.

We leave the car in the small parking lot, set out single file on the narrow footpath, and make our way to a prairie knoll overlooking the river far below. High in the sky, three pelicans glide southward, quite possibly late migrants from their breeding areas along the Upper Minnesota. These talismans from our Minnesota River exploration seem to be welcoming us to a new, yet familiar, river.

The knoll separates two ravines, evidence of feeder streams and springs that ate into the banks of the glacial River Warren. Yes, that monstrous flash flood of a river carved out the Mississippi River Valley from the confluence to Lake Pepin just as it carved out the Minnesota River Valley. Nowadays, the Minnesota River annually contributes anywhere from a little less than one-third to nearly one-half of the total volume of water at the confluence, depending on the amount of runoff from the respective watersheds.

Our view at Pine Bend Bluffs encompasses several miles up and down the river. Late autumn, when the leaves are off the trees and before snow blankets the ground, is a great time to observe a landscape. From this vantage point, we see the river slicing through a wide, saturated floodplain. Across the river is Grey Cloud Island (site of another scientific and natural area) and a gravel- or sand-mining operation. On our side of the river a couple of miles to the south, we can see the massive buildings of CF Industries, whose website proclaims its purpose: "Transforming natural gas into nitrogen, helping feed the crops that feed the world and supporting a cleaner and healthier future." Nature and industry sit side by side here, just as they do along the Minnesota.

I remind myself that the wide valley here was created by the same force that created the Minnesota River Valley and that much of the water is the Minnesota River. I decide this river should still be called the Minnesota, or, to be inclusive, the Minnissippi.

Just as the last stretch of the Minnesota River flows through a national wildlife refuge, so does this stretch of the Mississippi flow through the Mississippi National River and Recreation Area. Managed by the National Park Service, MNRRA extends seventy-two river miles north to south through the metropolitan area. Along the way are such attractions as the Coon Rapids Dam, Mill City Museum, Minnehaha Regional Park, Science Museum of Minnesota (site of the MNRRA Visitor Center), and the Bruce Vento Nature Sanctuary. While the Minnesota Valley National Wildlife Refuge has purchased its fourteen thousand–plus acres from willing landowners, a mere sixty-six acres of MNRRA are owned by the National Park Service. Stewardship is accomplished through education, advocacy, and collaboration.

We watch a towboat pushing a phalanx of a dozen barges downriver, perhaps transporting grain recently harvested in the Minnesota River Basin. Destination Galena? Hannibal? St. Louis? New Orleans and beyond? The procession slips silently from our view.[44]

The passage of the barges reminds us that the hardworking, gritty Minnesota River and the rich prairie soil in its basin have given much to sustain us and, via the Minnesota's convergence with the Mississippi, to share our bounty far and wide. In the basin, first wheat and now corn and soybeans have formed the base of Minnesota's economy; today, more than three hundred thousand Minnesota jobs are directly related to agriculture. The river moves not just grain but limestone, fertilizer, cement, coal, the list goes on. Strategically situated on the river's banks are grain terminals, cities and towns, gravel mines, landfills, sewage treatment plants, power plants, state parks, and national wildlife refuges. Life revolves around the river.

Also sustaining us is the spiritual nourishment derived from paddling on the river, sitting on the banks with fishing pole in hand, fixing binoculars on a skein of geese, soaking in a panoramic view, dreaming about what we have seen and hope to see.

The Minnesota River's story revolves around resources and land use. Native peoples vied for game, wild rice, and water routes. Season by season, they moved to different habitats in the basin to take advantage of what grew where and when, and they strategically used fire to maintain equilibrium in the prairies and Big Woods. White settlers outnumbered and overpowered the natives and took control of the land and the river. They cut down the Big Woods to provide building material and carve out farmland. Fertile prairie soils produced outstanding cash crops, so the settlers broke more and more sod until 99 percent of the prairie was gone. And they drained countless wetlands that held back water and provided wildlife habitat to make way for yet more commodity-based agriculture, until more than 90 percent of the wetlands were gone. Factories dumped their waste, and municipalities dumped their sewage (what we all flush down the toilet) into the river, such that by the 1950s, University of Minnesota fisheries expert (and my advisor in graduate school) Dr. James C. Underhill reported,

---

44. Back home, we learned about Ship Finder, an app for your phone or computer that provides real-time, detailed information about a ship, its route, and its cargo.

"Seine hauls frequently contained peas and carrots from canneries, human feces from untreated sewage, and not surprisingly, very few fish."

We have made a lot of progress since then, as DNR fish surveyors and recreational anglers can attest. Nets today are hauling in bass, walleye, and catfish, not poop, peas, and carrots. A major reason for the improvement is that cities and towns in the basin have installed proper sewage treatment plants. The conversion of floodplain farmland into perennial vegetative cover through programs like CREP is another.

A similar story can be told about the Mississippi River: In the metropolitan area, we used the Mississippi to dispose of human waste, and by the early 1930s, the pollution was so bad that there were virtually no fish in the stretch of the Mississippi River running through the Twin Cities. Toss in offal refuse from the stockyards in South St. Paul, and the Mississippi was one stinky stew of a river.

It is much cleaner today, thanks to a grassroots campaign spearheaded by the Minnesota Division of the Izaak Walton League and resulting construction project undertaken by the Works Project Administration. The Metropolitan Wastewater Treatment Plant in St. Paul (originally and still colloquially known as the Pig's Eye Plant in honor of Pierre "Pig's Eye" Parrant, first resident of what would become St. Paul) began separating waste from water in 1938. Within months, fish returned to the river. The treatment plant remains in operation today and is recognized as one of the most effective and reliable such systems in the nation.

* * *

If our vantage point at Pine Bend Bluffs allowed us to see just a little farther downriver, to Hastings, Minnesota, we would be looking at something quite unlike anything on the Minnesota River: a lock and dam. The lock is a narrow passageway with a gate on each end through which watercraft travel to get past the dam. The dam has a series of gates, which open when there is enough water in the river to fill a nine-foot channel (the depth required to float modern barges) and close when water levels are low, collecting the water flowing from upstream to form what's officially called a *pool* to make the channel deep enough. The lock and dam at Hastings features an observation deck that is well worth a visit. The river behind it, what Geri and I are viewing from the Pine Bends Bluff, is Pool 2.

In fact, the Mississippi River, from St. Anthony Falls in Minneapolis all the way to St. Louis, Missouri, is punctuated by twenty-eight lock-and-dam structures operated by the US Army Corps of Engineers. Authorized by Congress in 1930 to make it possible to maintain the nine-foot channel, this monumental construction project might have wrought ecological devastation in the Mississippi River floodplain. Fortunately, citizen activists had helped lay the foundation for using the river as a navigation channel while maintaining the floodplain as a wildlife mecca.

In the early 1920s, a man by the name of Will Dilg was one of a group of businessmen from Chicago who were avid anglers. They loved fishing the backwaters of the Mississippi, and they were alarmed at the degradation of the area from increasing industrial use of the river and over-harvesting from commercial fishing operations. So Will and his friends organized. They formed what became known as the Izaak Walton League of America and, astonishingly, persuaded Congress to authorize establishment of the Upper Mississippi River National Fish and Wildlife Refuge in 1924. The refuge extends from just south of Lake Pepin all the way to the Quad Cities on the Illinois-Iowa border. When the lock and dam construction was undertaken a few years later, preserving the floodplain for wildlife and recreation became a required part of the project. And to this day, the area is indeed a mecca for wildlife. Perhaps the most spectacular manifestation of this is the annual fall migration of tundra swans, which gather in their thousands throughout the refuge, especially in Pool 8 near Brownsville, Minnesota, a few miles south of Le Crescent, which is across the river from La Crosse, Wisconsin.

* * *

Of the twenty-eight pools on the Mississippi River, Pool 4 is unique; it's the beloved Lake Pepin, a naturally occurring wide spot in the river stretching about twenty-one miles, from just south of Red Wing (Bay City, on the Wisconsin side) to just north of Wabasha (Nelson, Wisconsin). The lake was formed about ten thousand years ago (after glacial River Warren had run its course), when sediment from Wisconsin's Chippewa River dumped into the Mississippi and formed a delta, or partial dam. Originally, the lake extended as far upstream as St. Paul, but sediment coming mostly from the Minnesota River has been filling in Pepin ever since. Sediment giveth, and sediment taketh away.

Today, some sediment is deposited in Pools 1, 2, and 3, but most—nearly one million tons a year, 80 percent of which comes from the Minnesota River Basin—settles at the upper end of placid Lake Pepin. It disrupts aquatic plant growth and fish habitat, produces high levels of turbidity, and reduces recreation values.

As I described earlier in this book (see "Ice"), sediment-producing erosion of the Minnesota River Valley is a natural phenomenon. What's not natural is the rate at which it's happening now; Lake Pepin is filling in ten times faster than it was before the Minnesota River Basin was converted to agriculture. In 2009, alarmed that they were losing their lake, activists from the upper end of the lake (where most of the sediment gets dropped) organized the Lake Pepin Legacy Alliance (LPLA) to help protect their precious resource. Their goals are to reduce the sediment load by half, monitor conditions at the head of Lake Pepin, and make sure government entities are aware of the problems and supportive of solutions. The inspirational voice of the Minnesota River, Patrick Moore, recognized that "upstreamers" from his part of the state around Montevideo and "downstreamers" from the LPLA had a common goal of a clean, sustainable Minnesota River and fostered amity and collaboration between the two traditionally contentious groups.

* * *

The Mississippi River watershed is the main source of fresh water flowing to the Gulf of Mexico. Unfortunately, the flow from the corn belt of Minnesota, Iowa, and other midwestern states contributes significant amounts of nutrients to the Gulf. The outcome is hypoxia, a condition in which the nutrients consume so much oxygen that there isn't enough for aquatic life to survive. An area where river meets gulf becomes what is known as a *dead zone*. Fish and shrimp die off, driving fishermen and shrimpers out of business. The size of the Gulf's dead zone varies from year to year; the average over the past five years is about 5,800 square miles. In 2017, we set the record at 8,776 square miles—more than half the size of the Minnesota River Basin. How do you think we Minnesotans would react if, say, North Dakota sent pollution our way that turned half the Minnesota River Basin into a dead zone?

A dozen Mississippi River state governments, including Minnesota's, are working with a coalition of nonprofit organizations to address the nutrient problem and other challenges in the Mississippi Basin. The goal is to reduce phosphorus by 35 percent and nitrogen by 20 percent.

* * *

From the top of Pine Bends Bluff, Geri and I take one last look at the river below. I feel as though I'm at least beginning to form an understanding of rock and ice, river and land, soil and lakes, and, for 11,500 years of humans, a communion of the whole. We turn back toward the parking lot at just the right time to see a pair of bald eagles flying high above the bluff. Within my

Bald eagles typically build their huge nests high in tall trees near lakes and rivers.

lifetime, I have witnessed the decline of eagles to the point of near extinction and the revival of their population to the point that they are a common sight along the Minnesota and Mississippi Rivers. We saved the bald eagle, and we can save the Minnesota River.

Epilogue: It's What We Do on Land

It's time we all understand

It's what we do on land

That makes our water what it is today

This simple fact is true

It's controlled by me and you

It's time to fix the mistakes of yesterday.

—SCOTT SPARLIN

Those lyrics by Voice of the River Scott Sparlin bear repeating. They remind us that as water runs off the land into lakes and streams, it carries with it parts of the land such as sediment and vegetative matter. This, of course, is a natural process; it's been happening all over planet Earth for as long as there have been water and land. But when people change the land, as we have done in the Minnesota River Basin by transforming the prairie-pothole and Big Woods ecosystems to agricultural purposes, we change the natural dynamic. So the question for us is, what mistakes have we made, and what are we doing to fix them?

The most distinctive natural resource in the Minnesota River Basin is the incredibly rich topsoil. By first driving out the bison and the indigenous human populations, who used the soil and the prairie it supported for different purposes, European American businessmen and the settlers they recruited used the soil to grow commodities. Minnesota River researcher Polly Fry writes, "The stockyards, grain elevators, lumberyards, and mills of the Twin Cities gathered the resources of the Minnesota River Basin and transformed them into altogether different products that would then flow to other places, including the basin itself. . . . The Twin Cities shaped the development of the Minnesota River Basin. In turn, the rich resources of the Minnesota River Basin literally fed the Twin Cities."

But transformation from prairie to crops marked the beginning of our water-quality problems. Deep-rooted, perennial prairie holds much more water than relatively shallow-rooted, annual crops. More runoff equals more erosion, which is to say more sediment carried into the river.

Sediment is a key component of what's called *total suspended solids* (TSS) in the water. The solids consist of particles of sediment as well as decaying plant and animal matter, industrial wastes, and sewage. A related measure, turbidity, refers to how well light passes through water—what we ascertain with a Secchi depth reading. Minnesota Pollution Control Agency research concludes that the main stem of the Minnesota River and its major tributaries are impaired for TSS and turbidity. These forms of pollution limit light availability to aquatic plants living on river bottoms and in backwaters, impact gill functioning of fish and aquatic invertebrates, and degrade spawning habitats. Turbidity also reduces the resource value for boating, canoeing, fishing, swimming, and tourism.

Studies show that the level of TSS from the upper end of the river at Ortonville to its bend at Mankato increases a thousandfold. The Le Sueur River watershed contributes 24–30 percent of the total suspended solids to the Minnesota River even though it comprises only about 7 percent of the river's watershed. The Blue Earth, Watonwan, Redwood, and Cottonwood Rivers and Sand, High Island, and Hawk Creeks are also major contributors. These tributaries are in the middle and lower portions of the basin, where the natural landscape is more prone to erosion and receives more precipitation (thus producing more runoff) than does the upper part of the basin.

We didn't just plow up the prairie of the Minnesota River Basin, we also drained 90 percent of the potholes. Water that used to flow into and stay in these wetlands and shallow lakes now runs off into the river. To early farmers, wetlands were viewed as an obstruction, the antithesis of a "resource." But wetlands prevent floods and reduce erosion by holding water on the landscape. They also provide habitat for a biologically diverse flora and fauna and offer recreational opportunities for duck hunters, bird watchers, and everyone who simply enjoys looking at something beautiful.

Tile drainage systems have been a boon to row-crop farmers in the basin because they quickly remove water from their fields, which facilitates operations such as tilling and prevents roots from becoming waterlogged. The downside is that all this "excess" water is quickly transported to streams and rivers, where it can erode the banks and cause flooding downstream.

Researchers—including Dr. Shawn Schottler, senior scientist at the St. Croix Watershed Research Station—have determined that the flow rate in the Minnesota River has increased 70 percent over the past sixty years. Further, the researchers found a significant increase in stream flow in agricultural watersheds from 1980 to 2009 as compared to the period from 1940 to 1979. Additional research by the Freshwater Society has found that the river has been widening throughout the watershed. It is washing away about eighty acres of riverbank every year, on average, which amounts to about six inches for each of the thirteen thousand individually owned parcels along the Minnesota River and its tributaries that have steep ravines, bluffs, and banks. Six inches may not sound like a lot, but it adds up: a foot of land lost every two years. That's ten feet in a generation, seventy feet by the seventh generation.

Climate change is contributing to the increased flow—the Minnesota River Basin is now receiving more frequent intense rains and more total annual precipitation than in years past. Erosion happens when water is high and the flow is swift.

Fertilizer, principally nitrogen and phosphorus, introduced a whole new problem beginning in the 1940s. Some of the nitrogen and phosphorus added to soil to increase crop yield washes into underground drainage systems, ditches, and natural streams, and seeps into groundwater. Fertilizers degrade water quality by encouraging algal growth; algae consume oxygen in the water and increase turbidity. Lakes and streams turn from clear to murky, leading to unhealthy conditions for fish and other aquatic organisms. We need fertilizer to grow corn, but we certainly don't need it in the water.

The Minnesota Pollution Control Agency has determined that 70 percent of nutrient pollution in the basin comes from cropland, as one might expect, considering that 80 percent of the land is agricultural. Most of the rest comes from wastewater treatment plants, malfunctioning private septic systems, and urban stormwater systems.

To farmers, fertilizer is money, and they want to spend it all on their crops. They do not want it to go down the drainage. Farmers do extensive soil testing to determine optimal fertilizer rates and apply fertilizer only when the crop needs it (and then hope an unexpected rainstorm doesn't wash it away). They plan tile spacing and depth; install controllable drainage systems that hold water in the tile; create grass waterways and terraces to soak up and slow down runoff; treat tile drainage water in bioreactors and saturated buffers; plant cover crops (such as radishes) on tilled fields; and, often with the help of government initiatives such as the federal Conservation Reserve Program or the state's Reinvest in Minnesota, construct and restore wetlands and convert marginal cropland to perennial vegetation.

By and large, wastewater treatment plants in the basin are now discharging water with very low phosphorus content. In the last twenty years or so, the plants in every incorporated city on the river have been brought up to standard. Fixing broken septic systems is an individual responsibility, and government financial assistance is often available. Urban stormwater systems are another matter. Just like tile drainage systems on farmland, stormwater systems in cities are designed to move water off the land as quickly as possible and discharge it into the nearest stream, river, or lake. Most do so without treating the water in any way. Often carrying nutrients in the form of fertilizer, grass clippings, and leaves, water runs off into the street, goes down a drain, travels through an underground pipe, and is discharged, untreated, into the body of water. Excess water and nutrients are just as much a problem in urban areas as they are in farm country.

Public health professionals are deeply concerned about the risks to safe drinking water that are created when nitrogen gets into rivers or percolates into groundwater, producing water that is not safe for human consumption. (Infants are particularly at risk; ten parts per million nitrogen can trigger the dangerous blue-baby syndrome.) Case in point: the City of St. Peter, on the river north of Mankato, obtains its water supply from wells that tap into groundwater, and testing in the mid-2000s revealed that the water was polluted with nitrates. The city was compelled to construct an expensive, reverse-osmosis treatment plant to remove the nitrogen and make their water safe to drink.

Yet another problem is bacteria, specifically the *E. coli* variety. It comes from animal waste from feedlots and grazing areas without a sufficient buffer along a body of water, and it also comes from humans who have deficient wastewater treatment plants or septic systems. For decades, bacteria counts in the Minnesota River have exceeded standards, making swimming unsafe.

Years ago, the state asked farmers to voluntarily establish vegetated buffer strips from the edge of a riverbank to the edge of a crop. Many farmers complied; some did not. The Minnesota Legislature passed a bill in 2015 to require a fifty-foot buffer.

I am heartened when I read this, in *The Farmer* magazine:

> In the end, the great buffer debate could lead to a better understanding of water quality issues and to establish enforceable, effective tillage setbacks. I also hope that farmers would be allowed and encouraged to work with their Soil and Water Conservation Districts to establish buffers wider than the required minimum, where necessary, through volunteer programs that lever the costs associated with retiring productive land for a public benefit. Let's hope that common sense and balance prevail.

I figure if farmers are required to establish buffer strips that reduce farmable land, we urbanites ought to do our part as well. A stream close to our house in the north metro carries its water to the Mississippi River. A number of homes line the attractive stream, but the city lacks a comprehensive approach to treating stormwater, and most homeowners do little on their own to protect water quality. Unfortunately, many residents are not aware of or not willing to do simple, inexpensive things to help slow down the water and reduce nutrient and sediment loads. But a growing number of municipalities and individual homeowners in the metro area are installing rain gardens, which capture runoff from roadways and rooftops into gardens composed of water-tolerant plants. These gardens soak up nutrient-rich water and allow it to seep slowly into the ground instead of rushing directly into stormwater pipes.

Geri and I have attended a number of agriculture conferences to better understand farmers' points of view. One conference in Mankato, with well over three hundred farmers in attendance, was particularly insightful. In a breakout session, an elderly farmer described his operation and, during the Q&A, conservation entered the discussion. He hesitated a moment before saying, "I'm in farming to make money." After another pause, he added, "But some young farmers seem more interested in conservation." Having met many conservation-minded farmers myself, I have a feeling that this old-timer may have been downplaying his and his peers' commitment to sustainability. Indeed, passing the business from one generation to the next is a mainstay of farming. Minnesota has a Century Farm program that recognizes farms that have been in the same family for at least one hundred years, and since the program was launched in 1976, more than ten thousand farms have been so recognized.

"What does all this mean?" conference attendee and Iowa farmer John Gilbert asked. "It means we may have created conditions for a perfect storm of water-quality problems. It also means we have much hard work to do, and everyone must pitch in. This problem is way past the denial stage, and the sooner that is understood, the sooner finding solutions can build momentum. Understanding causes is essential to finding workable solutions. The good news is the recommendations [cover crops, minimum tilling, et al.] do make a difference. Knowing what to do is the easy part. The hard part is changing attitudes."

In our many excursions on the waters and highways of the Minnesota River Basin, Geri and I have discovered that many people care deeply about the condition of the river and its watershed. I have tried to understand the issues and positions held by both environmental groups and farmers. Society needs to acknowledge farmers' care of the land and recognize the multiple challenges they face. For example: the selling price of commodities is determined not by producers but by private speculators in places such as the Chicago Board of Trade and public officials in the form of trade policies such as tariffs. Some years, prices yield a healthy profit; other years, prices fall short of the cost of production. Since peaking at just over $8/bushel in 2012, prices have steadily declined; as of summer 2018, the price was about $3.50/bushel. Farmers who can't turn a profit are in no position to invest in conservation practices such as taking land out of production.

Savvy environmental activists recognize that we cannot protect the river long term unless we work together with the agricultural community. Consensus is key, and knowledge is key to arriving at consensus. Scientists, including Minnesota Pollution Control Agency staff, are committed to keeping the public informed of restoration efforts and the status of the basin's resources. The University of Minnesota, with its campuses in the Twin Cities, Marshall, and Morris, and the Minnesota State College and University system (MNSCU), especially Minnesota State University–Mankato, are heavily involved in agricultural research and finding collaborative water-quality solutions. The university also operates agricultural research and outreach centers in the basin towns of Waseca, Lamberton, and Morris.

* * *

The Minnesota Agricultural Water Quality Certification Program, established in 2013, is an opportunity for farmers and landowners to demonstrate that they are conducting their operations in an environmentally responsible fashion and, in return, become exempt for ten years from new regulations that may be imposed on agricultural practices. To qualify, farmers must demonstrate that they have implemented best management practices for tillage, application of fertilizers, and several other categories.

Chuck Uphoff, one of the farmers participating in the program, said, "Conservation and agriculture work well together. The value of conservation is real, and I hope people can see that." Another, Glen Haag, said, "We're stewards of the land. We want to pass this on to the next generation." These farmers have modified their farming practices and have discovered that the new practices not only produce yields comparable to conventional farming but are also cost-effective.

The news that twelve farmers from Mower and Freeborn Counties have recently joined other basin farmers in the Minnesota Agricultural Water Quality Certification Program brings me hope. The Mower County Soil and Water Conservation District resource specialist says, "Agriculture and water quality can work together and this program shows that is possible." As of January 2017, the program had certified 306 farms statewide, comprising about 175,000 acres. Time—and meticulous data collection and analysis—will determine how impactful this program will be.

* * *

To this day, elected officials and agency professionals struggle to devise and implement land- and water-use practices based on those thin red lines demarcating townships and the equally artificial boundaries of counties rather than the natural, watershed-based boundaries of the landscape. More often than not, watershed boundaries overlap two or more county boundaries. Take, for example, the Chippewa River in western Minnesota. It runs through eight different counties, and the agency professionals in each of those counties are required to develop their own plans and acquire their own funding for projects in their section of the river.

In 1955, the State of Minnesota took a step in the right regulatory direction by creating something unique in the nation: watershed districts. They're a special-purpose unit of government whose jurisdictional boundaries are watershed boundaries—inherently different from county boundaries or the township boundaries mapped out by the US General Land Office surveys. Minnesota has eighty-one major watersheds (twelve in the Minnesota River Basin), and forty-six of them (eight in the basin) now have watershed districts. They are created by citizen petition (if you live in a watershed that doesn't have a district, you can initiate a petition to establish one), have taxing authority (check the fine print of your property tax statement), and a board of managers appointed by county commissioners (all citizens of the watershed are eligible to apply). Oversight is provided by the state's Board of Water and Soil Resources (BWSR), whose website explains, "The specific duties of Watershed Districts vary across the state— some focus mainly on flood damage reduction, while others have a broad range of programs and services to protect and improve water quality."

A further step in the right direction happened in 2016, when BWSR introduced a new, voluntary program called One Watershed, One Plan. Rather than requiring counties, watershed districts, soil and water conservation districts, and other agencies to develop local water plans independently, now these entities can collaborate on a single plan. As the BWSR website explains, "The program is designed to foster collaboration between upstream and downstream neighbors to work where it's most important in the watershed, not limited to county or other jurisdictional boundaries."

One giant leap in the right direction would be to adopt a recommendation made by the Minnesota River Citizens' Advisory Committee in 2004: to establish joint powers boards in each major watershed. All the public agencies and other organizations involved in water-quality issues would pool their human and financial resources to not just devise "One Plan" but put the plan into action.

**

What does the future hold for the Minnesota River? From my perspective, it depends on a broader appreciation for the river, how we use science and technology, and how well we work together.

Science and technology have made possible the dramatic changes we've made to our land and waters. Invention of the plow and ditchdiggers enabled us to convert the prairie-pothole region to commercial agriculture. The system of locks and dams on the Mississippi River made possible the economical, large-scale transport of agricultural commodities. New kinds of seeds and the introduction of fertilizers allowed us to greatly increase our agricultural output. In recent years, we have developed methods, such as controllable tile-drainage systems, saturated buffers, and cover crops, to slow the flow of water and decrease the amount of sediment and nutrients that pollute our water. We need to refine and more broadly implement these methods. We have also learned how to reestablish some of the 90 percent of wetlands and 99 percent of the prairie that we have lost. We need to do much, much more of that. While continuing research and development of sustainability practices is crucial, we know enough now to make significant progress toward a swimmable and fishable Minnesota River. We just need the will.

In this book, I have included brief stories about six "Voices for the River." I could have written about six hundred more. From our paddling adventures, road trips, and attendance at dozens of gatherings of people with diverse backgrounds and priorities, Geri and I have learned that passion for the river runs wide and deep in the basin's residents. This gives me great hope. Invariably, change occurs through what Margaret Mead famously referred to as "a small group of thoughtful, committed citizens." To make big changes happen (such as creating the Minnesota Valley National Wildlife Refuge or the Conservation Reserve Enhancement Program), citizens need to persuade elected officials to enact the changes and provide resources in the form of dollars and expertise from agency professionals. John Anfinson, superintendent of the Mississippi National River and Recreation Area, explains, "Without partners like the Izaak Walton League and others, we'd just be the voice of Big Government. But with them, it's a voice of constituents, not just here but nationwide." Only by working together will we make significant progress.

The old saying is true: Everybody lives downstream. But Minnesotans live farther upstream than almost everybody else, and we owe it to ourselves and our downstream neighbors to pass along water as clean as we would like our own water to be.

Another, much older saying is also true: Mní Wičhóni—water is life. We cannot continue to mistreat our water if we want our descendants to have a decent life.

Voice of the American Revolution Patrick Henry once said, "Since the achievement of our independence, he is the greatest patriot who stops the most gullies." Voice of the Minnesota River Patrick Moore puts it like this: "We need to make water walk, not run, off the land." Hear, hear. How we deal with water on the land determines the quality of the water in our lakes and rivers.

I spent my formative years on the Minnesota River and fell in love with it. And I have spent a good portion of my "retirement" years striving to get better acquainted with it, searching to understand why this river occupies such a powerful place in my heart and soul. There are places along the Minnesota River every bit as beautiful as anything I've seen in the Boundary Waters. Exploring the river by canoe is facilitated by numerous landing sites, campsites, and the detailed DNR water trails maps. The fishing is great! And the most significant events in the history of the state of Minnesota—the forced displacement of the native population and conversion of the landscape to the commodity-based agriculture that formed our economy—took place in the Minnesota River Basin. My motivation in writing this book has been to help people learn about and appreciate the river I love. Awareness comes first, which leads to appreciation, which leads to a commitment to act. I invite you to get out and spend some time on the Minnesota River. You might just fall in love.

A Note from Geri

In 2011, Darby was diagnosed with mild cognitive impairment. His first book, *For Love of Lakes,* came out that fall, and he and I embarked on a journey to 150-plus events over seven years promoting lake stewardship and the book. After the first two very busy years, Darby finally had time to delve into the research for and writing of this book. We made numerous trips to paddle, talk to people, visit historic sites, attend conferences and meetings, and browse local libraries. Between trips and during the winters, Darby frequented his backyard writing shack. As each chapter took shape, I would finally say, "Good first draft."

Darby completed the first draft of the complete manuscript in 2016. By that time, we were attending our Memory Café support group for people with memory loss and their caregivers. We had to acknowledge his condition had become Alzheimer's. His neurologist credited the hard mental work of writing this book as having slowed the progression of the disease.

For Love of Lakes went through countless revisions before Darby and I agreed it was ready to be published. Each refinement made the language more vivid and tightened it up. For this book, reasoning through organizational challenges and wording changes became increasingly difficult. Holding a thought long enough to evaluate whether one way of saying something was better than another was no longer possible.

Darby and I knew from the beginning that we were in a race against time and memory loss, and eventually we turned to our friend John Hickman to help us through the final stages of the book. John is a writer, editor, and film producer who shares our love for the Minnesota River. As he started revising the text, we were delighted to see how well his edits meshed with Darby's original manuscript. John had found Darby's voice. It was excruciating for Darby to release control, but in the end, we all agreed that the book's message was too important to not get published. So, to John goes our endless gratitude for his expertise, encouragement, wisdom, and sound counsel. This book would have stayed in a file on our computer if not for his walk with us at the end of this journey.

Acknowledgments

To our friends and fellow river enthusiasts who asked how the book was coming and encouraged and celebrated with us as we repeatedly reported, "We're getting really close": many thanks for your support.

Geologist and Freshwater Society policy director Dr. Carrie Jennings caught many a technical error and offered several insightful observations that enhanced the manuscript. Who knew that rounded rocks did not all get that way by bouncing around in water? Carrie, that's who!

Elizabeth Jarrett Andrew, writing mentor extraordinaire, read and commented on the manuscript in its early stages. Marlys and Jim Terrian edited two chapters and gave encouragement throughout.

To Scott Sparlin and Ted Suss, who organized the Minnesota River Congress meetings, thanks for keeping us up to date and for all your support. Duane Ninneman and Peg Furshong from Clean Up the River Environment (CURE) shared historical and current advocacy efforts.

Dan Engstrom and Shawn Schottler from the St. Croix Watershed Research Station shared their research on the Minnesota River. Warren Formo, executive director of the Minnesota Agricultural Water Resource Center, reviewed a chapter. Dale Schwie reviewed the information about Henry David Thoreau, and Larry Granger provided valuable input on the "War" chapter.

Helping us with logistics on our paddling excursions were Loran Kaardal from the Tatanka Bluffs Corridor, Dixie Tilden from CURE, Scott Sparlin from the Coalition for a Clean Minnesota River, Marj Fredrickson, and our daughter and granddaughter, Robin and Halle Daiker.

In addition to masterfully editing the manuscript, John Hickman organized discussions over lunch in St. Peter and Montevideo with people knowledgeable and passionate about the river, deepening our understanding of issues in the basin. Thanks to Mark Bosacker, Bob Finley, Scott Kudelka, Rick Moore, and Kim Musser in St. Peter, and Audrey Arner, Patrick Moore, Kylene Olson, Del and Shirley Wehrspann, and John White in Montevideo. Thanks also to Debbie and Loran Kaardal, as well as to Nicole

Elzenga, executive director of the Renville County Historical Society, for hosting a presentation about Darby's days in Morton and our Minnesota River experiences.

Our thanks to Beth Dale, whose photography we admired when we met her on the river, and who provided the lovely photo of the river at New Ulm. Thanks also to contributing photographers Ron Bolduan, John White, John Hickman, and the *Mankato Free Press*.

Pidamayaye (Thank you) to University of Minnesota Director of Dakota Language Program Çaŋte Máza (Neil McKay), for spelling and pronouncing the Dakota language words that appear in this book.

"Voices for the River" subjects Del Wehrspann, Patrick Moore, Scott Sparlin, and Ed Crozier were (and are!) alive to tell us their stories. Thanks to them and all the other voices, named and unnamed, for their activism to improve the health of the Minnesota River and its basin.

And, finally, to the staff at Beaver's Pond Press, who facilitated the publishing process with wisdom, expertise, and grace, our heartfelt thanks.

Working together!

Dakota Glossary

(n) the letter is pronounced very briefly

<n> a glottal: the letter is pronounced with exhalation through constricted throat

Dakota	English	Pronunciation
Mnísota Makhóčhe	Land Where the Waters Reflect the Clouds	M'NEE-sota Mah-KOH-chay
Mnísota Wakpá	Minnesota River	M'-NEE-sota Wahk-PAH
Íŋyaŋ ša	red stone	EE-yah(n) sha
Bdoté	the place where two waters meet	B'doh-TEYH
Ȟpu´Ȟpu	David Larsen	<H>-poo <H>-poo
Thaóyate Dúta	His Red Nation (Little Crow)	Tah-OH-yah-tay DOO-ta
Ziŋtkáda Ȟóta	Gray Bird	Zint-KAH-da <H>OH-ta
Waŋbdí Tháŋka	Big Eagle	Wahn-b'dee TAHN-ka
Thaŋpá yukháŋ	place of the white birch	Tawn-PAH yuh-KUH(N)
omníča	beans	oh-m'NEE-cha
wamnáheza	maize	oh-m'NAH-hay-zah
wamnú	squash	wah-m'NOO

Dakota	English	Pronunciation
waȟčázizi	sunflowers	wa<h>k-CHA-zee-zee
psiŋ	wild rice	(p)see(n)
mitákuyapi	my relatives	mih-TAH-kee-yah-pee
Phežíhutazizi Oyáte	Upper Sioux Indian Community	Pay-ZHEE-hoo-tah-zee-zee Oh-YAH-tay
Waŋbdí Wakita (?)	Looking Eagle	Wahn-b'DEE WAH-kee-tah (?)
Čháŋšayapi	where they marked the trees red	CHAH(N)-shah-yah-pee
thatháŋka	bison	ta-TAHN-kah
Bde Maġataŋka	Swan Lake	B'day Mah-<K>AH-tanka
Ištáȟba	Chief Sleepy Eye	Eesh-TA<H>K-pah
Mniópha	water falling twice	M'nee-OH-pah
Wókiksuye Makhóčhe	Land of Memories	OH-kay-soo-yeh Mah-KOH-chay
Makhátho Wakpá	Blue Earth River	Mah-KAH-toh Wahk-PAH
Oíyuweğe	the place of crossing	Oh-EE-uh-way-<h>ay
Mayáskadaŋ	White banks	My-OSS-kah-dah
Šaská or Čhaské	the number 6	Shahss-KAH or Chass-KEH
Mní Wičhóni	Water Is Life	M'ni Wih-CHO-nee

Selected Bibliography

Amato, Joseph. *Southwest Minnesota: The Land and the People*. Marshall, MN: Crossings Press, 2000.

Anderson, Gary Clayton. *Kinsmen of Another Kind: Dakota-White Relations in the Upper Mississippi Valley, 1650–1862*. St. Paul: Minnesota Historical Society Press, 1997.

Anderson, Gary Clayton, and Alan R. Woolworth, eds. *Through Dakota Eyes: Narrative Accounts of the Minnesota Indian War of 1862*. St. Paul: Minnesota Historical Society Press, 1988.

Anfinson, Scott F. *Southwestern Minnesota Archaeology: 12,000 Years in the Prairie Lake Region*. Minneapolis: University of Minnesota Press, 1997.

Barras, Colin. "Funeral Flowers: A Rite Since 11,000 BC." *New Scientist* 219 (2924): 14.

Bray, Martha Coleman, ed. *The Journals of Joseph N. Nicollet: A Scientist on the Mississippi Headwaters with Notes on Indian Life*. St. Paul: Minnesota Historical Society, 1970.

Cafaro, Kris Bronars. *Cloudy-Sky Waters: An Annotated Bibliography of the Minnesota River. The Rural & Regional Essay Series*. The Center for Rural and Regional Studies, Southwest Minnesota State University, Marshall Minnesota. Jackson, MN: Livewire, 2004.

Carver, Jonathan. *The Journals of Jonathan Carver and Related Documents, 1766–1776*. St. Paul: Minnesota Historical Society Press, 2004.

Christgau, John. *Birch Coulie: The Epic Battle of the Dakota War*. Lincoln: University of Nebraska Press, 2012.

Crampton, John. *IKEs Clean Up the Mississippi River in Twin Cities, 1930s.* Video, 2013.

Eddy, Samuel, and A. C. Hodson. *Taxonomic Keys of the Common Animals of the North Central States.* Minneapolis: Burgess Publishing Company, 1961.

Featherstonaugh, George W. *A Canoe Voyage up the Minnay Sotor: With an Account of the Lead and Copper Deposits in Wisconsin; of the Gold Region in the Cherokee Country; and Sketches of Popular Manners.* Vol. 2, 1847. Reprint. St. Paul: Minnesota Historical Society, 1970.

Folwell, William Watts. *History of Minnesota: Vol. 1,* 1921. St. Paul: Minnesota Historical Society.

Fry, Polly. "A River Runs Through It: Cultures, Economies and Landscapes within the Minnesota River Basin to 1900." PhD diss., University of Minnesota, 1999.

Gibbon, Guy. *Archaeology of Minnesota: The Prehistory of the Upper Mississippi River Region.* Minneapolis: University of Minnesota Press, 2012.

Gibbon, Guy. *The Sioux: the Dakota & Lakota Nations.* Malden, MA: Blackwell Publishing, 2003.

Gilman, Rhoda R., Carolyn Gilman, and Deborah St. Ulz. "The MN Valley Trail," Chap. 4 in *The Red River Trails: Oxcart Routes Between St. Paul and the Selkirk Settlement 1820–1870.* St. Paul: Minnesota Historical Society Press, 1979.

Goldich, Samuel S., Alfred O. Nier, Halfdan Baadsgaard, John H. Hoffman, and Harold W. Krueger. *The Precambrian Geology and Geochronology of Minnesota.* Minneapolis: University of Minnesota Press, 1961.

Grimm, Eric C. "Chronology and Dynamics of Vegetation Change in the Prairie-Woodland Region of Southern Minnesota, U.S.A." 1983. *New Phytologist* 93: 311–350.

Hazard, Evan B. *The Mammals of Minnesota*. Minneapolis: University of Minnesota Press (for the James Ford Bell Museum of Natural History), 1982.

Hickman, John. *River Revival: Working Together to Restore the Minnesota River*. Documentary film. John Hickman, executive producer; Jonathan Carlson, producer-photographer-editor, 2011.

Hickman, John. *Working Together: A Plan to Restore the Minnesota River*. Final report of the Minnesota River Citizens' Advisory Committee. Minnesota Pollution Control Agency, 1994.

Hudson, John C. *Making the Corn Belt: A Geographical History of Middle-Western Agriculture*. Indianapolis: Indiana University Press, 1994.

Long, Steven Harriman, and James Edward Colhoun. *The Northern Expeditions of Stephen H. Long: The Journals of 1817 and 1823 and Related Documents*. Edited by Lucile M. Kane, June Drenning Holmquist, and Carolyn Gilman. St. Paul: Minnesota Historical Society Press, 1978.

Metzer, David. *First People in a New World: Colonizing Ice Age America*. Berkeley: University of California Press, 2009.

Minnesota County Biological Survey, Division of Ecological Resources, Department of Natural Resources, St. Paul. "Native Plant Communities and Rare Species of the Minnesota River Valley Counties." September 2007. Biological Report No. 89.

Montgomery, David R. *Dirt: The Erosion of Civilizations*, 2nd ed. Berkeley: University of California Press, 2012.

Nelson, Darby. *For Love of Lakes*. East Lansing: Michigan State University Press, 2012.

Nicollet, Joseph N. *The Hydrographical Basin of the Mississippi River 1863*. St. Paul: Minnesota Historical Society Press, 1976.

Ojakangas, Richard W. *Roadside Geology of Minnesota*. Missoula Montana: Mountain Press Publishing Company, 2009.

Ojakangas, Richard W., and Charles L. Matsch. *Minnesota's Geology*. Minneapolis: University of Minnesota Press, 1982.

Parker, John, ed. *The Journals of Jonathan Carver and Related Documents, 1766–1770*. St. Paul: Minnesota Historical Society Press, 1976.

Pielow, E. C. *After the Ice Age: the Return of Life to Glaciated North America*. Chicago: University of Chicago Press. 1991.

Pierce, Richard L. *Lower Upper Cretaceous Plant Microfossils from Minnesota*. Minneapolis: University of Minnesota Press, 1961.

Queenan, Anne. *Voices of the River*. Queenanproductions.com, 2012.

Schwartz, George M., and George A. Thiel. *Minnesota's Rocks and Waters: A Geological Story*. Minneapolis: University of Minnesota Press, 1954.

Sims, P. K., and G. B. Morey, eds. *Geology of Minnesota: A Centennial Volume*. Minneapolis: Minnesota Geological Survey, 1972.

Smith, Corinne Hosfeld. *Westward I Go Free: Tracing Thoreau's Last Journey*. Sheffield, VT: Green Frigate Books, 2012.

Smith, Welby R. *Trees and Shrubs of Minnesota*. Minneapolis: University of Minnesota Press, 2008.

Svoboda, Frank D. *Looking Back: A History of Agriculture in Renville County, Minnesota*. Morton, MN: Renville County Historical Society, 1976.

Tester, John R. *Minnesota's Natural Heritage: An Ecological Perspective.* Minneapolis: University of Minnesota Press, 1995.

Waters, Thomas F. *The Rivers of Minnesota.* St. Paul: Riparian Press, 2010.

Waters, Thomas F. *The Streams and Rivers of Minnesota.* Minneapolis: University of Minnesota Press, 1977.

Westerman, Gwen, and Bruce White. *A Day at Lower Sioux.* St. Paul: Minnesota Historical Society Press, 2012.

Wingerd, Mary Lethert. *North Country: The Making of Minnesota.* Minneapolis: University of Minnesota Press, 2010.